ADVANCE PRAISE FOR *BAGHDAD BURNING*

"Passionate, frustrated, sarcastic, and sometimes hopeful. . . . Riverbend is most compelling when she gives cultural object lessons on everything from the changing status of Iraqi women to Ramadan, the Iraqi educational system, the significance of date palms and the details of mourning rituals. The blog . . . offers quick takes on events from a perspective too often overlooked, ignored, or suppressed." **—Publishers Weekly**

"In a voice that grips with drama and cuts to core with humor, Riverbend reports the personal side of war as no other account I know of does. Anyone who cares about the war in Iraq must read this book."
—Susan Sarandon

"I've learned more about the occupation of Iraq from Riverbend's blog than from just about any other news source. This 24-year-old Baghdad woman writes about everything from her house-proud neighbor, 'the Martha Stewart of Iraq,' to the rising toll of kidnappings, murders, and attacks on unveiled women by the religious fanatics whose empowerment is one of the many unintended consequences of the American invasion. With spiritedness and even humor, she writes about daily life under siege and families under incredible stress. Every American should read this book."
—Katha Pollitt

"Baghdad Burning is an amazing testimony from a young woman who reports from the front and center of the terrible occupation of her homeland. Riverbend makes an astute witness as her country is disassembled right by right and family by family by the self-righteous invaders who believe they are heroes taking what belongs to them by divine right. As I read her brilliant, honest daily account in her ongoing blog, I am often struck by déjà vu. I recognize the same basic stories of theft and destruction. It is all happening all over again." **—Joy Harjo,** poet and musician

"Sometimes the world has to wait years before the victims of war tell their stories. Riverbend's tale comes right at us, fresh, furious, and demanding. You are about to make a friend and you'll never watch the news the same way again. Thank you, Riverbend, for the generous gift of your words. Your dignity, irony, rage, and extravagant humanity may yet liberate us from denial: U.S. OUT OF IRAQ NOW." **—Laura Flanders, Air America Radio**

"Riverbend's online journal exposes what liberation is really like for the Iraqi people. She talks about the fear, uncertainty, and harassment that the Iraqis are living with, a story we don't see reported by the major media or the government/military. Her voice is especially unique because she is a young woman, and she tells what the occupation is like for young women, challenging our government's assertion that our invasion of Iraq has liberated women. Riverbend's journals let people in the United States and elsewhere read what it is like to live in Iraq and this helps us to better understand the resistance against our presence there and also to humanize and relate to the Iraqi people. Despite the ten months I spent in Iraq, and all of the contact I had with the people, I have learned more reading Riverbend's blog than I ever understood from the stunted communication I had with Iraqis while I was there. When I read Riverbend's journal entries, I'm struck that she seems like a normal person trapped in a very abnormal, difficult situation. Her writings should dispel the belief among Americans that the Iraqi people are somehow so different from us in every aspect of their lives, that it is impossible to understand them. Identifying with the Iraqi people is a crucial step in ending the occupation, and I think Riverbend's journals are an important way for people to gain insight into the lives of a people living under foreign occupation.

—**Kelly Dougherty,** cofounder, **Iraq Veterans Against the War**

Baghdad Burning

GIRL BLOG FROM IRAQ

by Riverbend

Foreword by Ahdaf Soueif
Introduction by James Ridgeway

MARION BOYARS
LONDON • NEW YORK

First published in Great Britain in 2005 by
MARION BOYARS PUBLISHERS LTD
24 Lacy Road, London SW15 1NL.
www.marionboyars.co.uk

Distributed in Australia and New Zealand by Peribo Pty Ltd
58 Beaumont Road, Kuring-gai, NSW 2080.

Printed in 2005
10 9 8 7 6 5 4 3 2 1
© Riverbend 2005
Foreword copyright © 2005 by Ahdaf Soueif
Introduction copyright © 2005 by James Ridgeway

First published in the United States of America in 2005 by The Feminist Press, New York.

A CIP catalogue record for this book is available from the British Library.

ISBN 0-7145-3118-9

Text design and composition by Lisa Force.

Printed in Canada by Transcontinental Printing.

"I wish," says Riverbend, towards the end of her blog, "every person who emails me supporting the war, safe behind their computer, secure in their narrow mind and fixed views, could actually come and experience the war live." *Baghdad Burning* brings us as close to the war in Iraq as it's possible to be. And "close" does not mean just knowing about electricity cuts and water shortages, about street battles and raids on homes; "close" means right inside the heart and mind of a young Baghdadi woman as she lives through the war.

Her career interrupted, her social life blown, "Riverbend" decides to reach out and "blog" her account of the war onto the Internet. "I looked for a 'rantlog,'" she says, "this is the best Google came up with." But *Baghdad Burning* is far from being a rant; it is an articulate, sensitive, often witty, always brave narrative of what it is like to be an Iraqi living in Iraq today.

It is a narrative authentic for being firmly embedded in the daily life of her family and friends. While her parents are kept in the shadows, Riverbend's beloved brother "E" is right there with her, sharing her tasks and her thoughts. And because Riverbend is responsive to questions and comments sent to her blog, she from time to time treats us to a potted introduction to particular subjects: Arab family ties, women and Islam, the hijab, Ramadan customs, saving and investment, relations between Muslims and Christians, relations between Sunnis and Shia, university education in Baghdad, and many others. A great many of the questions about Arabs that have so exercised the Western public over the last several years are answered here. For me, also an Arab woman, her accounts invariably ring true. None more so, perhaps, than the riposte to the insidious and recurring charge of "anti-Americanism": "When I hear talk about 'anti-Americanism,'" she writes, "it angers me. Why does America identify itself with its military and government? Why does being anti-Bush and anti-occupation have to mean that a person is anti-American? We watch American movies, listen to everything from Britney Spears to Nirvana and refer to every brown fizzy drink as 'Pepsi.'"

In fact, far from being anti anything, this book is firmly on the side of humanity and on the side of life. Even the invading troops were once seen as deserving of human sympathy: on May 7, 2004, fourteen months into the invasion, Riverbend writes: "There was a time when people here felt sorry for the troops. No matter what one's attitude was to the occupation, there were moments of pity towards the troops, regardless of their nationality. We would see them suffering under the Iraqi sun, obviously wishing they were somewhere else and somehow that vulnerability made them seem less monstrous and more human. That time has passed." The watershed was the publication of the now notorious torture photographs from Abu Ghraib. There have been other watersheds since, the destruction of Falloojeh being the most obvious.

There is, naturally, a fair amount of politics in this book. But it is never abstract or ideologically motivated; it stems from what is happening on the spot. From the invasion itself ("The frontline is our homes . . . the 'collateral damage' are our friends and families") to the appointment of the Iraqi Governing Council and the economy ("For sale: A fertile, wealthy country with a population of around 25 million . . . plus around 150,000 foreign troops and a handful of puppets") to the efforts at reconstruction, the (un)desirability of deploying Turkish troops in Iraq, the targeting of Iraqi intellectuals and academics, and the plans for elections—Riverbend's account is always intelligent and perceptive. Here, after a discussion of his flashy tie, is Riverbend's take on one aspect of Ahmad Chalabi: "I stare at him when he gives his speeches on television and cringe with the thought that someone out there could actually have thought he was representative of any faction of Iraqi society. I can hardly believe that he was supposed to be the one to target the Iraqi intellectuals and secularists. He's the tasteless joke Bush and Co. sent along with the soldiers . . ." This is pinpoint description of the feelings of the vast majority of Arabs toward the "leaders" selected for them by Western powers.

This book should shame all those with a lingering imperialist bent of mind who see Iraqis (or Arabs, or Muslims, or "third-worldeans") as somehow lesser or, at best, "developing." For in its astute observation, sharp analysis, and hard-headed interpretation of what is happening in Iraq, *Baghdad Burning* cannot be bested.

One charge that could be laid at the book's door is that it lacks geopolitical perspective. It rarely ventures outside Iraq and it does not offer a theory for why the Bush administration deemed it necessary to invade the country. I think it is fair to say that the world's media, mainstream and alternative, are not lacking in these kinds of analyses and theories. What they do lack is the voice of an "ordinary" Iraqi, resident in Iraq, to tell us what the invasion feels like. This is the function that *Baghdad Burning* fulfills uniquely and with power and elegance.

Baghdad Burning makes painful reading. It also makes enjoyable—even fun—reading. It is certainly necessary reading. Never naïve, never blinkered, it is a wise and disillusioned book—yet it is not cynical, for it insists on identifying and celebrating what is good and what is hopeful.

English-speaking readers are incredibly lucky that this young Iraqi woman has written her narrative straight into English, that they can hear and relate to her directly without the mediation of a translator. She should not, of course, have had to write this book at all. But now that she has written it, and written it so brilliantly, I hope English speakers everywhere will take Riverbend and *Baghdad Burning* to their hearts.

Ahdaf Soueif
London
December 2004

> # Introduction

This book is written by a young woman whom we know only by the name "Riverbend," who calls her blog "Baghdad Burning" and describes it simply as a "Girl Blog from Iraq." For more than a year, this anonymous "girl blog" has made the war and occupation real in terms that no professional journalist could hope to achieve.

We don't know much about Riverbend. She is in her mid-twenties and lives in what seems to be a middle-class section of Baghdad with her mother, father, and brother. Before the war she had a job involving computers. She writes in excellent English with a slight American inflection. New entries to her blog appear sometimes daily, sometimes days or even weeks apart. And to many of her readers, these entries have become perhaps the most important source of news from Iraq.

Riverbend's news has nothing to do with troop movements, casualty figures, or the latest from the Green Zone—the subjects of mainstream news reports. For Riverbend, war is something that is lived every day—and every night. She and her brother, "E," sit on the roof to watch Baghdad burning and have learned to identify different types of automatic weapons by the sound of their volleys. Occupation is a way of life. It means rounding up enough friendly armed men to take the kids to the store to buy crayons. It means trying to bury an elderly aunt in a city where the mosques are all overbooked for funerals and the cemeteries are full. It means jumping up in the middle of the night, when the electricity briefly comes on, in order to run the washing machine—or work on her blog.

Once you are into Riverbend, her war becomes your war. You begin to see things through her eyes and those of her family. You read in the news about a raid on a section of Baghdad, and immediately you want to check her blog, hoping her house wasn't on that block. You hear of an airstrike and nervously wonder whether her mother got E off of the roof in time. Whenever Riverbend and her family travel out of the neighborhood to a family gathering, you travel with her as she describes every turn the car takes, the tension as it rounds a corner, hoping there is not an American tank in the street. If she does not write for several days, maybe a week or more, you fear the worst—a bomb strike, a tank raid, imprisonment. Then she reappears, explaining that the electricity has been off, or sometimes that things were so depressing that she just couldn't bring herself to write.

Riverbend has plenty of well-informed, acid opinions on the follies of the Bush administration. She is scornful of the American "puppets" in the Iraqi interim government, and she brings readers fresh insight on the factions within the Iraqi populace. She despises the gangs of religious fundamentalists who make it impossible for women to hold jobs or walk alone in the streets. She slaps back at detractors on the net, sending out a tart response to their jibes. It's all darkly perceptive, and well worth reading. But what remains are her accounts of war as an experience lived day-by-day. It is both quotidian and absolutely riveting, and once you begin to read Riverbend, it's unlikely you will stop.

BACKGROUND

Riverbend's culture is rooted in one of the oldest and richest civilizations in the world. Her nation was created by Western colonialism, driven by a desire to control its most valuable natural resource.

The current political boundaries in the oil-producing regions of the Middle East go back to the opening years of the twentieth century. Even then plotting its strategy against the Germans in anticipation of

World War I, the British navy decided to change the fuel for its battleships from coal to oil, and Britain aggressively expanded its exploratory oil holdings in the Middle East. Its early stake in the region—and its victory in the war—left Britain well positioned in the power grab that came with the postwar breakup of the Ottoman Empire. In 1920, the League of Nations awarded the British a mandate to govern areas of the Middle East, including what is now Iraq.

Soon the British were awash in Middle East oil and sought to expand its market into the United States. Until that time, the U.S. oil business had been in the viselike grip of Rockefeller's Standard Oil Company. In reaction to the British strike at its market, the American oil industry came up with an aggressive plan of its own. The government and industry issued warnings to the public of the impending dire shortage of petroleum, paving the way for higher prices to support more U.S. exploration and development. Then the Americans pushed into the Middle East themselves, going toe-to-toe with the British. Eventually the competing companies worked out a cooperative agreement for divvying up the oil through an entity called the Iraq Petroleum Company.

This overall arrangement survived the end of the British mandate, years of coups and counter-coups in Iraq, and the rise of the Baath party, up to the growth of OPEC (Organization of the Petroleum Exporting Countries) in the early 1970s. It then underwent a series of transformations, with OPEC, made up of state companies, gaining more of a grip on the basic oil and gas resources, while Western companies continued to dominate the processing and transportation of the fuels.

British and French influence in the region gradually diminished as their colonial empires withered, while U.S. involvement grew. At the center of the new order was Aramco, the giant combine of American and Saudi interests that has dominated life in Saudi Arabia for decades. Saudi Arabia long has been the repository of the largest oil reserves in the world. It grew in importance during World War II as a source of fuel for the Allied Armies in the war against the Nazis. It also became an early outpost and resource bin for the United States in the Cold War and in its struggle against emerging Middle Eastern nationalism, which threatened the U.S.'s control of oil. The Saudis played a role in drawing Egypt away from the Soviet orbit. The United States persuaded the Saudis to help finance covert action against various enemies, most notably the Russians who had moved into Afghanistan. And in Iran, the United States fomented the 1953 coup that ousted a democratic, nationalist government and restored the Shah—and paved the road to the Iranian revolution in 1979.

The United States quickly turned to Iraq—and to its new president, Saddam Hussein—as a counterweight to Iran. American agricultural exports to Iraq were stepped up, along with various forms of aid. This included substantial military aid to Saddam during the Iran-Iraq War of the 1980s. It also may have included the export of components for gas warfare, which Saddam used both on the Iranians and on Iraq's own Kurdish minority.

Everything changed in an instant for U.S.-Iraq relations—and for the well-being of the Iraqi people—when Saddam invaded Kuwait in 1990, and the United States responded with a brief but deadly war.

THE GULF WAR AND AFTER

The Iraq in which Riverbend grew up was an Iraq shaped by the 1991 Persian Gulf War. (She would have been just entering her teens when the war took place.) The full effect of this first war, and of a twelve-year period of economic sanctions, on the 26 million people who live in Iraq is difficult to gauge. And few government or mainstream media sources have even attempted to do so.

We know that in the first Gulf War, 293 American military personnel were killed. (Our allies lost 50 more.) Beth Osborne Daponte, a respected demographer now at Yale University, estimated in 1993 that 56,000 Iraqi soldiers and 3,500 Iraqi civilians died during the fighting. Daponte estimated that additional conflicts in the immediate postwar period, which included a Shiite uprising in southern Iraq, killed 5,000 more soldiers and 30,000 civilians. (The figures provided by Daponte, who at the time was working for the U.S. Census Bureau, were controversial, in part because she had contradicted then Pentagon boss Dick Cheney. He had declared at the end of the war, "We have no way of knowing precisely how many casualties occurred . . . [and we] may never know.")

The war's "indirect" effects took a much larger toll. According to Daponte, by the end of 1991—ten months after the February cease-fire—health problems caused by the war led to 111,000 more deaths, of which 70,000 were children under 15.

In fact, the damage had only just begun. The 1991 Gulf War left Saddam Hussein in power and punished the Iraqis for that fact by also leaving in place the UN sanctions that had been imposed in 1990, when Saddam invaded Kuwait. Richard Garfield, a Columbia University nursing professor whose work is also highly regarded, estimates in a report completed in 2003 that there were from about 345,000 to 530,000 excess deaths of children under five between 1990 and 2002. That comes down to about 100 children a day dying due to the Gulf War and the subsequent sanctions. Garfield's figures do not include the second, or 2003, war.

From 1990 through 1996, the sanctions meant that Iraq could not sell oil to generate income. A 2004 Commerce Department study noted that historically oil was responsible for three-quarters of Iraq's GDP and over 90 percent of its foreign exchange income. The sanctions extended and exacerbated the humanitarian crisis generated by the Gulf War's destruction of Iraq's infrastructure.

The 1991 war crippled the electric power system, reducing generating capacity from around 5 gigawatts to 1.8 gigawatts, according to a report in *Middle East Economic Survey*. This affected not only civilian life in Iraq's cities and towns, but also its agricultural production, which depended on electric power for its irrigation systems. Food supplies were reduced, and by the mid-1990s, one-third of the country's children under the age of five were malnourished. Supplies of clean drinking water were initially reduced by half as Iraq's system of pumping stations crashed.

The activities of the public health system were cut in half by the war and remained compromised under sanctions. The number of diarrhea episodes in children below the age of five quadrupled from 1991 to 1996. Garfield reports that "informal estimates suggest that 70 percent of child deaths in the mid-1990s were due to preventable diarrheal or respiratory diseases." Before the first Gulf War, virtually all children—including girls—went to grammar school. After the war, school attendance fell and the literacy rate quickly declined.

The UN's Oil for Food program, which began in 1996, permitted some export. The program generated $27 billion for humanitarian purposes, providing the financial equivalent of 50 cents a day for every Iraqi. The income might have been much higher, but the United States extracted reparations for the 1991 war. The program did help feed Iraq's people and rebuild some of its infrastructure, but the country's basic standard of living never returned to pre-Gulf War levels. By the end of 2004 details of the alleged corruption that surrounded the Oil for Food program were just beginning to be widely known. Charges of corruption from investigations launched by, among others, the U.S. Congress, culminated in Republican right-wing calls for the resignation of Kofi Annan and demands for the U.S. to block further payments to the international organization. In short, alleged corruption was immediately put to political use in the U.S. by a right wing that has always detested the UN and sought for years to get rid of it.

THE 2003 WAR

The Bush administration appears to have determined to go to war against Saddam as a primary foreign policy goal well before 9/11. Claims of faulty UN inspections, weapons of mass destruction, and a tenuous connection to 9/11 were the publicly stated reasons for the attack; all have been proven clearly false.

The war as defined by the administration—the "mission" that was declared "accomplished" on May 2, 2003—was destructive, but brief. It has now been overshadowed by the occupation, a scene of ongoing fighting, ongoing casualties among both "coalition" forces and Iraqi and foreign civilians, and ongoing destruction to Iraq's infrastructure and civil society. It is this scene that Riverbend describes so vividly in her blog.

From the start, the occupation was at best a clumsy affair—and at worst, a folly of near-criminal proportions. The United States never gained enough control to restore any sort of order. And of course, the wild welcome—and ongoing support and cooperation—expected from the Iraqi street never materialized. The U.S. occupiers allowed large stocks of heavy explosives mysteriously to slip through their hands. They said they would build up an Iraqi police force that could exercise control sufficient to allow a withdrawal of American troops, but were unable to recruit adequate numbers of these new security forces or equip them with sufficient vehicles, weapons, body armor, and radios.

"Days after Iraq regained 'sovereignty,' the White House revealed some startling details about the reconstruction: just 2 percent of the $18.4 billion earmarked for the urgent reconstruction of Iraq had been spent. Not a penny was spent on healthcare or water and sanitation, two of the more urgent needs for Iraqis," wrote Pratap Chatterjee in his book *Iraq, Inc.* Most of the money coming out of U.S. taxpayers' pockets went for military operations, not reconstruction. And the reconstruction often involved soldiers handing out wads of $100 bills in the streets for repairs. As one administration official told the *New York Times*, "You want to hire everybody on the street, put money in their pockets and make them like you." But as time went on, major reconstruction contracts were handed out predominantly to U.S. companies, while, as Riverbend notes, Iraq's accomplished engineers were shut out of work.

As for the human casualties of war, *The Lancet*, the respected British medical journal, sent researchers throughout the country to gauge the effect of the war on the civilian population. The startling findings are summarized in an October 2004 article by the magazine:

A cluster sample survey was undertaken throughout Iraq during September, 2004. 33 clusters of 30 households each were interviewed about household composition, births, and deaths since January, 2002. In those households reporting deaths, the date, cause, and circumstances of violent deaths were recorded. We assessed the relative risk of death associated with the 2003 invasion and occupation by comparing mortality in the 17.8 months after the invasion with the 14.6-month period preceding it.

The risk of death was estimated to be 2.5-fold. . . . higher after the invasion when compared with the preinvasion period. Two-thirds of all violent deaths were reported in one cluster in the city of Falloojeh. If we exclude the Falloojeh data, the risk of death is 1.5-fold higher after the invasion. . . . The major causes of death before the invasion were myocardial infarction, cerebrovascular accidents, and other chronic disorders whereas after the invasion violence was the primary cause of death. Violent deaths were widespread, reported in

15 of 33 clusters, and were mainly attributed to coalition forces. Most individuals reportedly killed by coalition forces were women and children. The risk of death from violence in the period after the invasion was 58 times higher than in the period before the war.

Making conservative assumptions, we think that about 100,000 excess deaths, or more, have happened since the 2003 invasion of Iraq. Violence accounted for most of the excess deaths and air strikes from coalition forces accounted for most violent deaths.

The numbers cited by *The Lancet* are considerably higher than any cited by earlier reports. The Iraqbodycount.net project, run by a collective of US and British academics, put the maximum number of civilian deaths at 17,000 by late October of 2004.

In Beth Osborne Daponte's view, "High-quality data has not yet become available" for the second U.S. war in Iraq. What makes the task especially difficult, she says, is the fact that the situation is too volatile. "I don't think Americans have the full picture of the war's impact on the Iraqi population." The number of civilians—and of children—who already have died or will die because of the American invasion and occupation is unknown. The availability of electricity will be key in determining what happens. "Everything hinges on it," said Colin Rowat, a lecturer in economics at the University of Birmingham in Great Britain and an Iraq expert in May 2003. "Food and medicine cannot be properly preserved without electricity."

In fact, more than a year and a half after the invasion, Iraq's infrastructure—which had never fully recovered from the Gulf War and sanctions—remained badly compromised. Once again, oil production, the basis for Iraq's economy, fell steeply. Crude oil exports for May 2004 averaged 1.6 million barrels a day. The U.S. Commerce Department's "Iraq Investment and Reconstruction Taskforce" reported that it did not foresee Iraq fulfilling its potential production capacity of 6 million barrels a day for many years (until sometime "after 2010") and emphasized the need for "sizable" investment just to get oil fields functioning properly—a boon for U.S. companies like Halliburton, but a sorry state of affairs for millions of Iraqis, who by late 2004 had yet to feel any benefits from these investments.

Agriculture historically accounted for a bit more than one-quarter of Iraq's GDP and provided 20 percent of all employment. Beginning in 1990, the industry declined and scarcity of food became a serious worry for perhaps half of the country's population. (The UN Oil for Food program was little help in this area, as it increased dependence on imported foodstuffs.) Agriculture in Iraq suffered from the lack of water supplies for irrigation. While U.S. government officials rhapsodized in 2004 about the sector's "potential for the future" in the post-invasion period, the figures told a different story: recovery costs for 2004 alone were estimated by the World Bank at $3.6 billion, exceeding the funding earmarked for agriculture in the Iraqi budget by over a billion.

Before the Gulf War, Iraq produced more than enough electricity to meet the country's needs. Through patchwork repairs, it had partially rebuilt its electricity grid—but the 2003 invasion cut capacity in half. Only after 18 months of rebuilding has production come close to pre-invasion levels. And even at these levels, there is not enough electricity to meet current and future predicted demands. Clean drinking water also remains in short supply in many parts of the country. Iraq's sewage treatment system, never fully rebuilt after the Gulf War, was further damaged, and as of summer 2004, raw sewage was flowing into the Tigris River at Baghdad.

According to August 2004 reports, some 1,000 Iraqi schools need to be rebuilt as a result of damage and looting; almost 20 percent of the country's 18,000 school buildings need comprehensive or partial repair. The BBC reported at the end of 2003 that most of Iraq's 2004 education budget would need to be spent for salaries alone, with little left over for investment in physical infrastructure. Even where schools exist, some parents are afraid to allow their children to attend, not wanting to expose them to the dangers of stray bullets or rampant kidnappings. Meanwhile, among adults the unemployment level remains, by various estimates, somewhere between 25 and 50 percent.

The Iraqi health care system is suffering from chronic shortages of all kinds. According to the World Health Organization, unsafe streets impeding the mobility of health workers and the transport of supplies is one of the roots of the problem. Doctors in major hospitals continue to complain of shortages of drugs used in surgery and emergency operations, anti-inflammatory and cancer drugs, and vital antibiotics.

Electricity shortages and a lack of clean water further compound the problems faced by hospitals: when generators break down, patients can die on the operating table, while unsanitary conditions lead to deadly infections. Equipment shortages are also crippling, with doctors attempting to do their work without sufficient or effective X-ray machines and cardiac monitors. U.S. administrator L. Paul Bremer himself was reported to have said, in February 2004, that spending on reconstruction was "not nearly enough to cover the needs in the healthcare field." While millions have been "committed" to the health sector in the Iraq budget, a September 2004 State Department weekly report showed that next to nothing was being "disbursed."

THE PUPPET SHOW

Riverbend's blog returns repeatedly to the ongoing saga of the United States' efforts to establish what she calls a pro-American "puppet" government. While the most visible civilian ruler of the occupation was L. Paul Bremer, Presidential Envoy and CPA (Coalition Provisional Authority) Administrator, the administration made no secret of its hope that the nation would soon be turned over to Ahmed Chalabi of the exiled Iraqi National Congress and his pro-American followers. Chalabi, to say the least, cuts an odd figure. He is a former banker who was convicted in absentia by a Jordanian court and sentenced to twenty-two years in prison for his role in wrecking a bank. He left Iraq as a child, and had not lived there since 1956.

In 1996 the CIA bankrolled Chalabi in an unsuccessful bid to overthrow Saddam with Kurdish fighters from the north. By that time, he had become the darling of the U.S.-sponsored Iraqi resistance in exile and had succeeded in getting the Iraqi National Congress named recipient of taxpayer funds under the 1998 Iraq Liberation Act. The American right, in its fascination with Chalabi, went so far as to portray him as some sort of liberator and to float plans calling for Chalabi himself, accompanied by Special Forces, to invade Iraq from the south and on landing wait for the promised uprising.

Chalabi's exile group never had seemed to amount to much, but he successfully insinuated himself among the neo-conservative foreign policy advisers in the Defense Department and elsewhere. It was

Chalabi who sold Bush a bill of goods in the form of bogus intelligence purportedly showing Saddam's arsenal and factories for making weapons of mass destruction. The existence of WMDs became Bush's main rationale for going to war after 9/11—but since accounts from former Bush insiders now show that Bush had decided to invade Iraq earlier in his administration, it remains unclear just who was manipulating whom.

After the invasion, the United States made Chalabi a member of the IGC—the Iraqi Governing Council—which initially ran the country for the Americans. But when the IGC transferred power to the UN-sponsored interim government in June 2004 to pave the way for elections, Chalabi was not included. Chalabi's underlings had been insinuated into the workings of the IGC, and his nephew Salem Chalabi was the man in charge of organizing Saddam's trial. But by that time, Salem had been charged with murder and Chalabi's group fell out of favor.

Chalabi was a dud. He never had any power base in Iraq, and his promised throngs of supporters never materialized. Instead, he became an embarrassment to the administration, charged in 2004 with spying for the government of Iran by informing the Iranians that the United States had their codes. In response to the accusations, Chalabi said the CIA was now out to smear him. He began playing politics on the side of the Shia political coalition.

With the decline in the stature of Chalabi, the Bush government began to support the interim prime minister, Ayad Allawi, the head of a six-party coalition made up of secular Sunni and Shia leaders. The people around Allawi largely hailed from his Iraqi National Accord, a CIA-backed group which was created while Allawi was in exile in London. The leaders were former Baathists who had split with Saddam.

LIBERATED IRAQ

As Riverbend points out, among the most disturbing features of the "liberated" Iraq is the rise of religious fundamentalism in what was once among the Arab world's most secular societies. Where women once enjoyed something approaching equal rights, they are now being barred from the scarce supply of jobs. As a young, educated woman who once worked as a computer "geek" and moved freely about her city, Riverbend is particularly poignant in relating what has happened since the war: the loss of her own job, the fear she and other women now feel walking in the streets without men, the risks of stepping outside with her head uncovered.

Postwar Iraq has seen the formation of gangs inspired by Islamic fundamentalism, that have made a habit of kidnapping women who in their eyes flaunted Islamic law in clothing and behavior. Soon they were capturing men and offering them for ransom, and kidnapping became a fact of daily life. Groups claiming association with Al Qaeda held foreigners for ransom and to demand other political goals; in many cases, the victims were executed.

The Bush administration's purported plan to establish a Western-style democracy in Iraq seems as doomed to failure as its bloody occupation and inept "reconstruction." Riverbend shows an understanding far more sophisticated than the Americans' when it comes to the various religious and ethnic factions that make up Iraq, and must collectively shape its future or carry it into civil war.

Saddam is a Sunni Muslim, and his political apparatus was largely managed by a middle class of educated Sunnis, most of whom lived in an area around Baghdad referred to as the "Sunni Triangle." But Sunni Muslims are a minority in Iraq, accounting for only about 20 percent of the population. In the north are the Kurds, dwelling in a sort of semi-autonomous no-man's land. They have been savaged by Saddam over the years, most famously in chemical gas attacks in the 1980s. Shia Muslims account for 60 percent of nation's population, and as such stand to be the majority factor in any democratically elected government. After the Gulf War, while Bush's father sat by, Saddam brutally put down and punished a Shia uprising inspired by the war. Both Kurds and Shia are concentrated around the twin centers of the nation's oil industry, Kirkuk in the north and Basra in the south.

Ever since the Iranian revolution of 1979, the United States has viewed the Shia as allies of the Ayatollah Khomeini and as part of an expanding mob of extremists determined to turn the entire region into some sort of unspeakable medieval theocracy. But the Shia are not monolithic by any means. As Riverbend recounts, Shiites marry Sunnis and large Iraqi families, like families elsewhere in the world, are conglomerations of different ethnic groups and religions. Within the Shia, there are those who believe the state should be governed by clerics according to religious rules, and others who desire a separation of religion and state. Their religious leaders cover the spectrum of political ideas, from Al-Sistani's aloof removal from politics to the young Moqtada Al-Sadr's fiery radicalism. Shiites are more likely than not to be Arabs, but Kurds, Turkomen, and others also identify with this branch of Islam. Ethnicity, as well as other divisions—region, class—play a role in Shia politics.

All in all, the American invasion and occupation of Iraq at the end of 2004 appears to have pushed the country to the brink of a sort of civil war, with a strong Sunni insurgency making security impossible in key parts of the country. At the same time, the Shia leaders, reportedly with the help of Iran, successfully pulled together the majority of Shia in a political coalition. With Americans unable to maintain security in the face of the continuing insurgency, the country reeled towards civil war and conceivably a breakup over the long term.

James Ridgeway
Washington, D.C.
December 2004

Editor's Note

The content of this book reproduces the first year's worth of Riverbend's writing as it appears in her blog, without any abridgements.
Words that are spelled using a mix of numerals and letters, for
instance "burgu3" (burqa), are intentional and transliterate Arabic
terms using standard computer keystrokes. Select material from the
blog's hyperlinks is included here to illustrate Riverbend's commentary and appears set off in boxes.

Riverbend's ongoing additions to her blog can be read online at
http://riverbendblog.blogspot.com/.

Three months after President Bush declared victory on May 2, 2003 and said major hostilities were "over," the fighting continues. The press cites terrorist attacks, but gradually, the reporters begin to talk about an "insurgency." No one seems quite sure who is in the insurgency, but everyone gets the picture: the Iraqis are uniting to get the Americans out. Casualties begin to climb. US combat and non-combat casualties approach 300 in August. Suicide bombers attack the Jordanian embassy in Baghdad, killing 11. Resisting pressure from the US, which had heretofore ignored them, diplomats at the UN try to avoid awarding Iraq's new American-appointed government any sort of formal recognition. Instead the United Nations Security Council passes a resolution "welcoming" the new Iraqi Governing Council. Five days later the UN headquarters in Baghdad is bombed. Twenty-two people are dead, 100 injured. Among the dead is UN Special Envoy Sergio Vieira de Mello, a gifted diplomat, highly regarded on all sides, and widely viewed as the one man who might weld together the complex politics of the war-torn nation. The UN bombing leads to the international organization abandoning its headquarters and leaving the country.

Attacks increase. At the end of August, a car bomb explodes in the holy city of Najaf, killing 95. Among the dead is one of the most important Shia clerics in Iraq, Ayatollah Mohammed Baqir Al-Hakim, who opposed the occupation but saw the possibility of establishing some form of democracy. In a tour of Iraq, Secretary of Defense Donald Rumsfeld seeks to emphasize the positive aspects of post-war occupation, comparing Baghdad to Chicago.

In September, UN Chief Weapons Inspector Hans Blix tells Australian radio he doubts the coalition will find any weapons of mass destruction. On September 25, Dr. Aqila al-Hashimi, one of three women on the Iraqi Governing Council [IGC], dies after being shot several days earlier.

In October, the UN formally recognizes the IGC but also sees the need to pass full control to Iraqis as soon as possible. From the point of view of the US this is a step forward, since recognition of the IGC means institutional status for the man it wants to play the key part in forming a new democratic government. He is Ahmed Chalabi, a former Iraqi banker, who has not been in Iraq since he was 12 and for the last decade has operated in London and the US out of his Iraqi National Congress. He is seen as the most important lobbyist for the invasion, and a man who stands to gain from Saddam's overthrow. Bush now says he needs more money to assure security and begin reconstruction in Iraq. David Kay, the top US weapons inspector in Iraq, thought to be more amenable to Bush's insistence on the existence of weapons of mass destruction, presents in an interim report that he cannot find any.

The US meets with resistance to its pleas for financial assistance from the world community. Eighty nations gather in Madrid to put together an aid package for Iraq, but only pledge $15 billion to add to the $19 billion already pledged by the US. These amounts fall far short of the $55 billion goal set by the World Bank, the International Monetary Fund, the Coalition Provisional Authority, and the UN. In bombings that target the International Committee of the Red Cross and several police stations, 35 are killed, 224 wounded. Suicide bombings by now are a regular occurrence.

November turns into the deadliest month of the post-war period to date for US troops as rebels shoot down a US helicopter, killing 16 soldiers and wounding at least 80 others. During this month, 80 US soldiers die. The US Congress passes $87.5 billion for Iraq, and Bush drops in for a photo-op Thanksgiving dinner among troops in Baghdad. Insurgents increase their attacks, killing 4 US soldiers and begin to target members of the US coalition. A bomb explodes at an Italian military police base, killing 14 Italians and 8 Iraqis. By month's end Bush reverses policy and agrees to turn over power to an interim Iraqi government in early 2004. There is a sense things are getting further and further out of control, and with the election approaching, Bush needs some sort of resolution.

Economic matters worsen. Paul Wolfowitz, deputy secretary of defense, causes a furor in December when he bans France, Germany, Russia, and other countries that did not back the war from bidding on contracts for rebuilding Iraq.

On December 13, the US captures Saddam Hussein, who is hiding near his hometown of Tikrit. The arrest, elaborately portrayed on TV around the world, seems to have little effect. The insurgency continues.

—James Ridgeway

THE BEGINNING . . .

So this is the beginning for me, I guess. I never thought I'd start my own weblog . . . All I could think, every time I wanted to start one was "but who will read it?" I guess I've got nothing to lose . . . but I'm warning you—expect a lot of complaining and ranting. I looked for a "rantlog" but this is the best Google came up with.

A little bit about myself: I'm female, Iraqi, and 24. I survived the war. That's all you need to know. It's all that matters these days anyway.

Riverbend **posted by river @ 7:36 PM**

WAKING UP

Waking up anywhere in Iraq these days is a trial. It happens in one of two ways: either slowly, or with a jolt. The slow process works like this: you're hanging in a place on the edge of consciousness, mentally grabbing at the fading fragments of a dream . . . something creeps up around, all over you—like a fog. A warm heavy fog. It's the heat . . . 120 F on the cooler nights. Your eyes flutter open and they search the dark in dismay—the electricity has gone off. The ceiling fan is slow-ing down and you are now fully awake. Trying to sleep in the stifling heat is about as productive as trying to wish the ceiling fan into motion with your brain. Impossible.

The other way to wake up is to be jolted into reality with the sound of a gun-shot, explosion, or yelling. You sit up, horrified and panicked, any dream or nightmare shattered to oblivion. What can it be? A bur-glar? A gang of looters? An attack? A bomb? Or maybe it's just an American midnight raid? **posted by river @ 8:02 PM**

Monday, August 18, 2003

ANOTHER DAY . . .

Normal day today. We were up at early morning, did the usual "around the house things," you know—check if the water tank is full, try to determine when the electricity will be off, checked if there was enough cooking gas . . .

You know what really bugs me about posting on the internet, chat rooms or message boards? The first reaction (usually from Americans) is "You're lying, you're not Iraqi." Why am I not Iraqi, well because, a. I have internet access (Iraqis have no internet), b. I know how to use the inter-net (Iraqis don't know what computers are), and c. Iraqis don't know how to speak English (I must be a Liberal). All that shouldn't bother me, but it does. I see the troops in the streets and think, "So that's what they thought of us before they occupied us . . . that may be what they think of us now." How is it that we're seen as another Afghanistan?

The best part of the last two days was watching tv yesterday—the latest news from our rotating presidential council: Jordan is trying to get Washington to hand Ahmad Al-Chalabi over to authorities in Amman!! That was great to watch . . . you know what? He's my favorite out of the whole interim government hand-picked by Bremer. If Bremer has learned anything about the Iraqi people he's been attempting to govern these last few months, he would hand Chalabi over to Jordanian authorities with a red ribbon around his neck (as a sign of good will). I haven't seen anyone who likes the rat (and his buddy Qambar is even worse).

6

For those who don't know, the interim governing council chosen by Bremer to "represent" the Iraqi people couldn't decide which of the power-hungry freaks should rule Iraq, soooooo . . . Bremer decided that 3 people would govern (as temporary presidents) until the Americans could set up elections. The three people were Al-Hakim (as a representative of the Supreme Council for the Islamic Revolution), Bahr Al-Uloom (another Shi'ite cleric), and Adnan Al-Pachichi. Naturally, the other members of the governing council objected . . . why should Iraq only have 3 presidents?! And the number became nine. Each of the nine (including Adnan Al-Pachichi, Ahmad Al-Chalabi, Al-Hakim, and various others) get to "rule" for a month. You know, Iraq just needs more instability—all we need is a new president each month . . . anyway, our current "Flavor of the Month" is Ibraheim Al-Jaffari, who is the head of the infamous Al-Daawa Party (responsible for various bombings in Iraq before and during the Saddam era). I'll talk more about him later . . .

The funny thing is that the 9 get to govern Iraq alphabetically (according to the Arabic alphabet). The only reason for this seems to be that Bremer found them all equally ingratiating, dishonest, and incompetent so he was hard-pressed to make a decision. The way it will work is that each one will have their chance at governing Iraq, and at the end of the nine-month period, Bremer will decide which one of them best represents American assets in the region and he will become "The Chosen One." They'll set up some fake elections and "The Chosen One" will magically be rewarded with . . . Iraq. I just hope Adnan Al-Pachichi makes it long enough to get his chance on the occupation throne—he looks ready to fall over any minute.

email me: riverbend@popmail.com **posted by river @ 9:12 PM**

Tuesday, August 19, 2003

TIRED.

How is it possible to wake up tired? It feels like I've been struggling in my sleep . . . struggling with nightmares, struggling with fears . . . struggling to listen for gunshots or tanks. I'm just so tired today. It's not the sort of "tired" where I want to sleep—it's the sort of tired where I just want to completely shut down . . . put myself on standby, if you will. I think everyone feels that way lately.

Today a child was killed in Anbar, a governorate northwest of Baghdad. His name was Omar Jassim and he was no more than 10 years old, maybe 11. Does anyone hear of that? Does it matter anymore? Do they show that on Fox News or CNN? He was killed during an American raid—no one knows why. His family is devastated—nothing was taken from the house because nothing was found in the house. It was just one of those raids. People are terrified of the raids. You never know what will happen—who might be shot, who might react wrong—what exactly the wrong reaction might be . . . Things are getting stolen too—gold, watches, money (dollars) . . . That's not to say ALL the troops steal—that's unfair. It's like saying all of Iraq was out there looting. But it really is difficult having to worry about looters, murderers, gangs, militias, and now American troops. I know, I know— someone is saying, "You ungrateful Iraqis! They are doing this for YOU . . . the raids are for YOU!" But the truth is, the raids only accomplish one thing: they act as a constant reminder that we are under occupation, we are not independent, we are not free, we are not liberated. We are no longer safe in our own homes—everything now belongs to someone else.

I can't see the future at this point, or maybe I don't choose to see it. Maybe we're just blocking it out like a bad memory or premonition. Eventually it will creep up on you, though. We're living, this moment, the future we were afraid to contemplate 6 months ago. It's like trying to find your way out of a nightmare. I just wish they would take the oil and go . . .

email me: riverbend@popmail.com **posted by river @ 3:50 PM**

UNBELIEVABLE . . .

The UN building explosion is horrible . . . terrifying and saddening. No one can believe it has happened . . . no one understands why it was chosen. For God's sake these people are supposed to be here to help.

I'm so angry and frustrated. Nothing is moving forward—there is NO progress and this is just an example. The media is claiming Al-Qaeda. God damn, we never HAD Al-Qaeda before this occupation . . . fundamentalists kept their heads down. Now they are EVERYWHERE—they "represent" the Iraqi people on Bremer's puppet council . . .

You know what? Something like this could never happen to the Ministry of Oil. The Ministry of Oil is being guarded 24/7 by tanks and troops. It has been guarded ever since the fall of Baghdad and will continue under Bremer's watchful eye until every last drop of oil is gone. Why couldn't they have put a tank in front of the UN building? Why? Why? Why? We know the Pentagon's planning has been horrid up until now, but you'd think they would have seen this one coming from a mile away . . . **posted by river @ 9:14 PM**

Wednesday, August 20, 2003

DAZED

Sergio de Mello's death is catastrophic. We are all a little bit dazed. He was, during these last few months, the best thing that seems to have happened to Iraq. In spite of the fact that the UN was futile in stopping the war, seeing someone like de Mello gave people some sort of weak hope. It gave you the feeling that, no, the Americans couldn't run amuck in Baghdad without the watchful of eye of the international community.

Bremer is trying to link it to "resistance" and Al-Qaeda . . . this is a new type of attack. *This* is terrorism, Mr. Bush . . . not the attack of occupying forces—that's resistance. Attacking humanitarian organizations you could not, or would not, protect. A type of terrorism Iraqis hadn't seen until this occupation—we never had people bombing the UN or embassies, no matter how difficult things got. The UNSCOM [UN Special Commission] were definitely unloved here, but they were protected. America, as an occupying power, is responsible for the safety and security of what is left of this country. They are responsible for the safety and security of any international humanitarian organizations inside of the country to help the people. They have been shirking their duties horribly . . . but you would think someone like Sergio de Mello could have gotten better.

9

...

Somehow I'm terrified. If someone like de Mello couldn't, or simply wasn't, protected—what's going to happen to the millions of people needing protection in Iraq? How could this have been allowed to happen?

Some news channel was just saying that when Bremer got the news, he broke down and cried . . . I don't know why. It certainly wasn't his loss . . . it was Iraq's.   **posted by river @ 1:32 PM**

Thursday, August 21, 2003

EMAILS

Wow. Dozens of emails were the result of being on Salam's blog. I was astounded. I guess I never thought so many people would end up reading the blog. It has made me appreciative and nervous all at the same time.

Most of the emails moved me to . . . gratitude. Thank you for understanding . . . no, thank you for even *trying* to understand. Other emails, on the other hand, were full of criticism, cynicism, and anger. You really don't have to read my blog if you don't want to and you certainly don't have to email me telling me how much you hate it. It's great to get questions and differing opinions—but please be intelligent about it, and above all, creative—if I want to hear what Fox News has to say, I'll watch it.

And keep one thing in mind—tanks and guns can break my bones, but emails can be deleted.   **posted by river @ 3:13 PM**

MY NEW TALENT

Suffering from a bout of insomnia last night, I found myself in front of the television, channel-surfing. I was looking for the usual—an interesting interview with one of the council, some fresh news, a miracle . . . Promptly at 2 am, the electricity went off and I was plunged into the pitch black hell better-known as "an August night with no electricity in Iraq." So I sat there, in the dark, trying to remember where I had left the candle and matches. After 5 minutes of chagrined meditation, I decided I would "feel" my way up the stairs and out onto the roof. Step by hesitant step, I stumbled out into the corridor and up the stairs, stubbing a toe on the last step (which wasn't supposed to be there).

(For those of you who don't know, people sleep up on the roof in some of the safer areas because when the electricity goes off, the houses get so hot, it feels like you are cooking gently inside of an oven. The roof isn't much better, but at least there's a semblance of wind.)

Out on the roof, the heat was palpitating off of everything in waves. The strange thing is that if you stand in the center, you can feel it emanating from the walls and ground toward you from all directions. I stood there trying to determine whether it was only our area, or the whole city, that had sunk into darkness.

A few moments later, my younger brother (we'll call him E.) joined me—disheveled, disgruntled and half-asleep. We stood leaning on the low wall enclosing the roof watching the street below. I could see the tip of Abu Maan's cigarette glowing in the yard next door. I pointed to it with the words, "Abu Maan can't sleep either . . ." E. grunted with the words, "It's probably Maan." I stood staring at him like he was half—wild—or maybe talking in his sleep. Maan is only 13 . . . how is he smoking? How can he be smoking?

"He's only 13." I stated.

"Is anyone only 13 anymore?" he asked.

I mulled the reality of this remark over. No, no one is 13 anymore. No one is 24 anymore . . . everyone is 85 and I think I might be 105. I was too tired to speak and, in spite of his open eyes, I suspected E. was asleep. The silence was shattered a few moments later by the sound of bullets in the distance. It was just loud enough to get your attention, but too far away to be the source of any real anxiety. I tried to determine where they were coming from . . .

E: How far do you think that is?

Me: I don't know . . . 'bout a kilometer?

E: Yeah, about.

Me: Not American bullets—

E: No, it's probably from a . . .

Me: Klashnikov [Kalishnikov].

E (impressed): You're getting good at this.

No—I'm getting great at it. I can tell you if it's "them" or "us."

I can tell you how far away it is. I can tell you if it's a pistol or machine-gun, tank or armored vehicle, Apache or Chinook . . . I can determine the distance and maybe even the target. That's my new talent. It's something I've gotten so good at, I frighten myself. What's worse is that almost everyone seems to have acquired this new talent . . . young and old. And it's not something that anyone will appreciate on a resume . . .

I keep wondering . . . will an airplane ever sound the same again?

posted by river @ 3:15 PM

AL-CHALABI . . . NO STRINGS ATTACHED!

So I just saw Al-Chalabi on tv. He was interviewed by a prominent reporter for Al-Arabiya. I missed it last night and this morning. But my cousin, who has a generator, kindly recorded it for me (she knows Al-Chalabi is one of the few "politicians" that can make me laugh).

What can I say? He is incredible in interviews—almost as good as Bush (comically infuriating). I can see why the Pentagon adopted him—he would be fun to train, a pet monkey of sorts . . .

Anyway, the interview started out more or less reasonably—he was shining all over (I could swear there was lip-gloss). He really doesn't know how to talk. I think Bremer should forbid him from giving interviews from now until elections—and if they decide to make him president, someone can just write his speeches for him. But he really is an embarrassment to the CIA at this point.

The most amusing part of the interview was when they showed one of his former bodyguards (who he denied knowing with a vengeance worthy of an Oscar). The ex-bodyguard was complaining how when the INC [Iraqi National Congress] first came into Baghdad, and began recruiting people, they seemed reasonable enough. Suddenly, they had overtaken the "Sayd Club," a recreational club (not exclusive to the past regime) and turned the INC into a militia.

They were hijacking cars in the middle of Baghdad during April, May and June, claiming that the cars they were "confiscating" at gunpoint were "looted" (hence, property of Al-Chalabi?). The cars were kept in the "headquarters" and smuggled out of Iraq and to the Kurdish territory. The nicer ones were split amongst the "members" of the INC. Someone or another who wasn't getting a piece of the action complained to the CPA [Coalition Provisional Authority] and Al-Chalabi & Co. were given a collective slap on the wrist and told not to do it again.

After this was brought up, Ahmad Al-Chalabi was just charming—he promptly sneered and told the reporter that it was all LIES! LIES! LIES! And just how much had they paid that witness!? Then he continued to insult the reporter, telling him that they had stooped to a new low (Al-Chalabi's specialty) or in7i6a6 (in Arabish)! The reporter asked him about Jordanian allegations and the Jordanian parliament wanting to bring him to justice . . . he said that it was all LIES! And the Jordanian parliament was a disgrace to the people, etc. He wasn't a crook, he wasn't a thief, he wasn't a puppet. The Iraqis and Jordanians are collectively deranged and ridiculous . . .

In my opinion, the reporter was asking the wrong questions. He should have asked him how he spent the INC funds given to him by the CIA (certainly not on his wardrobe).

The whole interview brought to mind the Associated Press report from August 11 (by Mark Fritz). Especially the first line:

> Iraq is swimming in oil, but anybody who thinks that such natural wealth translates into a fat and happy middle class is in for a crude awakening.

. . . well naturally—we'll have to pay off Ahmad Al-Chalabi's debtors first—can't really expect anything to be left for the people, can we?
posted by river @ 4:58 PM

Friday, August 22, 2003

SETTING THE RECORD STRAIGHT

I'm going to set the record straight, once and for all.

I don't hate Americans, contrary to what many people seem to believe. Not because I love Americans, but simply because I don't hate Americans, like I don't hate the French, Canadians, Brits, Saudis, Jordanians, Micronesians, etc. It's that simple. I was brought up, like millions of Iraqis, to have pride in my own culture and nationality. At the same time, like millions of Iraqis, I was also brought up to respect other cultures, nations and religions. Iraqi people are inquisitive, by nature, and accepting of different values—as long as you do not try to impose those values and beliefs upon them.

Although I hate the American military presence in Iraq in its current form, I don't even hate the American troops . . . or wait, sometimes I do:

—I hated them all through the bombing. Every single day and night we had to sit in terror of the next bomb, the next plane, the next explosion. I hated them when I saw the expression of terror, and remembrance, on the faces of my family and friends, as we sat in the dark, praying for our lives, the lives of our loved ones and the survival of Iraq.

—I hated them on April 11—a cool, gray day: the day our family friend lost her husband, her son and toddler daughter when a tank hit the family car as they were trying to evacuate the house in Al-A'ad-hamiya district—an area that saw heavy fighting.

—I hated them on June 3 when our car was pulled over for some strange reason in the middle of Baghdad and we (3 women, a man and a child) were made to get out and stand in a row, while our handbags were rummaged, the men were frisked and the car was thoroughly checked by angry, brisk soldiers. I don't think I'll ever be able to put into words the humiliation of being searched.

—I hated them for two hours on July 13. As we were leaving Baghdad, we were detained with dozens of other cars at a checkpoint in the sweltering, dizzying heat.

—I hated them the night my cousin's house was raided—a man with a wife, daughter and two young girls. He was pushed out of the house with his hands behind his head while his wife and screaming daughters were made to wait in the kitchen as around 20 troops systematically searched the house, emptying closets, rummaging underwear drawers and overturning toy boxes.

—I hated them on April 28 when they shot and killed over a dozen kids and teenagers in Fallojeh [Falluja]—a place west of Baghdad. The American troops had taken over a local school (one of the only schools) and the kids and parents went to stand in front of the school in a peaceful demonstration. Some kids started throwing rocks at the troops, and the troops opened fire on the crowd. That incident was the beginning of bloodshed in Falloojeh.

On the other hand . . .

—I feel terrible seeing the troops standing in this merciless sun—wearing heavy clothes . . . looking longingly into the air-conditioned interiors of our cars. After all, in the end this is Baghdad, we're Iraqi—we've seen this heat before.

—I feel bad seeing them stand around, drinking what can only be lukewarm water after hours in the sun—too afraid to accept any proffered ice water from "strange Iraqis."

—I feel pity watching their confused, frightened expressions as some outraged, jobless, father of five shouts at them in a language they can't even begin to understand.

—I get hopeless, seeing them pointing their guns and tanks at everyone because, in their eyes, anyone could be a "terrorist" and almost everyone is an angry, frustrated Iraqi.

—I feel sympathy seeing them sitting bored and listless on top of their tanks and in their cars—wishing they were somewhere else.

So now you know. Mixed feelings in a messed up world.

I talk about "American troops" because those are the only ones I've come into contact with—no British soldiers, no Italians, no Spaniards . . . I don't know—maybe they feel the same towards the British in the south.

Someone wrote that I was naïve and probably spoiled, etc. and that "not one single American soldier deserves to die for you." I completely agree. No one deserves to die for me or for anyone else.

This war started out a war on WMD [weapons of mass destruction]. When those were not found, and proof was flimsy at best, it turned suddenly into a "War against Terrorism." When links couldn't be made to Al-Qaeda or Osama Bin Laden (besides on Fox and in Bush's head), it turned into a "Liberation." Call it whatever you want—to me it's an occupation.

My suggestion? Bring in UN peace-keeping forces and pull out the American troops. Let the people decide who they want to represent them. Let the governing council be composed of Iraqis who were suffering the blockade and wars *inside* of Iraq. People are angry and frustrated and the American troops are the ones who are going to have to bear the brunt of that anger simply because the American administration is running the show, and making the mistakes.

It always saddens me to see that the majority of them are so young. Just as it isn't fair that I have to spend my 24th year suffering this whole situation, it doesn't seem fair that they have to spend their 19th, 20th, etc. suffering it either. In the end, we have something in common—we're all the victims of decisions made by the Bush administration.

On the other hand . . . they'll be back home, safe, in a month, or two or three or six . . . and we'll be here having to cope with the mess of a homeland we have now.   **posted by river @ 7:51 PM**

EMAILS

I'm having a few problems with my mailbox, so could everyone please send emails to riverbend@velocall.com until further notice? Thanks . . .

Also, I'm probably going to have a "comments" box starting tomorrow . . . so everyone can see everyone else's comments. **posted by river @ 11:06 PM**

Saturday, August 23, 2003

WE'VE ONLY JUST BEGUN . . .

Females can no longer leave their homes alone. Each time I go out, E. and either a father, uncle, or cousin has to accompany me. It feels like we've gone back 50 years ever since the beginning of the occupation. A woman, or girl, out alone, risks anything from insults to abduction. An outing has to be arranged at least an hour beforehand. I state that I need to buy something or have to visit someone. Two males have to be procured (preferably large) and "safety arrangements" must be made in this total state of lawlessness. And always the question: "But do you have to go out and buy it? Can't I get it for you?" No you can't, because the kilo of eggplant I absolutely have to select with my own hands is just an excuse to see the light of day and walk down a street. The situation is incredibly frustrating to females who work or go to college.

Before the war, around 50% of the college students were females, and over 50% of the working force was composed of women. Not so anymore. We are seeing an increase of fundamentalism in Iraq which is terrifying.

For example, before the war, I would estimate (roughly) that about 55% of females in Baghdad wore a hijab—or headscarf. Hijabs do not signify fundamentalism. That is far from the case—although I, myself, don't wear one, I have family and friends who do. The point is that, before, it didn't really matter. It was *my* business whether I wore one or not—not the business of some fundamentalist on the street.

For those who don't know (and I have discovered they are many more than I thought), a hijab only covers the hair and neck. The whole face shows and some women even wear it Grace Kelly style with a few locks of hair coming out of the front. A "burqa" on the other hand, like the ones worn in Afghanistan, covers the whole head—hair, face, and all.

I am female and Muslim. Before the occupation, I more or less dressed the way I wanted to. I lived in jeans and cotton pants and comfortable shirts. Now, I don't dare leave the house in pants. A long skirt and loose shirt (preferably with long sleeves) has become necessary. A girl wearing jeans risks being attacked, abducted, or insulted by fundamentalists who have been . . . liberated!

Fathers and mothers are keeping their daughters stashed safe at home. That's why you see so few females in the streets (especially after 4 pm). Others are making their daughters, wives, and sisters wear a hijab. Not to oppress them, but to protect them.

I lost my job for a similar reason. I'll explain the whole depressing affair in another post. Girls are being made to quit college and school. My 14-year-old cousin (a straight-A student) is going to have to repeat the year because her parents decided to keep her home ever since the occupation. Why? Because the Supreme Council of the Islamic Revolution in Iraq overtook an office next to her school and opened up a special "bureau."

Men in black turbans (M.I.B.T.s as opposed to M.I.B.s) and dubious, shady figures dressed in black, head to foot, stand around the gates of the bureau in clusters, scanning the girls and teachers entering, the secondary school. The dark, frowning figures stand ogling, leering and sometimes jeering at the ones not wearing a hijab or whose skirts aren't long enough. In some areas, girls risk being attacked with acid if their clothes aren't "proper."

The Supreme Council for the Islamic Revolution in Iraq (SCIRI—but I prefer "SCAREY") was established in 1982 in Tehran. Its main goal is to import the concept of the "Islamic Revolution" from Iran to Iraq. In other words, they believe that Iraq should be a theocracy led by Shi'a Mullahs. Abdul Aziz Al-Hakim, the deputy leader of SCIRI, is a part of the nine-member rotating presidency and will soon have a go at ruling Iraq.

The SCIRI would like to give the impression that they have the full support of all Shi'a Muslims in Iraq. The truth is that many Shi'a Muslims are terrified of them and of the consequences of having them as a ruling power. Al-Hakim was responsible for torturing and executing Iraqi POWs in Iran all through the Iran-Iraq war and after. Should SCIRI govern Iraq, I imagine the first step would be to open the borders with Iran and unite the two countries. Bush can then stop referring to the two countries as a part of his infamous "Axis of Evil" and can just begin calling us the "Big Lump of Evil and Bad North Korea" (which seems more in accord with his limited linguistic abilities).

Ever since entering Iraq, Al-Hakim has been blackmailing the CPA in Baghdad with his "major Shi"a following." He entered Iraq escorted by "Jaysh Badir" or "Badir"s Army." This "army" is composed of thousands of Iraqi extremists led by Iranian extremists and trained in Iran. All through the war, they were lurking on the border, waiting for a chance to slip inside. In Baghdad, and the south, they have been a source of terror and anxiety to Sunnis, Shi'a, and Christians alike. They, and some of their followers, were responsible for a large portion of the looting and the burning (you'd think they were going to get reconstruction contracts . . .). They were also responsible for hundreds of religious and political abductions and assassinations.

The whole situation is alarming beyond any description I can give. Christians have become the victims of extremism also. Some of them are being threatened, others are being attacked. A few wannabe Mullahs came out with a "fatwa," or decree, in June that declared all females should wear the hijab and if they didn't, they could be subject to "punishment." Another group claiming to be a part of the "Hawza Al Ilmia" decreed that not a single girl over the age of 14 could remain unmarried—even if it meant that some members of the Hawza would have to have two, three, or four wives. This decree included females of other religions. In the south, female UN and Red Cross aides received death threats if they didn't wear the hijab. This isn't done in the name of God—it's done in the name of power. It tells people—the world—that "Look—we have power, we have influence."

Liquor stores are being attacked and bombed. The owner usually gets a "threat" in the form of a fatwa claiming that if they didn't shut down the store permanently, there would be consequences. The consequences are usually either a fire or a bomb. Similar threats have been made to hair-dressers in some areas in Baghdad. It's frightening and appalling, but true.

Don't blame it on Islam. Every religion has its extremists. In times of chaos and disorder, those extremists flourish. Iraq is full of moderate Muslims who simply believe in "live and let live." We get along with each other—Sunnis and Shi'a, Muslims and Christians, and Jews and Sabi'a. We intermarry, we mix and mingle, we live. We build our churches and mosques in the same areas, our children go to the same schools . . . it was never an issue.

Someone asked me if, through elections, the Iraqi people might vote for an Islamic state. Six months ago, I would have firmly said, "No." Now, I'm not so sure. There's been an overwhelming return to fundamentalism. People are turning to religion for several reasons.

The first and most prominent reason is fear. Fear of war, fear of death, and fear of a fate worse than death (and yes, there are fates worse than death). If I didn't have something to believe in during this past war, I know I would have lost my mind. If there hadn't been a God to pray to, to make promises to, to bargain with, to thank—I wouldn't have made it through.

Encroaching Western values and beliefs have also played a prominent role in pushing Iraqis to embrace Islam. Just as there are ignorant people in the Western world (and there are plenty—I have the

emails to prove it . . . don't make me embarrass you), there are ignorant people in the Middle East. In Muslims and Arabs, Westerners see
suicide bombers, terrorists, ignorance, and camels. In Americans,
Brits, etc. some Iraqis see depravity, prostitution, ignorance, domina-
tion, junkies, and ruthlessness. The best way people can find to
protect themselves, and their loved ones, against this assumed threat
is religion.

Finally, you have more direct reasons. 65% of all Iraqis are
currently unemployed for one reason or another. There are people who
have families to feed. When I say "families" I don't mean a wife and
2 kids . . . I mean around 16 or 17 people. Islamic parties supported by Iran, like Al-Daawa and SCIRI, are currently recruiting followers by offering "wages" to jobless men (an ex-soldier in the army, for
example) in trade of "support." This support could mean anything—
vote when the elections come around, bomb a specific shop, "confis-
cate," abduct, hijack cars (only if you work for Al-Chalabi . . .).

So concerning the anxiety over terror and fundamentalism—I
would like to quote the Carpenters—worry? "We've only just begun . . .
we've only just begun . . ." **posted by river @ 6:20 PM**

ABOUT RIVERBEND

A lot of you have been asking about my background and the reason
why my English is good. I am Iraqi—born in Iraq to Iraqi parents, but
was raised abroad for several years as a child. I came back in my early
teens and continued studying in English in Baghdad—reading any
book I could get my hands on. Most of my friends are of different ethnicities, religions, and nationalities. I am bilingual. There are thousands in Iraq like me—kids of diplomats, students, expatriates, etc.

As to my connection with Western culture . . . you wouldn't
believe how many young Iraqi people know so much about
American/British/French pop culture. They know all about Arnold
Schwarzenegger, Brad Pitt, Whitney Houston, McDonalds, and M.I.B.s
. . . Iraqi tv stations were constantly showing bad copies of the latest
Hollywood movies. (If it's any consolation, the Marines lived up to the

Rambo/Terminator reputation which preceded them.)

But no matter what—I shall remain anonymous. I wouldn't feel free to write otherwise. I think Salam and Gee are incredibly brave . . . who knows, maybe one day I will be too. You know me as Riverbend, you share a very small part of my daily reality—I hope that will suffice.   **posted by river @ 11:33 PM**

WILL WORK FOR FOOD . . .

Over 65% of the Iraqi population is unemployed. The reason for this is because Bremer made some horrible decisions. The first major decision he made was to dissolve the Iraqi army. That may make sense in Washington, but here, we were left speechless. Now there are over 400,000 trained, armed men with families that need to be fed. Where are they supposed to go? What are they supposed to do for a living? I don't know. They certainly don't know.

They roam the streets looking for work, looking for an answer. You can see perplexity and anger in their stance, their walk, their whole demeanor. Their eyes shift from face to face, looking for a clue. Who is to answer for this mess? Who do you think?

Bremer also dissolved the Ministry of Information and the Ministry of Defense. No matter what the excuses, these ministries were full of ordinary people with ordinary jobs—accountants, janitors, secretaries, engineers, journalists, technicians, operators . . . these people are now jobless. Companies have been asked to "cut down" their staff. It no longer has anything to do with politics. The company my uncle works in as an engineer was asked by the CPA to get rid of 680 of the 1,500+ employees—engineers, designers, contractors, mechanics, technicians, and the administration were all involved.

Other companies, firms, bureaus, factories, and shops shut down as a result of the looting and damage done in the post-war chaos— thousands of other workers lost their jobs. Where to go? What to do?

It isn't any easier for employed people . . . the standard $50 being given out in various ministries and hospitals is not nearly enough to support a single person, let alone a family. But at least it is work. At least it is a reason to wake up every morning and accomplish something.

Someone asked why the thousands of Iraqi men roaming the

streets don't go out and get work. For weeks, after the occupation, men would line up daily by the thousands outside of the "Alwiyah Club" filling out papers, begging for work. But there is no work. Men were reluctant to apply to the Iraqi police force because they weren't given weapons! The Iraqi police were expected to roam and guard the hellish cities without weapons . . . to stop looters, abductors, and murderers with the sheer force of an application to their warped sense of morality.

The story of how I lost my job isn't unique. It has actually become very common—despondently, depressingly, unbearably common. It goes like this . . .

I'm a computer science graduate. Before the war, I was working in an Iraqi database/software company located in Baghdad as a programmer/network administrator (yes, yes . . . a geek). Every day, I would climb three flights of stairs, enter the little office I shared with one female colleague and two males, start up my PC and spend hours staring at little numbers and letters rolling across the screen. It was tedious, it was back-breaking, it was geeky and it was . . . wonderful.

When I needed a break, I'd go visit my favorite sites on the internet, bother my colleagues, or rant about "impossible bosses" and "improbable deadlines."

I loved my job—I was *good* at my job. I came and went to work on my own. At 8 am I'd walk in lugging a backpack filled with enough CDs, floppies, notebooks, chewed-on pens, paperclips and screwdrivers to make Bill Gates proud. I made as much money as my two male colleagues and got an equal amount of respect from the manager (that was because he was clueless when it came to any type of programming and anyone who could do it was worthy of respect . . . a girl, no less—you get the picture).

What I'm trying to say is that no matter *what* anyone heard, females in Iraq were a lot better off than females in other parts of the Arab world (and some parts of the Western world—we had equal salaries!). We made up over 50% of the working force. We were doctors, lawyers, nurses, teachers, professors, deans, architects, programmers, and more. We came and went as we pleased. We wore what we wanted (within the boundaries of the social restrictions of a conservative society).

During the first week of June, I heard my company was back in business. It took several hours, seemingly thousands of family meetings, but I finally convinced everyone that it was necessary for my sanity to go back to work. They agreed that I would visit the company (with my two male bodyguards) and ask them if they had any work I could possibly take home and submit later on, or through the internet.

One fine day in mid-June, I packed my big bag of geeky wonders, put on my long skirt and shirt, tied back my hair and left the house with a mixture of anticipation and apprehension.

We had to park the car about 100 meters away from the door of the company because the major road in front of it was cracked and broken with the weight of the American tanks as they entered Baghdad. I half-ran, half-plodded up to the door of the company, my heart throbbing in anticipation of seeing friends, colleagues, secretaries . . . just generally something familiar again in the strange new nightmare we were living.

The moment I walked through the door, I noticed it. Everything looked shabbier somehow—sadder. The maroon carpet lining the hallways was dingy, scuffed and spoke of the burden of a thousand rushing feet. The windows we had so diligently taped prior to the war were cracked in some places and broken in others . . . dirty all over. The lights were shattered, desks overturned, doors kicked in, and clocks torn from the walls.

I stood a moment, hesitantly, in the door. There were strange new faces—fewer of the old ones. Everyone was standing around, looking at everyone else. The faces were sad and lethargic and exhausted. And I was one of the only females. I weaved through the strange mess and made my way upstairs, pausing for a moment on the second floor where management was located, to listen to the rising male voices. The director had died of a stroke during the second week of the war and suddenly, we had our own little "power vacuum." At least 20 different men thought they were qualified to be boss. Some thought they qualified because of experience, some because of rank, and some because they were being backed by differing political parties (SCIRI, Al-Daawa, INC).

I continued upstairs, chilled to the bone, in spite of the muggy heat of the building which hadn't seen electricity for at least 2 months. My little room wasn't much better off than the rest of the building. The desks were gone, papers all over the place . . . but A. was there! I couldn't believe it—a familiar, welcoming face. He looked at me for a moment, without really seeing me, then his eyes opened wide and disbelief took over the initial vague expression. He congratulated me on being alive, asked about my family and told me that he wasn't coming back after today. Things had changed. I should go home and stay safe. He was quitting—going to find work abroad. Nothing to do here anymore. I told him about my plan to work at home and submit projects . . . he shook his head sadly.

I stood staring at the mess for a few moments longer, trying to sort out the mess in my head, my heart being torn to pieces. My cousin and E. were downstairs waiting for me—there was nothing more to do, except ask how I could maybe help? A. and I left the room and started making our way downstairs. We paused on the second floor and stopped to talk to one of the former department directors. I asked him when they thought things would be functioning, he wouldn't look at me. His eyes stayed glued to A.'s face as he told him that females weren't welcome right now—especially females who "couldn't be protected." He finally turned to me and told me, in so many words, to go home because "they" refused to be responsible for what might happen to me.

Ok. Fine. Your loss. I turned my back, walked down the stairs and went to find E. and my cousin. Suddenly, the faces didn't look strange—they were the same faces of before, mostly, but there was a hostility I couldn't believe. What was I doing here? E. and the cousin were looking grim, I must have been looking broken, because they rushed me out of the first place I had ever worked and to the car. I cried bitterly all the way home—cried for my job, cried for my future and cried for the torn streets, damaged buildings and crumbling people.

I'm one of the lucky ones . . . I'm not important. I'm not vital. Over a month ago, a prominent electrical engineer (one of the smartest females in the country) named Henna Aziz was assassinated in front of her family—two daughters and her husband. She was threatened by some fundamentalists from Badir's Army and told to stay at home because she was a woman, she shouldn't be in charge. She refused—the country needed her expertise to get things functioning—she was brilliant. She would not and could not stay at home. They came to her house one evening: men with machine-guns, broke in and opened fire. She lost her life—she wasn't the first, she won't be the last. **posted by river @ 11:36 PM**

Tuesday, August 26, 2003

LET'S PLAY MUSICAL CHAIRS . . .

The nine-member rotating presidency is a failure at first sight. It's also a failure at second, third, fourth . . . and ninth sight. The members of the rotating presidency, composed of 4 Shi'a Muslims, 2 Sunni Muslims and 2 Kurds, were selected on a basis of ethnicity and religion.

It is a way of further dividing the Iraqi population. It is adding confusion to chaos and disorder. Just the concept of an ethnically and religiously selected council to run the country is repulsive. Are people supposed to take sides according to their ethnicity or religion? How, nine months down the line, are they going to select one president . . . or will we always have 9 presidents to govern the country? Does every faction of the Iraqi population need a separate representative? If they do, then why weren't the Christians represented? Why weren't the Turkomen represented? Would two more members to add to the nine really have made that big a difference?

The nine dancing puppets—excuse me, rotating presidents— were exclusively selected from the "Governing Council," an interim council chosen by the CPA. The first thing the 25-member Governing Council did to alienate itself from the people was the fatal decision to make April 9 the new Iraqi National Day. People were incredulous when Bahr Ul Iloom (one of the nine puppets) read out the announcement.

April 9, 2003 was a nightmare beyond anyone's power to describe. Baghdad was up in smoke that day—explosions everywhere, American troops crawling all over the city, fires, looting, fighting, and killing. Civilians were being evacuated from one area to the other, houses were being shot at by tanks, cars were being burned by Apache helicopters . . . Baghdad was full of death and destruction on April

9. Seeing tanks in your city, under any circumstance, is perturbing. Seeing foreign tanks in your capital is devastating.

But back to rotating presidents . . . Insiders say that all 9 members of the council hate each other. Meetings sometimes end in shouting, name-calling, and insults. The one thing they do agree on is that Bremer is God. His word is Scripture.

It was decided that each one of them would get a chance to govern their adoring Iraqi population a month. After several arguments and, I imagine, threats, ultimatums, and tantrums, it was decided that each one of the members would get their turn in alphabetical order (the Arabic alphabet).

So here is the cast of the most elaborate puppet show Iraq has ever seen (in order of appearance).

The Puppet: Ibraheim Al-Jaffari
56-year-old head of the Islamic Daawa Party who was living in Iran and London. The Al-Daawa Islamic Party debuted in 1958 as the most prominent Shi'a political movement. Al-Daawa "activists" learned their techniques from an extremist Iranian group known as "Fida'yeen El-Islam" and were distinctive for their use of explosives to make political statements. Universities, schools, and recreational centers were often targets.

Ibraheim Al-Jaffari makes me uncomfortable. He isn't very direct or coherent. He speaks in a suspiciously low voice and has a shifty gaze that never seems to settle on the camera.

The Puppet: Ahmad Al-Chalabi
This guy is a real peach. He is the head of the Iraqi National Congress and heavily backed by the Pentagon. He was a banker who embezzled millions from the Petra Bank in Jordan. My favorite part of his life story is how he escaped from Jordan in the trunk of a car . . . a modern-day Cleopatra, if you will. When asked if he thinks the war on Iraq was justified, even if WMD aren't found, he immediately (and rather huffily) replies, "Of course—*I* wouldn't be sitting here in Iraq if it weren't for the war . . ." As if he's God's gift to humanity. He's actually America's gift to the Iraqi people—the crowning glory of the war, chaos and occupation: the looter of all looters.

The Puppet: Iyad Allawi

A former Iraqi intelligence officer, and former Ba'ath member, who was sent to London on a scholarship from the former Ba'athist government. Rumor has it that when the scholarship ran out, he denounced his Ba'ath membership and formed the Iraqi National Accord [INA]. He has been living in London ever since 1971.

The Puppet: Jalal Talabani

Head of the Patriotic Union of Kurdistan (PUK). The PUK controls the southeastern part of the autonomous Kurdish area in the north. Scintillating rumor on the street: before he became a "leader," he had a nightclub in Turkey where he was running an illegitimate . . . umm . . . we'll call it an "escort service." The truth is that he is the rival of Massoud Berazani, the other leader in the autonomous Kurdish region, and their rivalry would often lead to bloodshed between their supporters. His famous quote: "Politics is a whore."

The Puppet: Abdul Aziz Al-Hakim

Deputy leader of SCIRI (Supreme Council of the Islamic Revolution in Iraq). He has been in Iran for decades and is the commander of "Badir's Army," or what is also known as the Badir Brigade—responsible for a lot of the post-war chaos. The frightening thing is that there are rumors of negotiations between SCIRI and the CPA about allowing the Brigade to be in charge of "security" in some regions.

The Puppet: Adnan Al-Pachichi

A Sunni Arab who is—brace yourself—81 years old (some say it's 84). He was foreign minister for 2 years in the '60s. My grandfather remembers him *vaguely*. I'm sorry, but he just looks too weary to be running Iraq. It will be amazing if he makes it to elections. He has been outside of Iraq ever since the late '60s and seems to know as little about modern Iraq as the Iraqis know about him.

The Puppet: Mohsen Abdul Hamid

The secretary of the Islamic Party—a Sunni fundamentalist Islamic group (a branch of the Islamic Brotherhood). Yet another fundamentalist group, but this one was chosen to keep the Sunni fundamentalists quiet.

The Puppet: Mohammed Bahr Ul Iloom

Otherwise known as "Mohammed Bahr Ul—who???" Very few people seem to have heard of him. He is a Shi'a Muslim cleric who fled Iraq in 1991. He was in exile in London. He is also in his 80s and his only political qualification seems to be the fact that he fled and considered himself in exile. He promptly squelched any chance he had at gaining popularity by being the one selected to declare April 9 the Iraqi National Day.

The Puppet: Massoud Berazani

The head of the Kurdistan Democratic Party and rival of Jalal Talabani. He was backed by the US in north Iraq. His conflicts with Talabani have resulted in the deaths of thousands of Kurds in bloody battles and assassinations and the exile of others. To see them sitting at the same table, staring adoringly at "Father Bremer," you would think they had always been the best of friends—it's a fascinating lesson in politics. A question poses itself: if they couldn't control a few provinces in the north, how do they expect to be able to govern all of Iraq?

The two Kurdish leaders also control an armed militia known as "Bayshmarga." The Bayshmarga are multitalented. They act as bodyguards, and smugglers. They were caught smuggling cars, currency and artifacts. These last two days there have been clashes between them and the Turkomen in Kirkuk.

The most infuriating thing is hearing Bremer talk about how the members of the rotating presidency represent the Iraqi people. In reality, they represent the CPA and Bremer. They are America's Puppets (some of them are Iran's). They do not govern Iraq or Iraqis in any way—they are merely very highly paid translators: Bremer gives the orders and they translate them to an incredulous public. The majority of them were trained using American tax dollars, and now they are being "kept" by the CPA using Iraqi oil money.

It's a bad start to democracy, being occupied and having your government and potential leaders selected for you by the occupying powers . . . On the other hand, could we really expect more from a country whose president was "appointed" by the Supreme Court?
posted by river @ 9:33 PM

NATIONAL DAY

For me, April 9 was a blur of faces distorted with fear, horror, and tears. All over Baghdad you could hear shelling, explosions, clashes, fighter planes, the dreaded Apaches and the horrifying tanks heaving down streets and highways. Whether you loved Saddam or hated him, Baghdad tore you to pieces. Baghdad was burning. Baghdad was exploding . . . Baghdad was falling. April 9 is the American Occupation Day. I can understand why Bush was celebrating—I can't understand how anyone who values independence would celebrate it.

April 9, I woke to the sound of a huge explosion at around 6 am, only 2 hours after I had fallen into a fitful sleep. I was sitting up stiff in bed, even before I had my eyes open. The room was warm, but I sat in bed, still in my jeans of the night before, my teeth chattering, clutching at the covers, groping my consciousness for sanity.

We had been sleeping in our clothes for the last few nights with pockets stuffed with identification papers and money because we kept expecting the house to come crumbling down around us . . . we wanted to be out the door as soon as it was necessary.

I listened to the noise that had become as common as crickets in the summer—the constant drone of helicopters and fighter planes . . . explosions and shelling.

We spent the early hours of that morning watching each other silently and solemnly—the only human voice in our midst was coming from the radio, crackling and fading. It told us what we already knew—what we had been dreading for what felt like an eternity—the American tanks were in Baghdad. There had been some resistance, but the tanks were all over Baghdad.

And that was the start of "National Day" . . .

April 9 was a day of harried neighbors banging on the door, faces so contorted with anxiety they were almost beyond recognition. "Do we leave? Do we evacuate?! They sound so close . . ."

It was a day of shocked, horrified relatives, with dilated pupils and trembling lips, dragging duffel bags, spouses and terrified children needing shelter. All of us needing comfort that no one could give.

It was the day we sat at home, bags packed, fully dressed, listening for the tanks or the missile that would send us flying out of the house and into the streets. We sat calculating the risks of traveling from one end of Baghdad to the other or staying in our area and waiting for the inevitable.

It was the day I had to have "the talk" with my mother. The day she sat me down in front of her and began giving me "instructions"— just in case.

"In case of what, mom?"

"In case something happens to us . . ."

"Like what, like maybe we get separated?"

"Fine, ok. Yes. Separated, for example . . . you know where the money is, you know where the papers are . . ."

Yes, I know. But it won't matter if anything happens to you, or dad, or E.

It was a day of stray dogs howling in the streets with fear, flocks of birds flying chaotically in the sky—trying to escape the horrible noises and smoke.

It was a day of charred bodies in blackened vehicles.

It was a grayish-yellow day that burns red in my memory . . . a day that easily rises to the surface when I contemplate the most horrible days of my life.

That was the "National Day" for me. From most accounts, it was the same for millions of others.

Maybe come April 9, 2004, Bremer and the Governing Council can join Bush in the White House to celebrate the fall of Baghdad . . . because we certainly won't be celebrating it here.
posted by river @ 9:41 PM

Thursday, August 28, 2003

THE OPPOSITE DIRECTION

The Scene: Family Living Room
The Mood: Gloomy
We were sitting around—two families . . . ours and my uncle's. Adults were sitting neatly on couches and us "kids" sprawled out on the cool "kashi" (tiles) on the floor, watching tv. Everyone was feeling

depressed because we had just seen Nada Domani (head of the Red Cross in Iraq) telling the world they had decided to pull out some of their personnel and send them to Jordan because they were expecting attacks.

I am praying that whoever tipped them off was very wrong. Who would attack the Red Cross? Everyone needs the Red Cross . . . The Red Cross isn't simply administering aid in the form of medication or food, they are acting as mediators between the POWs and detainees and the CPA. Before the Red Cross got involved, the families of the detainees knew nothing about them. During raids or at checkpoints, people would be detained (mainly men and boys) and they would simply disappear. Relatives of the detainees would stand for hours in front of the hotels where there were American security authorities begging for some information—some clue—as to where they could find a father, an uncle, a son . . .

What will we do without the Red Cross?

So we were sitting there, trying to figure out what was happening, what was becoming of the whole situation, when I suddenly muted the tv—I heard a voice calling E.'s name from outside. E. immediately got up, picked up the loaded gun and stuck it in his jeans in the back. We went to the kitchen to see what/who it was. E. opened the screen door and stepped outside while I stuck my face to the glass, trying to see out into the dark.

It was our neighbor—R. All I could see was his head, looking at us over the wall that separated our gardens. "Are you watching Al-Jazeera??? You should watch it!" And his head disappeared once more behind the wall. That's it? That's all? You don't call out a person's name, at night—in post-war Iraq, to tell them to watch Al-Jazeera . . . someone remind me to raise the wall.

On Al-Jazeera was the program "Al-Itijah Al-Mu3akis," or "The Opposite Direction." For non-Arabs, it's a program that takes up political and social issues important in the Middle East and has two guests attacking the issues from opposite directions. The viewers get to comment by phone and email and there's also a vote as to which speaker they think is doing better.

The surprise wasn't the issue which was us, Iraq, as usual. The surprise was one of the guest speakers—Intifadh Qambar—second man after Ahmad Al-Chalabi and spokesman for the INC! The moment Qambar's hard, sly face appeared on the screen, the gloomy living room lit up with hoots, howls, clapping, and whistling. He brings mirth to many Iraqis.

Only an Arab can fully appreciate Qambar. I guess, since he's spokesman, he's supposed to be the "diplomat" of the INC. He was there to represent the rotating presidents and the Governing Council. He was their downfall—Ahmad Al-Chalabi should kill himself.

He sat stiff, in a suit that was a shade of brown similar to that of caked, dry mustard. He wore a white shirt, a black, yellow-striped tie and fluorescent yellow handkerchief with charming black spots. His hair was greased back with something or another to show a broad, furrowed brow over tiny, hard eyes. He did not look like he was on some political talk show—he looked like he was being persecuted.

He sat for over an hour, taking a verbal beating from just about everyone who called (including Iraqis)—being called a thief, a traitor, an Americanized thug, a murderer, and some other terms almost as colorful as his tie. His "defense" of the council was worse than the actual accusations being thrown at him. He more or less said that the whole war was justified, the sanctions were justified, America was justified, and what did it matter how many people died during the sanctions? What did it matter how many people were dying now? Saddam was gone—the council was here—that was all that mattered. And all this in a shrill, ugly voice. After he finishes something he imagines particularly clever, he ends up looking smug and haughty.

The other guest speaker (editor of Al-Quds Al-Arabi newspaper) was astounded, to say the least. He just looked at him like he couldn't believe this guy was being sent to represent the new government. If this was the "smooth talker" of the group, we are in a lot of trouble.

Qambar has no political or cultural scruples. He stoops to vulgarity when he can find no legitimate argument. During one debate on Abu Dhabi tv, he was arguing with another politician named Wamidh Nadhmi. Now, Wamidh Nadhmi is an old respected man who is neither Baathist nor loyalist. In fact, he used to speak against Saddam and the whole government long before the war. He was against the war as a way of regime change and against the occupation—that was the whole argument. So after an hour of futilely arguing that the

Americans were right and everyone was wrong, Qambar started getting insulting. Wamidh kept his cool but told Qambar that Ahmad Al-Chalabi was a crook and any group being led by someone so infamous was bound to be a failure . . . suddenly Qambar jumped up and *attacked* Wamidh on tv! I'm serious—he attacked the man. The poor presenter, Jassim Al-Azzawi, found himself caught in the middle of a scuffle being fought over his head, and as he tried to separate them, he kept screaming "What is this?! Gentlemen . . . what is this?!" So you can see why we enjoy Qambar (almost as much as Al-Chalabi).

So what are the options? The options to people like that are Iraqis who were living with the people, inside of Iraq. Iraqis who were *not* affiliated with Saddam, but also not affiliated with the CIA. Bush was wrong when he said, "You are either with us or against us." The world isn't in black and white—there are plenty of people who were against this war, but also against Saddam. They aren't being given a chance. Their voices aren't heard because they weren't in Washington or London or Teheran [Tehran].

There are intelligent, cultured people—professors, historians, linguists, lawyers, doctors, engineers in Iraq who can contribute to running the country. They understand the Iraqi mentality after over a decade of sanctions and three different wars—they know what the people want to hear and what needs to be done . . . they are competent. They aren't acceptable to the CPA because it can't be sure of their "loyalty" to America. The Puppet Council is perfect because they were brought in on American tanks, they were installed using American force—they can be rooted out if—or when—it becomes necessary . . .

There's a famous Arabic saying: "Al ba3*lu bayn al 7ameer raka9*" which basically means—"A camel in the midst of donkeys is a fast runner." It is said to describe someone who is considered "the best of a bad bunch." If Qambar and Chalabi are the camels of the INC (perhaps of the whole council), I wonder what the donkeys are like . . . **posted by river @ 1:48 AM**

THE PROMISE AND THE THREAT

The Myth: Iraqis, prior to occupation, lived in little beige tents set up on the sides of little dirt roads all over Baghdad. The men and boys would ride to school on their camels, donkeys, and goats. These schools were larger versions of the home units and for every 100 students, there was one turban-wearing teacher who taught the boys rudimentary math (to count the flock) and reading. Girls and women sat at home, in black burkas, making bread and taking care of 10-12 children.

The Truth: Iraqis lived in houses with running water and electricity. Thousands of them own computers. Millions own VCRs and VCDs. Iraq has sophisticated bridges, recreational centers, clubs, restaurants, shops, universities, schools, etc. Iraqis love fast cars (especially German cars) and the Tigris is full of little motor boats that are used for everything from fishing to water-skiing.

I guess what I'm trying to say is that most people choose to ignore the little prefix "re" in the words "rebuild" and "reconstruct." For your information, "re" is of Latin origin and generally means "again" or "anew."

In other words—there was something there in the first place. We have hundreds of bridges. We have one of the most sophisticated network of highways in the region: you can get from Busrah, in the south, to Mosul, in the north, without once having to travel upon those little, dusty, dirt roads they show you on Fox News. We had a communications system so advanced, it took the Coalition of the Willing 3 rounds of bombing, on 3 separate nights, to damage the Ma'moun Communications Tower and silence our telephones.

Yesterday, I read how it was going to take up to $90 billion to rebuild Iraq. Bremer was shooting out numbers about how much it was going to cost to replace buildings and bridges and electricity, etc.

Listen to this little anecdote. One of my cousins works in a prominent engineering company in Baghdad—we'll call the company H. This company is well-known for designing and building bridges all over Iraq. My cousin, a structural engineer, is a bridge freak. He spends hours talking about pillars and trusses and steel structures to anyone who'll listen.

As May was drawing to a close, his manager told him that someone from the CPA wanted the company to estimate the building costs of replacing the New Diyala Bridge on the South East end of Baghdad. He got his team together, they went out and assessed the damage, decided it wasn't too extensive, but it would be costly. They did the necessary tests and analyses (mumblings about soil composition and water depth, expansion joints and girders) and came up with a number they tentatively put forward—$300,000. This included new plans and designs, raw materials (quite cheap in Iraq), labor, contractors, travel expenses, etc.

Let's pretend my cousin is a dolt. Let's pretend he hasn't been working with bridges for over 17 years. Let's pretend he didn't work on replacing at least 20 of the 133 bridges damaged during the first Gulf War. Let's pretend he's wrong and the cost of rebuilding this bridge is four times the number they estimated—let's pretend it will actually cost $1,200,000. Let's just use our imagination.

A week later, the New Diyala Bridge contract was given to an American company. This particular company estimated the cost of rebuilding the bridge would be around—brace yourselves—$50,000,000!!

Something you should know about Iraq: we have over 130,000 engineers. More than half of these engineers are structural engineers and architects. Thousands of them were trained outside of Iraq in Germany, Japan, America, Britain, and other countries. Thousands of others worked with some of the foreign companies that built various bridges, buildings, and highways in Iraq. The majority of them are more than proficient—some of them are brilliant.

Iraqi engineers had to rebuild Iraq after the first Gulf War in 1991 when the "Coalition of the Willing" was composed of over 30 countries actively participating in bombing Baghdad beyond recognition. They had to cope with rebuilding bridges and buildings that were originally built by foreign companies, they had to get around a lack of raw materials that we used to import from abroad, they had to work around a vicious blockade designed to damage whatever infrastructure was left after the war . . . they truly had to rebuild Iraq. And everything had to be made sturdy, because, well, we were always under the threat of war.

Over a hundred of the 133 bridges were rebuilt, hundreds of buildings and factories were replaced, communications towers were rebuilt, new bridges were added, electrical power grids were replaced . . . things were functioning. Everything wasn't perfect—but we were working on it.

And Iraqis aren't easy to please. Buildings cannot just be made functionary. They have to have artistic touches—a carved pillar, an intricately designed dome, something unique . . . not necessarily classy or subtle, but different. You can see it all over Baghdad—fashionable homes with plate glass windows, next to classic old "Baghdadi" buildings, gaudy restaurants standing next to classy little cafes . . . mosques with domes so colorful and detailed they look like glamorous Faberge eggs . . . all done by Iraqis.

My favorite reconstruction project was the Mu'alaq Bridge over the Tigris. It is a suspended bridge that was designed and built by a British company. In 1991 it was bombed and everyone just about gave up on ever being able to cross it again. By 1994, it was up again, exactly as it was—without British companies, with Iraqi expertise. One of the art schools decided that although it wasn't the most sophisticated bridge in the world, it was going to be the most glamorous. On the day it was opened to the public, it was covered with hundreds of painted flowers in the most outrageous colors—all over the pillars, the bridge itself, the walkways along the sides of the bridge. People came from all over Baghdad just to stand upon it and look down into the Tigris.

So instead of bringing in thousands of foreign companies that are going to want billions of dollars, why aren't the Iraqi engineers, electricians, and laborers being taken advantage of? Thousands of people who have no work would love to be able to rebuild Iraq . . . no one is being given a chance.

The reconstruction of Iraq is held above our heads like a promise and a threat. People roll their eyes at reconstruction because they know (Iraqis are wily) that these dubious reconstruction projects are going to plunge the country into a national debt only comparable to that of America. A few already rich contractors are going to get richer, Iraqi workers are going to be given a pittance and the unemployed Iraqi public can stand on the sidelines and look at the glamorous buildings being built by foreign companies.

I always say this war is about oil. It is. But it is also about huge corporations that are going to make billions off of reconstructing what was damaged during this war. Can you say Haliburton? (which, by the way, got the very first contracts to replace the damaged oil infra-structure and put out "oil fires" way back in April).

Well, of course it's going to take uncountable billions to rebuild Iraq, Mr. Bremer, if the contracts are all given to foreign companies! Or perhaps the numbers are this frightening because Ahmad Al-Chalabi is the one doing the books—he *is* the math expert, after all. **posted by river @ 6:46 PM**

Friday, August 29, 2003

CHAOS

"[Iraq] is not a country in chaos and Baghdad is not a city in chaos."
—Paul Bremer ("Iraq "Needs Tens of Billions"," BBC News, August 27, 2003, http://news.bbc.co.uk/1/hi/world/middle_east/3183979 .stm)

Where is this guy living? Is he even in the same time zone??? I'm incredulous . . . maybe he's from some alternate universe where shooting, looting, tanks, rape, abductions, and assassinations aren't considered chaos, but it's chaos in *my* world.

Ever since the occupation there have been 400 females abducted in Baghdad alone and that is only the number of recorded abductions. Most families don't go to the Americans to tell about an abduction because they know it's useless. The male members of the family take it upon themselves to search for the abducted female and get revenge if they find the abductors. What else is there to do? I know if I were abducted I'd much rather my family organize themselves and look for me personally than go to the CPA.

By BBC's accounts there are 70 cars a day being hijacked in Baghdad alone . . .

And now we've just had some shocking news—Mohammed Baqir Al-Hakim was assassinated in the holy city of Najaf! Mohammed Baqir Al-Hakim was the head of SCIRI (Supreme Council of the Islamic Revolution in Iraq). They don't know who was behind it, but many believe it is one of the other Shi'a religious factions. There has been some tension between Al-Sadir's followers and Al-Hakim's followers. Another cleric, Al-Sistani, also had some interesting things to say against Al-Hakim . . .

What most people choose to forget is the fact that the Shi'a in the south lost hundreds of thousands of lives to the war against Iran—fighting the very regime that is backing SCIRI now—the Islamic Revolution in Teheran. Al-Hakim does have a strong backing from many Shi'a fundamentalists sympathetic with Iran, true enough, but he also has people who hate him (and Badir's Brigade) with a vengeance.

I hated this guy for what he represented—a puppet and a supporter of a fundamentalist Islamic government, but this wasn't the way to deal with it. This is going to result in more bloodshed and fighting. He is the second Shi'a cleric to be assassinated in Najaf—the first was Al-Kho'i who also came from Teheran (back in April).   **posted by river @ 6:40 PM**

Saturday, August 30, 2003

POSITION OPEN

Everyone is still discussing the death of Al-Hakim. Al-Hakim isn't particularly popular with moderate Shi'a. One of my cousins, and his wife, are Shi'a and when he heard the news, he just shrugged his shoulders and said he didn't like him much anyway—power-hungry clerics (of any religion) make people nervous, I guess. No one I know personally seems very traumatized with his death, but everyone is horrified with the number of casualties. 126 people dead and over 300 wounded—some of them dying.

They're saying on the news that they've caught the assassins who set up the bomb—supposedly some branch of Al-Qaeda currently functioning from Iraq (they too were "liberated").

A political analyst in Iraq says that there's a chance some of Al-Hakim's followers were actually involved in the bombing. That *would* explain how 700 kg of explosives found their way through his literal army (Badir's Brigade) and next to his black SUV. The analyst said that there were many prominent members of SCIRI who had turned against Al-Hakim ever since his return from Iran. It seems that upon his return "home" he decided to change the game plan and some of his followers didn't like the new arrangements—namely, his brother on the council. On the other hand, it is hard to believe that any Islamic group would engineer such a vicious attack at one of the holiest religious sites in Iraq—the shrine of Imam Ali.

An interesting development on the much-shaken puppet council—Bahr Ul Uloom has suspended his membership in the council. The elderly cleric claimed, in an interview, that America was doing such a bad job of keeping the Iraqi people secure, he didn't want to be a part of the council anymore. I wonder if he's going to return to London. That makes a council of only 8 members now . . . we need a new nominee otherwise we will have four months of the year without leadership. Maybe if Bush doesn't get re-elected, Bremer will give the position to him. Love to have him in Baghdad . . . **posted by river @ 11:43 PM**

ROAD TRIP

My brother, E., was out at 8 am this morning getting gasoline for the car. He came home at 12 pm in a particularly foul mood. He had waited in line of angry, hostile Iraqis for 3 hours. Gasoline lines drive people crazy because, prior to the war, the price of gasoline in Iraq was ridiculously low. A liter of gasoline (unleaded) cost around 20 Iraqi dinars when one US dollar equaled 2,000 Iraqi dinars. In other words, 1 liter of gasoline cost one cent! A liter of bottled water cost more than gasoline. Not only does it cost more now, but it isn't easy to get. I think they're importing gasoline from Saudi Arabia and Turkey.

We (a cousin, his wife, my mom and I) dragged E. out of the house, at 12:30 to go visit my aunt on the other end of the city. We heard the usual instructions before we left—stop at checkpoints, return before dark, and if anyone wants the car, give them the keys—don't argue, don't fight it.

The moment I had a foot out the door, the heat almost forced me back inside. Our sun, at noon, isn't a heavenly body—it's a physical assault. I could swear that at noon, in Iraq, the sun shuts out the rest of the world from its glory and concentrates its energies on us. Everything looks like it's traveling on waves of heat—even the date palms look limp with the exhaustion of survival.

We climbed into a battered, old, white 1984 Volkswagen—people are avoiding using "nice" cars that might tempt hijackers ("nice" is anything made after 1990). I mentally debated putting on sun glasses but decided against it—no need to attract any undue attention. I said a little prayer to keep us safe as I rummaged around in my bag, checking for my "weapon." I can't stand carrying a pistol so I carry around a big, red, switchblade hunting knife—you don't want to mess with Riverbend . . .

Being out in the streets is like being caught in a tornado. You have to be alert and ready for anything every moment. I sat in the backseat, squinting into the sun, trying to determine if a particular face was that of a looter, or abductor, or just another angry countryman. I craned my neck looking at the blue SUV, trying to remember if it had been behind us for the last kilometer or longer. I held my breath nervously every time the cousin slowed down the car because of traffic, willing the cars in front of us to get a move on.

I caught site of two men fighting. A crowd was beginning to gather and a few people were caught in the middle, trying to separate them. My cousin clucked angrily and started mumbling about ignorant people and how all we needed, on top of occupation, was hostility. E. told us not to keep staring and anxiously felt for the pistol under his seat.

The ride that took 20 minutes pre-war Iraq took 45 minutes today. There were major roads completely cut off by tanks. Angry troops stood cutting off access to the roads around the palaces (which were once Saddam's but are now America's palaces). The cousin and E. debated alternative routes at every checkpoint or roadblock. I stayed silent because I don't even know the city anymore. Now, areas are identified as "the one with the crater where the missile exploded," or "the street with the ravaged houses," or "the little house next to that one where that family was killed."

The looting and killing of today has changed from the looting and killing in April. In April, it was quite random. Criminals were working alone. Now they're more organized than the CPA (Coalition Provisional Authority) and the troops combined. No one works alone anymore—they've created gangs and armed militias. They pull up to houses in minivans and SUVs, armed with machine-guns and sometimes grenades. They barge into the house and demand money and gold. If they don't find enough, they abduct a child or female and ask for ransom. Sometimes the whole family is killed—sometimes only the male members of the family are killed.

For a while, the men in certain areas began arranging "lookouts." They would gather, every 6 or 7 guys, in a street, armed with Klashnikovs, and watch out for the whole area. They would stop strange cars and ask them what family they were there to visit. Hundreds of looters were caught that way—we actually felt safe for a brief period. Then the American armored cars started patrolling the safer residential areas, ordering the men off the streets—telling them that if they were seen carrying a weapon, they would be treated as criminals.

Most of the gangs, at least the ones in Baghdad, originate from slums on the outskirts of the city. "Al-Sadir City" is a huge, notorious slum with a population of around 1.5 million. The whole place is terrifying. If you lose a car or a person, you will most likely find them there. Every alley is controlled by a different gang and weapons are sold in the streets . . . they'll even try out that machine-gun you have your eye on, if you pay enough. Americans don't bother raiding the houses in areas like that . . . raids are exclusively for decent people who can't shoot back or attack. Raids are for the poor people in Ramadi, Ba'aquba, and Mosul.

By the time we got to my aunt's house, every muscle in my body was aching. My eyes were burning with the heat and the strain. E.'s brow was furrowed with the scenes we had left behind us on the street and the cousin's hands were shaking almost imperceptibly—knuckles still white with tension. My mother said a prayer of gratitude for our safe arrival and the cousin's wife, T., swore she wasn't going to leave my aunt's house for another three days and if we planned to go home today, we could do so without her because God needed to look out for other people today, not just us . . . **posted by river @ 11:45 PM**

Sunday, August 31, 2003

MADE ME LAUGH . . .

One of the readers of the blog (you know who you are) led me to this page and I've been laughing at it for the last 5 minutes—I am forever grateful! To access the page, type "Weapons of mass destruction" in the google.com search and click the "I'm Feeling Lucky" bar. Read the standard-looking error page CAREFULLY!

ⓘ These Weapons of Mass Destruction cannot be displayed

The weapons you are looking for are currently unavailable. The country might be experiencing technical difficulties, or you may need to adjust your weapons inspectors mandate.

Please try the following:

- Click the 🔁 Regime change button, or try again later.
- If you are George Bush and typed the country's name in the address bar, make sure that it is spelled correctly. (IRAQ).
- To check your weapons inspector settings, click the **UN** menu, and then click **Weapons Inspector Options**. On the **Security Council** tab, click **Consensus**. The settings should match those provided by your government or NATO.
- If the Security Council has enabled it, The United States of America can examine your country and automatically discover Weapons of Mass Destruction.
  If you would like to use the CIA to try and discover them, click 🔍 Detect weapons
- Some countries require 128 thousand troops to liberate them. Click the **Panic** menu and then click **About US foreign policy** to determine what regime they will install.
- If you are an Old European Country trying to protect your interests, make sure your options are left wide open as long as possible. Click the **Tools** menu, and then click on **League of Nations**. On the Advanced tab, scroll to the Head in the Sand section and check settings for your exports to Iraq.
- Click the 💣 Bomb button if you are Donald Rumsfeld.

Cannot find weapons or CIA Error
Iraqi Explorer
Bush went to Iraq to look for Weapons of Mass Destruction and all he found was this lousy T-shirt.

posted by river @ 12:01 AM

Monday, September 01, 2003

BLOG FIGHTS . . .

Sorry to disappoint, but it's not going to be much of a blog fight because I agree with most of what you say, Salam, though not all of it.

Salam Pax, http://dear_raed.blogspot.com/, August 31, 2003

> *Today we shall have a world premier. An Iraqi blog-fight. Roll up your sleeves Riverbend, let's talk about Al-Hakim's death.*
>
> *Look regardless of what he stood for and the fact that he and his party are very good buddies with Iran, the significance and the gravity of what happened is not to be overlooked. I agree with you, if SCIRI had its way we would end up as an Iran clone. But he is a religious leader, he is a "Marji'I," and at least for the moment they are playing by the rules. They are adopting a more lenient line, they talk about a constitution . . .*

Al-Hakim's assassination is very significant, you're right. It will be used as an excuse for vendettas, faction fighting, and more violence between Shi'a and Shi'a and Sunnis and Shi'a. Already his followers are swearing to avenge his death and I shudder to think of the next group of victims. It is extremely frightening to think of what the consequences of this will be.

People are blaming America because a. America is responsible for the security of this country—when you dissolve the army and pull down the police force, *you* become responsible and, b. there is a sense that the CPA is furthering the divide between Iraqis by encouraging and emphasizing religious, factional and ethnic differences. I know more about the different factions after this war than I ever knew and it's the same thing with everyone else. This heightened awareness is the result of labeling people as either "Arab Sunni" or "Shi"a Turkoman," or "Assyrian Christian" . . . you *have* to belong somewhere now—you can't just be a Kurd or Christian or Muslim or simply an *Iraqi*.

People believe that the ancient "divide and conquer" is being employed. Instead of having Iraqis, Shi'a and Sunnis and Christians, united in a struggle (peaceful or otherwise) against occupation, it's easier to have Iraqis fighting each other. The resulting sentiment will be that occupation forces are not only desirable, but that they are vital for "keeping the peace." I'm not blaming Americans, specifically— it's the oldest trick in the book. The British attempted it before them (factional differences), and the Ottomans practiced it for hundreds of years (ethnical differences).

And no, people—don't bother writing that email telling me to "stop blaming America" and why can't " . . . you mozlem freaks get your act together and stop killin' eachother . . ." Every society has its extremists and every nation has its potential for civil war. When there's no law and order, people will do strange and horrible things.

You don't know how hard I pray that we, as a people, are above religious differences. I seriously hope that this was done, as they are claiming, by Al-Qaeda or some outside forces because it will be horribly disappointing to see that after hundreds of years of putting religious differences aside, various groups of thugs and fanatics will be able to reap the benefits of even more chaos and killing. **posted by river @ 11:37 PM**

PUPPET OF THE MONTH

Today, September 1, 2003, is an important day. Ahmad Al-Chalabi has finally achieved the epitome of his political aspirations. All the years of embezzlement, conniving, and scheming have paid off: he is the current rotating president. He has officially begun his "presidential term."

To be quite honest, I've been waiting for this. I watch all his interviews and read any article I can get in an attempt to comprehend what hidden charms, or buried astuteness, made the Pentagon decide to so diligently push him forth as a potential leader. If I didn't know any better, I'd say he was some sort of elaborate, inside joke in Washington: "We're blighted with Bush—you deserve no better."

So I sat around waiting for an interview on Al-Jazeera. They said it would be on at 6:05 Baghdad time—I began watching at 6:00. I had to wait, impatiently, a full 20 minutes before he made his appearance, but it was worth it. He sat, wearing a black suit, striped shirt, and black tie. He was polished, and smug.

The interview, like most of his interviews, began well. He showed appropriate solemnity when asked about his views on the assassination of Al-Hakim. The smug look vanished from his face momentarily. When the reporter asked him who he thought was behind the assassination, he shrewdly narrowed it down to: extremists, loyalists, terrorists, Ba'athists, and people from neighboring countries.

The Governing Council, though, was a touchy subject. When asked about just how much power the Governing Council actually had, he immediately began foaming and spluttering—claiming they had all the power to govern Iraq. So the wily reporter asked about the American presence in Iraq—how long would it take for them to leave? Al-Chalabi instantaneously stated that the American presence in Iraq was completely in the hands of the Iraqis, like himself, and that Bremer had told them that if they wanted the Americans out, they would be out tomorrow!

When asked if he would nominate himself for "president" come elections, he denied having any political ambition and claimed he was there "to help the Iraqi people" (like he helped the Jordanian people?!).

He blamed the neighboring countries for any terrorism going on in Iraq. He said they should "close all the borders" because the Iraqi army couldn't currently secure its own border (apparently someone forgot to send him the memo about dissolving the army). I wish the reporter had posed the following question: Mr. Chalabi, if the neighboring countries close their borders, how will you make your stunning, historical flight in the trunk of a car when it becomes necessary?

I was a bit disappointed with it all. For the last week, I was anticipating some sort of . . . I don't know—elaborate inauguration ceremony? No, not really . . . maybe more of a festivity, worthy of the solemn occasion, marking his ascent to power. A circus-themed gala, perhaps, where Bremer can play the ring-master and Chalabi can jump through red, white, and blue hoops to mark this historical day. Qambar can serve the cocktails . . . **posted by river @ 11:40 PM**

HAVE YOU FORGOTTEN?

September 11 was a tragedy. Not because 3,000 Americans died . . . but because 3,000 humans died. I was reading about the recorded telephone conversations of victims and their families on September 11. I thought it was . . . awful, and perfectly timed. Just when people are starting to question the results and incentives behind this occupation, they are immediately bombarded with reminders of September 11. Never mind Iraq had nothing to do with it.

I get emails constantly reminding me of the tragedy of September 11 and telling me how the "Arabs" brought all of this upon themselves. Never mind it was originally blamed on Afghanistan (who, for your information, aren't Arabs).

I am constantly reminded of the 3,000 Americans who died that day . . . and asked to put behind me the 8,000 worthless Iraqis we lost to missiles, tanks and guns.

People marvel that we're not out in the streets, decking the monstrous, khaki tanks with roses and jasmine. They wonder why we don't crown the hard, ugly helmets of the troops with wreaths of laurel. They question why we mourn our dead instead of gratefully offering them as sacrifices to the Gods of Democracy and Liberty. They wonder why we're bitter.

But, I *haven't* forgotten . . .

I remember February 13, 1991. I remember the missiles dropped on Al-Amriyah shelter—a civilian bomb shelter in a populated, residential area in Baghdad. Bombs so sophisticated, that the first one drilled through to the heart of the shelter and the second one exploded inside. The shelter was full of women and children—boys over the age of 15 weren't allowed. I remember watching images of horrified people clinging to the fence circling the shelter, crying, screaming, begging to know what had happened to a daughter, a mother, a son, a family that had been seeking protection within the shelter's walls.

I remember watching them drag out bodies so charred, you couldn't tell they were human. I remember frantic people, running from corpse to corpse, trying to identify a loved-one . . . I remember seeing Iraqi aid workers, cleaning out the shelter, fainting with the unbearable scenes inside. I remember the whole area reeked with the smell of burnt flesh for weeks and weeks after.

I remember visiting the shelter, years later, to pay my respects to the 400+ people who died a horrible death during the small hours of the morning and seeing the ghostly outlines of humans plastered on the walls and ceilings.

I remember a family friend who lost his wife, his five-year-old daughter, his two-year-old son, and his mind on February 13.

I remember the day the Pentagon, after making various excuses, claimed it had been a "mistake."

I remember 13 years of sanctions, backed firmly by the US and UK, in the name of WMD nobody ever found. Sanctions so rigid, we had basic necessities, like medicine, on waiting lists for months and months before they were refused. I remember chemicals like chlorine, necessary for water purification, being scrutinized and delayed at the expense of millions of people.

I remember having to ask aid workers, and visiting activists, to "please bring a book" because publishing companies refused to sell scientific books and journals to Iraq. I remember having to "share" books with other students in college in an attempt to make the most of the limited resources.

I remember wasted, little bodies in huge hospital beds—dying of hunger and of disease; diseases that could easily be treated with medications that were "forbidden." I remember parents with drawn faces peering anxiously into doctors' eyes, searching for a miracle.

I remember the depleted uranium. How many have heard of depleted uranium? Those are household words to Iraqi people. The depleted uranium weapons used in 1991 (and possibly this time too) have resulted in a damaged environment and an astronomical rise in the cancer rate in Iraq. I remember seeing babies born with a single eye, 3 legs, or no face—a result of DU [depleted uranium] poisoning.

I remember dozens of dead in the "no fly zones," bombed by British and American planes claiming to "protect" the north and south of Iraq. I remember the mother, living on the outskirts of Mosul, who lost her husband and 5 kids when an American plane bombed the father and his sons in the middle of a field of peaceful, grazing sheep.

And we are to believe that this is all being done for the sake of the people.

"Have you forgotten how it felt that day
To see your homeland under fire
And her people blown away?"

No . . . we haven't forgotten—the tanks are still here to remind us.

A friend of E.'s, who lives in Amiriyah, was telling us about an American soldier he had been talking to in the area. E's friend pointed to the shelter and told him of the atrocity committed in 1991. The soldier turned with the words, "Don't blame me—I was only 9!" And I was only 11.

American long-term memory is exclusive to American traumas. The rest of the world should simply "put the past behind," "move forward," "be pragmatic," and "get over it."

Someone asked me whether it was true that the "Iraqi people were dancing in the streets of Baghdad" when the World Trade Center fell. Of course it's not true. I was watching the tv screen in disbelief—looking at the reactions of the horrified people. I wasn't dancing because the terrified faces on the screen, could have been the same faces in front of the Amiriyah shelter on February 13 . . . it's strange how horror obliterates ethnic differences—all faces look the same when they are witnessing the death of loved ones.   **posted by river @ 6:08 PM**

THE NEW CABINET

Two days ago, the Governing Council declared that the new Iraqi cabinet had been selected. The composition of the Iraqi cabinet is identical to that of the Governing Council: 13 Shi'a Muslims, 5 Sunni Muslims, 5 Kurds, 1 Christian, and 1 Turkoman.

After a long, tedious speech given this morning by Ibraheim Al-Jaffari, the ministers were "sworn in." Correct me if I'm wrong, isn't there supposed to be a constitution the ministers should swear to uphold? Apparently not.

Only 16 of the ministers were sworn in today because 9 of them couldn't be there for "technical reasons" (i.e. they're still outside of the country). I don't know how the ministries are going to function when the majority of the "ministers" were living abroad for most of their lives. There's going to be an American "advisor" for each of the ministries, which is supposed to help. I hope the American advisors are better than the ones Bush stocks the White House with . . .

Some points of interest . . .

—Ahmad Al-Chalabi, Jalal Talabani, and Ibraheim Al-Jaffari were swearing in the ministers.

—There is one female minister—Nisreen Mustafa Bawari. After she was sworn in, she started shaking the hands of Al-Chalabi, Talabani and Al-Jaffari, like her male counterparts. Al-Jaffari refused to shake her hand because Al-Da'awa consider it a "sin" to touch a female who isn't a direct relation.

—Mohammed Jassim Khudhair (Minister of Expatriates and Immigration) wasn't wearing a tie. Many Muslim fundamentalists (like the ones in Iran) don't wear ties because they believe that along with the head and arms, there's symbolism of a "cross" and a cross symbolizes Christianity and . . . well, you get the picture.

—The Minister of Oil is . . . Ibraheim Mohammed Bahr Ul-lloom—the son of Mohammed Bahr Ul-lloom of the Governing Council (the one who suspended his membership in the 9-member rotating presidency). Can anyone say nepotism? Brilliance must run in the family . . . **posted by river @ 6:30 PM**

Saturday, September 06, 2003

BAD, BAD, BAD DAY . . .

Bad #1: Mosque shooting.
Bad #2: No water.
Bad #3: Rumsfeld.

Today in Al-Sha'ab area, a highly populated area of Baghdad, armed men pulled up to a mosque during morning prayer and opened fire on the people. It was horrific and chilling. Someone said 3 people died, but someone else said it was more . . . no one knows who they are or where they're from, but it's said that they were using semiautomatic machine-guns (not a part of the army arsenal, as far as I know). And these were just ordinary people. It's incomprehensible and nightmarish . . . if you are no longer safe in a shrine or a mosque, where *are* you safe?

No running water all day today. Horrible. Usually there are at least a few hours of running water, today there's none. E. went out and asked if there was perhaps a pipe broken? The neighbors have no idea. Everyone is annoyed beyond reason.

A word of advice: never take water for granted. Every time you wash your hands in cold, clean, clear water—say a prayer of thanks to whatever deity you revere. Every time you drink fresh, odorless water—say the same prayer. Never throw out the clean water remaining in your glass—water a plant, give it to the cat, throw it out into the garden . . . whatever. Never take it for granted.

Luckily, yesterday I filled all the water bottles. We have dozens of water bottles, both glass and plastic. Every time there's even a semblance of running water, we put something under the faucet to catch the precious drops. We fill bottles, pots, thermoses, buckets—anything that will hold water. Some days are better than others.

The problem is this: when the electricity is off, the municipal water pumps don't work—the water pressure is so low, the water won't go up the faucet. When there *is* electricity, everyone starts up their own, personal water pumps to fill the water tanks on the roof and the water pressure drops again.

Washing clothes is a trial. Automatic washers are obsolete—useless. The best washers to use are those little "National" washers. They look like small garbage bins. You fill them with water and detergent and throw the clothes in. The clothes rotate and swish for about 10 minutes (there has to be electricity). We pull them out, rinse them in clean water, s and wring out the excess water. The excess water goes back into the washer. After the washing is done, the dirty soap water is used to wash the tiled driveway.

Washing dishes is another problem. We try to limit the use of dishes to what is absolutely necessary. Most of the water we store in buckets and tubs is used to wash people. We wash using the old-fashioned way—a smallish tub full of water, a ladle, a loofah, soap, and shampoo. The problem is that because of the heat, everyone wants to wash at least twice a day. The best time to wash is right before going to bed because for a few heavenly minutes after you wash, you feel cool enough to try to sleep. I have forgotten the delights of a shower . . .

Before the war, many people dug wells in their gardens. These wells don't look like your traditional well—a circular, stone wall with a bucket hanging in the middle. They are merely small, unpretentious holes in the ground to which mechanical pumps are attached. They provide a more or less decent water supply. The water has to be boiled or chlorinated to be used for drinking.

To make matters worse, Rumsfeld is in Iraq. It's awful to see him strutting all over the place. I hate the hard, smug look that seems plastered on his face . . . some people just have cruel features. The reaction to seeing him on tv differs from the reaction to seeing Bremer or one of the puppets. The latter are greeted with jeers and scorn. Seeing Rumsfeld is something else—there's resentment and disgust. It feels like he's here to add insult to injury . . . you know, just in case anyone forgets we're an occupied country.

And now he's going to go back to America and give a speech about how he doesn't know what anyone is talking about when they say "chaos" (*he* was safe in the middle of all his bodyguards) . . . how electricity and water are functioning (after all, his air-conditioner was working *fine*) . . . how the people are gloriously happy and traffic is frequently at a stand-still because the Iraqis are dancing in the streets . . . how the "armed forces" are cheerful and *grateful* to be on this heroic, historical mission . . . how kids wave at him, troops cheer him, dogs wag their tails in welcome and doves hover above his head . . .

To hell with him.

And no. I'm not whining—I'm ranting. You can't see me right now, but I'm shaking my fist at the computer screen, shaking my fist at the television, and heaping colorful, bilingual insults on Rumsfeld's head (hope the doves crap on him) . . . I'm angry. **posted by river @ 12:07 AM**

. . .

S u n d a y .   S e p t e m b e r   0 7 .   2 0 0 3

THIS JUST IN . . .

I just heard some interesting news! Apparently as Rumsfeld's plane was leaving Baghdad Airport to take him to Kuwait, missiles were fired at his plane and they missed! Hoping to hear more about it—but I just had to share.

The puppet-master met with Bremer and the puppets but the picture wasn't complete—Bush wasn't there.

I *love* Donald Rumsfeld's latest comment on Iraq . . . " . . . It's like Chicago."

Wow. This guy is funny.

You know what? I agree with him—he just didn't finish the statement properly. What he actually should have said was, "It's like Chicago . . . during the 1920s, when Al Capone was running it: gangs, militias, fighting, looting, vendettas, dubious business dealings, and shady figures in dark corners."

Except instead of Al Capone, we have Al-Jaffari, Al-Chalabi, Al-Hakim and L. Paul Bremer.

There were several attacks on the American forces today. The most prominent ones were in Baquba and Mosul, and a couple of hours ago there were two in Baghdad. We haven't seen the Baghdad ones on tv, but we heard a dull explosion and one of the neighbors told E. about an armored car burned.

Another comment: of the dozens of emails I got sympathizing with my feelings towards Rumsfeld, the *only* one I got defending him had a few choice sentences in it I thought I would share . . .

Basically it tells me that Rumsfeld is a heroic and very compassionate man and then continues to say that we ungrateful Iraqis should be ashamed of ourselves, etc. It also claims that I must be a Ba'athist because, of course, who else *except* a Ba'athist would be against this noble war?! (Sad, sad, *old* argument.)

Another fun line:

You should be thanking your lucky stars that Rumsfeld, and not Saddam, was in the Pentagon when your asshole buddies flew into it. Otherwise you and your whole family would be radioactive dust right now.

Apparently, I should be grateful Little Dougie, as I am fond of calling him, wasn't in the Pentagon either, because he finishes his compassionate email with the following:

If it were up to me I would have vaporized you ten minutes after the Trade center attacks.

The whole thing cheered me up because it simply confirmed my suspicions of Rumsfeld and his followers. His emails, compared to more intelligent emails, work to remind me of the diversity of blog readers. I am honored that people like Little Dougie take time off of watching Fox News to check out my blog. Thank you Little Dougie, *you* have made my day!

On the other hand, it could have been Rumsfeld personally emailing me . . . either way, I'm flattered—keep reading the blog! **posted by river @ 3:33 AM**

Monday, September 08, 2003

UNDER THE PALM LEAVES

The water was off and on again today. We filled all the bottles and containers. The water pressure was really low and evidently, our super-low garden faucet is one of the only ones in the area dribbling water at intervals. The neighbors have all sent buckets, pots, and messages of love and gratitude . . . perhaps I have found a job.

The sun was just beginning to set and the sky was a combination of blue, orange, and gray. I was standing, in the warm, dry grass, waiting for a pot to fill with water, when I heard someone knocking the garden gate. It was Ihsan, our ten-year-old neighbor across the street. He was holding freshly made "khubz" (something like whole-wheat pita bread) and squinting across the street at his next-door-neighbor's house.

Ihsan: They found Abu Ra'ad . . .

Me: What?! Did they? Is he . . .

Ihsan: He's dead. Ra'ad and his sisters are at my house.

I looked at the house across the street and saw that three cars were lined up in front of it, as if in a funeral procession. Ihsan followed my gaze and shook his head solemnly, "They didn't bring him home—they'll bury him tomorrow at dawn." He handed me the bread and turned to run back home. As he darted away to cross the street, he lost a flip-flop. He squealed as his foot hit the hot asphalt and hopped around on one leg like some bizarre stork.

I continued watching the late Abu Ra'ad's beige, stucco house with sadness and relief. The once green creeper all along the sides was yellow and decaying. The curtains were drawn on dusty windows and the whole house looked almost abandoned. The only signs of life were the shiny tiles of the driveway, washed daily by well-meaning neighbors.

They had finally found Abu Ra'ad.

Abu Ra'ad (meaning "father of Ra'ad") was a lawyer with his own private practice . . . if it could be called that. It was an office in a crowded, mercantile area in Baghdad large enough for three desks: one secretary and a partner.

On April 10, in the middle of the chaos, Abu Ra'ad left his house, his wife, and three children to go check on his parents, whom he had lost contact with a week earlier. At 10 am, he got into an old Toyota, said a prayer, and headed out to seek his family. He never came back.

For 3 days, Umm Ra'ad (mother of "Ra'ad") thought he was held up at his parents' house for some reason. Perhaps her husband had found his family hurt? Maybe he had found a parent dead—after all, his father was very sick and old . . . Maybe the fighting was so heavy, he couldn't make it out of their area? The possibilities were endless. Finally, one of the other neighbors delivered a note to Umm Ra'ad's brother asking him to please visit Abu Ra'ad's family and find out if he was okay. After a long day, Umm Ra'ad's brother visited her home, grim—Abu Ra'ad wasn't at his parents' home. He never made it and no one knew where he was.

For 7 days, everyone thought he was being detained by the Americans. We heard that hundreds of civilians were taken prisoner simply for being in the wrong place at the wrong time. Abu Ra'ad's younger brother, and his brother-in-law, visited authorities every day. They went to the various hotels, they visited the two or three remaining hospitals, and went over endless lists of detainees and POWs in search of Abu Ra'ad.

By the end of April, his family had resigned themselves to Abu

Ra'ad's death. His 35-year-old wife was wearing black from head-to-toe in anticipation of the news she knew she was bound, sooner or later, to receive.

I remember visiting her for the first time in early May. It was an awkward visit because we wanted to hold out hope, yet we knew there was none to give. She sat, very small and dark, on a couch in the living room, shredding tissues listlessly and listening vaguely to the words of commiseration and sympathy that, obviously, brought little or no comfort. Her 3 children, aged 1, 4, and 10, sat near her, unbearably quiet and calm. They sat gauging the situation by their mother's expression. She knew he was dead, but she couldn't bring herself to cry.

And still, they didn't give up the search. They traced his route from his home to Al-Jami'a Quarter, where his parents lived, pausing at every burnt vehicle to examine it and asking the people in the surrounding areas whether they had seen a white 1985 Toyota being driven by a 40-year-old man? Maybe it had been fired at by a tank? Maybe it was hit by an Apache? People were sympathetic, but helpless. No white Toyota—a blue Kia with 6 passengers, a red Volkswagen with a mother, father, and two kids . . . but no white Toyota. Every single time, they were referred to the makeshift graves along the main roads and highways. The temporary graves, for several weeks, lined the main roads of Baghdad.

As the tanks and Apaches invaded the city, they shot left and right at any vehicle in their path. The areas that got it worst were Al-Dawra and Al-A'adhamiya. People in residential areas didn't know what to do with the corpses in the burnt vehicles that had come from other parts of the city. They were the corpses of people and families who were trying to get away from the heavy fighting in their own areas, some of them had been officially evacuated.

The corpses sat decomposing in the heat, beyond identification. Some people tried asking the troops to help deal with them, but the reaction was mainly, "That's not my job." Of course not, how silly . . . your job is to burn the cars, we bury the corpses.

Finally, the people began to bury the corpses along the roadside—near the burnt vehicles so that family members looking for the car would find their loved ones not very far off.

...

For several weeks, you could see little piles of dirt all over Baghdad, and along the highways leading outside of the city, marked with bricks, or stones, or signs and, always, with palm leaves. The drying, wilting palm leaves were buried, standing up, to mark the graves. Some of the graves had little cardboard placards stuck carefully under a pile of stones to help family members: adult male, adult female, 2 children in black Mercedes. Adult male, small boy in a white pick-up.

Sometimes the graves were marked by the license plate of the car the victims were in. But most of them were marked with the palm leaves.

For several weeks, there would be people stooping, all along the way, trying to decide if they knew, or recognized, any of the dead. That's what Abu Ra'ad's family did, all through May, June, July, and August.

Finally, 3 days ago, an old man in Abu Ra'ad's parents' neighborhood told them how the roads were blocked to their area for a couple of days, and people coming from the other end of the city had had to detour. There were several burnt cars in an area on the suburbs, in their own makeshift graveyard. They should look there; maybe they would find their son.

They finally found him, this morning, in an area outside his expected course. One of the several burnt cars, dragged into a dusty field, was a white 1985 Toyota with the skeleton of a car-seat in the back. Not far off were the graves. They located the "adult male in the white Toyota" and with the help of some sympathetic men in the neighborhood, unearthed Abu Ra'ad for identification.

We went to give our condolences to Umm Ra'ad. The children were at Ihsan's house and she was surrounded by relatives and family members, grieving. Kerosene lamps and candles were lit in the darkened living room; they threw light all over the drawn, grief-stricken faces. She was finally crying.

Tomorrow, at dawn, he will be exhumed by his family and officially buried in the over-crowded family graveyard, under one of the dozens of palm trees, in the place reserved for his father.   **posted by river @ 1:54 AM**

T u e s d a y , S e p t e m b e r 0 9 , 2 0 0 3

FRIENDS, AMERICANS, COUNTRYMEN . . .

I heard/read Bush's speech yesterday. I can't watch him for more than a minute at a time—I hate him that much. He makes me sick. He stands there, squinting his eyes and pursing his lips, going on and on with such blatant lies. And he looks just plain stupid.

I listened for as long as I could tolerate his inane features and grating voice, then turned off the television. Then turned it back on. Then turned the channel. Then turned it back. Then almost threw a cushion at the screen. Then thought better and decided he wasn't worth it. Is it possible that someone like that is practically running the world? Is it possible he might see another term in the White House? God forbid . . .

His whole speech was just an idiotic repetition of what he's been saying ever since Afghanistan, "Give me more money, give me more power—I'm doing this for you. Bechtel and Halliburton have nothing to do with it." Doesn't he ever get tired of saying the same words? Don't people ever get tired of hearing them?

The one thing I agreed with was this: there are terrorists in Iraq. It's true. Ever since the occupation, they've been here by the hundreds and thousands. They are seeping in from neighboring countries through the borders the "Coalition of the Willing" could not protect and would not let the Iraqi army protect. Some of them are even a part of the Governing Council now. Al-Da'awa Party is responsible for some of the most terrible bombings in Iraq and other countries in the region.

Yes. I blame America for that. We never had Al-Qaeda or even links to Al-Qaeda. Ansar Al-Islam are supposed to be linked to Al-Qaeda, but they were functioning in the northern territory with the two Kurdish leaders' knowledge and blessings.

Then there's this:

> The attacks you have heard and read about in the last few weeks have occurred predominantly in the central region of Iraq, between Baghdad and Tikrit—Saddam Hussein's former stronghold. The north of Iraq is generally stable and is moving forward with reconstruction and self-government. The same trends are evident in the south, despite recent attacks by terrorist groups.

Is he serious? Only yesterday an American armored vehicle was burned in front of the University of Mosul in the north. There have been an increasing number of attacks on British troops in the south— we hear about them everyday. As for Baghdad . . . it has become a common occurrence. Baghdad Airport is constantly under missile attack and we hear of similar attacks all over Baghdad . . . or maybe the person who gave him that little fact is the same one who told him where to find the WMD . . .

Since the end of major combat operations, we have conducted raids seizing many caches of enemy weapons and massive amounts of ammunition, and we have captured or killed hundreds of Saddam loy- alists and terrorists.

Yes, we know all about the "raids." I wish I had statistics on the raids. The "loyalists and terrorists" must include Mohammed Al- Kubeisi of Jihad Quarter in Baghdad who was 11. He went outside on the second floor balcony of his house to see what the commotion was all about in their garden. The commotion was an American raid. Mohammed was shot on the spot. I remember another little terrorist who was killed four days ago in Baquba, a province north-east of Bagh- dad. This terrorist was 10 . . . no one knows why or how he was shot by one of the troops while they were raiding his family's house. They found no weapons, they found no Ba'athists, they found no WMD. I hope America feels safer now.

On top of it all, the borders between Iraq and Iran have been given to Badir's Brigade to guard. Badir's Brigade. Unbelievable. I thought the borders needed guarding to prevent armed militias like Badir's Brigade from entering the country. We have a proverb in Arabic: "Emin il bezooneh lahmeh," which means "Entrust a cat with meat." Yes, give the Iranian borders to Badir's Brigade. Right on.

Just a couple of days ago, two female school principals were "exe- cuted" by Badir's Brigade in Al-Belidiyat area in Baghdad. They were warned to resign their posts so that a "sympathetic" principal could replace them. They ignored the threat, they were shot. It's that simple these days. Of course, that's not terrorism because the targets are Iraqi people. Terrorism is when the Coalition of the Willing are targeted.

Everyone is asking, "What should be done?." Pull out the American troops. Take them home. Bring in UN peace-keeping troops under the Security Council—not led by America.

Let real Iraqis be involved in governing Iraq. Let Iraqis who actually have *families* living in Iraq be involved in governing their country. Let Iraqis who have something to lose govern the country. They aren't being given a chance. As long as any Iraqi isn't affiliated with one of the political groups on the Governing Council, no one bothers to listen.

We have thousands of competent, intelligent, innovative people who are eager to move forward, but it's impossible under these circumstances. There's no security, there's no work and there's no incentive. AND THERE'S NO ONE WHO WILL LISTEN. If you're not a part of the CPA or one of Ahmad Al-Chalabi's thugs, then you're worthless. You can't be trusted.

I read Bush's speech . . . just like I've read/heard what feels like a thousand different speeches these last few months. Empty words, meaningless phrases.

The abridged version of the speech . . .

"Friends, Americans, Countrymen, lend me your ears . . . lend me your sons and daughters, lend me your tax dollars . . . so we can wage war in the name of American national security (people worldwide are willing to die for it) . . . so I can cover up my incompetence in failing to protect you . . . so I can add to the Bush and Cheney family coffers at your expense and the expense of the Iraqi people. I don't know what I'm doing, but if you spend enough money, you'll want to believe that I do." **posted by river @ 10:43 PM**

Friday, September 12, 2003

TURNING TABLES . . .

I've been following TurningTables ever since someone pointed it out to me two weeks ago. "Moja" somehow puts a human face on the troops in Iraq. I read his blogs and look at the troops and wonder, could that be him? It's strange to read stories from the "other side" . . .

I'm glad he's going to be able to go home, safely.

. . . to many i'm sure that it would appear that i can not see the "macro" good that is attempting to come through with this war . . . the bigger picture . . . but i do . . . i know that saddam was a horrendous tyrant . . . capable of anything . . . holding his country at knife point . . . slaughtering . . . kidnapping . . . freighting . . . this country was not free . . . and it was being taken advantage of . . . it was being reaped . . . and it seems as though only a few would see the rewards . . . those in favor with the big guy . . . america liked him . . . with the old adage of "the enemy of my enemy . . . " . . . but that adage is not the best to ever come out of someone's mouth . . . and it creates problems . . . just like in afghanistan . . . we create problems . . . we have to deal with them . . . it's not fair . . . but that is the way it is . . . i look at iraq now . . . and i know that they were not in a black hole . . . they lived somewhat normal lives in comparison to us . . . the u.s . . . they did not have some very basic freedoms that we take for granted . . . i read an article by salam . . . he actually feared for his life while writing his journal . . . he feared for his family . . . and he risked their lives by putting his feelings out there . . . the feelings that we all could relate to . . . the feelings that said . . . "we aren't so different . . . you and i" . . .

i do think that iraq will one day be better . . . i do think that this country will enjoy basic freedoms . . . and i hope they will be able to take advantage of them . . . with out intervention from any outside source . . . they deserve it . . . because they are not all terrorists/freedom fighters/militants/what ever . . . they are people . . . and they hurt . . . and they worry . . . and they sweat . . . and they work . . . and they provide as best they can . . . that's what we do . . . all of us . . .

and maybe that is why the "micro" problems hurt me so . . . because i see now . . . like i've never seen before . . . the blinders are off . . . the eyes are wide . . . my heart is open . . . gut wrenching . . . and horrible . . . a problem we caused . . . that we have to end . . . and i wonder . . . at what cost . . . how many more will die . . . how many more will fight . . . how many more will feel the unquenched disbelief at this new situation . . . this situation that isn't exactly panning out like we might have imagined . . . i hear the small arms fire . . . i feel the explosions . . . the "micro" has slapped me in the face everyday that i woke up here . . . it has affected me . . . it will continue to affect for the rest of my life . . . i know all too well

> *that people . . . iraqis . . . and americans . . . are dying everyday . . .*
> *i see the smoke from the car bombs . . . i feel the hurt in my*
> *heart . . .*
> *they are dying here . . . these people . . . humans . . . us . . .*
>
> [Note: The U.S. soldier who was maintaining this blog returned
> home in September of 2003.]

posted by river @ 6:05 PM

LATELY . . .

I haven't been writing these last few days because I simply haven't
felt inspired. There's so much happening on a country-wide scale and
so little happening personally. Everything feels chaotic. Seeing what
we're supposed to be living on television differs drastically from actually living it. The moment you hear about something terrible happening somewhere, you let it sink in, then "take stock" and try to figure
out who you have living there and how you can contact them.

Three days ago there was a huge explosion in Arbil (one of the
northern Kurdish areas). They say it was a suicide bomber in a car
in front of the American intelligence headquarters. The number of
casualties varied from news network to news network, but one thing
is sure—a child in a house across from the headquarters was killed.
Horrible.

There was also an attack on Mosul Hotel in central Mosul where
American troops are staying. This was yesterday and no one is giving
the number of casualties.

There were attacks on troops in Ramadi and Falloojeh yesterday.
In fact, in Khaldiah (an area between Ramadi and Falloojeh) they say
there was actual fighting and gunfire lasted over an hour and a half.

In Falloojeh, the police were shot at by American troops this morning. I'm not sure how many died but the whole "accident" was atrocious. They say up to 7 Iraqi policemen were killed in some "mistake"
made by the troops. This is going to be horrible for Falloojeh—there's
already so much bitterness against the Americans there because of the
shooting incidents in April and May.

There's still some fighting in Kirkuk (the Turkomen dominated area). The reason is because the Bayshmarga (Kurdish militia) have been assigned to that area. There has always been a sort of hostility between Turkomen and Kurds and having the Bayshmarga running the show isn't making things any better. Turkey wants to send in "peace-keeping" troops to help secure Kirkuk, but the Kurds are refusing adamantly.

And then there's Baghdad. What is there to say about Baghdad? Baghdad is a mess. In Zayunah, an elegant area in east Baghdad, there was gang fighting yesterday. People were being shot in the streets, caught between gang crossfire. The scene was frightening and terrible.

We see Iraqi police every once in a while, but their numbers are ridiculous compared to the situation. They wear light blue shirts, dark pants, and these black arm badges with IP written on them and the flag. They get to carry around these little 7 mm Berettas that look tiny in their hands. And the guns are always drawn—they try to guide traffic waving a gun, try to stop cars waving a gun, try to stop fights waving a gun—it's the best means of communication these days—a tank works even better (but you can't wave it around).

In another area, a 12-year-old boy was shot in his garden while play-ing. The Americans say he was caught in the crossfire between them and someone else. His mother was almost tearing her hair out and his father was beating the ground and moaning. He looked ready to kill.

People talk about the future and how five years from now, ten years from now, fifty years from now things are going to be better. Some people no longer have a "future." The parents of that boy no longer care about the future of Iraq or the future of America or any-thing else. They buried their "future" last night. I'm sure the future means as much to them as it does to the parents of the soldiers dying in Iraq on a daily basis.

When Bush "brought the war to the terrorists," he failed to men-tion he wouldn't be fighting it in some distant mountains or barren deserts: the frontline is our homes . . . the "collateral damage" are our friends and families.   **posted by river @ 6:16 PM**

A MODERN-DAY FAIRY TALE

Someone asked me why I didn't write anything yesterday mentioning September 11. I'll be perfectly honest—I had forgotten about it until around 2 pm. I woke up to no electricity, washed up, and went into the kitchen to help out with breakfast.

I found my mother struggling with the gas cylinder, trying to roll it around on the ground in front of the stove. The cylinder was almost empty and the bright blue flames were orange at the tips, threatening to go out any minute. I stood nervously in the doorway of the kitchen—gas cylinders make me very nervous. After the war, when there wasn't enough cooking gas to go around, people who sell the gas began mixing kerosene with the cooking gas which resulted in some horrific explosions. Every time we change cylinders, I have a crazy urge to run out of the kitchen and wait to see if it explodes.

My mother looked at me helplessly as the flames began dying away. "E. will have to go see if they're selling cooking gas at the station."

"But E. was up until 4 am yesterday . . ." I remonstrated.

"Ok then—you guys don't need to drink tea or coffee."

And that was the beginning of a series of difficulties: almost no water, relatives who dropped by for a lunch that couldn't be cooked, and a wasp's nest that was terrorizing anyone who ventured into the garden.

By 2 pm, the electricity was back on and I was sitting in front of the tv watching one of the Arabic stations. Suddenly, they showed American troops standing solemnly in a 9/11 Memorial Service being held in . . . Tikrit (where Saddam was born)!!

I sat watching, confused. I assume it was done in that specific place so some oblivious person can, five years down the line, hold it up as testimony to the world that this whole war was, indeed, about terror and Osama bin Laden and 9/11 and WMD. It was done in that particular place so that someone, a week from now, can write to me and say, "Of course there was a link between Osama and Saddam and that's why we attacked you. The proof is this: the 9/11 Memorial Service was held in Tikrit."

This famous "missing link" between Iraq and the war on terror is like, how I imagine, a fairy might look—small, flighty, almost transparent and . . . nonexistent. Shortly after 9/11, this fairy was caught by the Pentagon and stashed in a cage for all the world to see.

Almost like the Emperor's new clothes, anyone who could not see this enigmatic creature was accused of being an Enemy of Freedom, a Saddam sympathizer or—horror of horrors!—unpatriotic. They were promptly indicted and burned at the metaphorical stake.

So most people chose to see the fairy. Some people, in fact, really thought they *could* see it. Everyone certainly tried. Unfortunately, the fairy soon began growing smaller and paler under the burning scrutiny of millions of curious eyes.

So what did they decide to do? Bush, Rumsfeld, and the rest made a critical decision: the fairy must be protected by a great wall. Plans were drawn up, the toughest bricks were selected, and contractors from Fox News, CNN, and others were assigned. And with every fresh news story, a brick was laid, until the wall was so high and strong, it became a fortress . . . and everyone forgot what lay behind it . . . which was the alleged fairy . . . who may, or may not have, existed. But it no longer mattered anymore, anyway—the wall itself was there . . .

And the fairy? The fairy dug an escape tunnel to Iran . . . or perhaps Syria . . . or maybe North Korea. Time will tell—she will be caught again. **posted by river @ 6:22 PM**

Tuesday, September 16, 2003

GIRL POWER AND POST-WAR IRAQ

I've been a bit sick these last few days. I seem to have come down with something similar to the flu that has left me red-eyed, runny-nosed, and feverish. I didn't actually realize I was sick until the electricity went off the day before yesterday: there was a collective groan as the heat instantly settled down upon us like a wool blanket and all I could say was, "What heat?!"

The family looked at me like maybe I was crazy—or feverish—and it finally hit me why the room took to dancing around before my eyes every few minutes . . . why the sunlight made me wince and squint in pain, rather like a bat.

So I spent yesterday on a couch in the living room, surrounded by tissues and Flu-Out (a favorite Iraqi flu medication). I watched tv whenever it was available and even managed to drag myself to the computer two or three times. The screen would move in waves in front of my bleary eyes so I'd give up trying to make sense of the dancing letters after a few minutes.

At night I focused enough to watch "For Females Only," a weekly program on Al-Jazeera. It left me feeling enraged and depressed. The subject was, as usual, Iraq. The program was hosting three Iraqi females: Dr. Shatha Jaffar, Yanar Mohammed, and Iman Abdul Jabar.

Yanar Mohammed is an architect who has been living in Canada ever since 1993, as far as I know. She is the founder of the "Organization of Women's Freedom in Iraq," which was based in Canada until a couple of months ago. Dr. Shatha Jaffar I haven't heard of. I think she left Iraq at the age of 15 (she is now in her 40s) and is also heading some sort of Iraqi women's movement, although the caption under her name said, "Women's Rights Activist." Iman Abdul Jabar was apparently representative of some sort of Islamic women's movement and was, as far as I could tell, living in Iraq the whole time.

Iman and Yanar both had a distinctive advantage over Shatha because they were both actually living in Iraq. The discussion was regarding how much women's rights in Iraq had been affected after the occupation—how females were being abducted, raped, and forced into a certain form of dress or action.

Yanar claimed that women's equality couldn't be achieved except through a secular government because an Islamic government would definitely hurt women's rights. I don't necessarily agree with that. If there were an Islamic government based purely on the teachings of Islam, women would be ensured of certain nonnegotiable rights like inheritance, the right to an education, the right to work and earn money, the right to marry according to her will, and the right to divorce her husband. Of course, there would be limitations in the way females dress and other restrictions.

Islamic government doesn't work because the people running the show usually implement certain laws and rules that have nothing to do with Islam and more to do with certain chauvinistic ideas in the name of Islam—like in Iran and Saudi Arabia.

Iman Abdul Jabar was taking Rumsfeld's attitude to the situation—see no evil, hear no evil, speak no evil. She claimed that she knew nothing about any extremists belonging to Al-Sadr and Al-Hakim coming into schools during the exams, pulling "safirat" (girls without hijab) out of tests and threatening that they wouldn't be allowed to come to school anymore if they didn't wear a hijab. She says she has heard nothing of all the signs and banners hanging all over colleges and universities in Baghdad condemning females who didn't wear what is considered the traditional Islamic dress. I say "considered" because there is nothing specifying exactly what is Islamic dress. Some people feel that a hijab is more than enough, while others claim that a burka or pushi are necessary . . .

Shatha was full of self-righteous blabbering. She instantly lost any point she was trying to make by claiming that girls in Iraq were largely ignorant and illiterate due to the last 30 years. She said that Iraqis began pulling their daughters out of school because non-Ba'athists weren't allowed an education.

Strangely enough, I wasn't a Ba'athist and I got accepted into one of the best colleges in the country based solely on my grades in my final year of high school. None of my friends were Ba'athists and they ended up pharmacists, doctors, dentists, translators, and lawyers . . . I must have been living somewhere else.

Every time Shatha was onscreen, I threw used tissues at her. She feeds into the usual pre-war/post-occupation propaganda that if you weren't a Ba'athist, you weren't allowed to learn. After 35 years that would mean that the only literate, sophisticated, and educated people in Iraq are Ba'athists.

Something you probably don't know about Iraq: We have 18 public universities and over 10 private universities, plus 28 technical schools and workshops. The difference between private and public colleges is that the public colleges and universities (like Baghdad University) are free, without tuition. The private colleges ask for a yearly tuition which is a pittance compared to colleges abroad. Public colleges are preferred because they are considered more educationally sound.

Arab students come from all over the region to study in our colleges and universities because they are the best. Europeans interested in learning about Islamic culture and religion come to study in the Islamic colleges. Our medical students make the brightest doctors and our engineers are the most creative . . .

In 6th year secondary school (12th grade), Iraqi students are made to take a standardized test known as the Bakaloriah. The students are assigned 9-digit numbers and taken to a different school with random examination supervisors to watch over the testing process. For "science students" the subjects required for examination are math, physics, English, Arabic, chemistry, Islam (for Muslim students only), French (for students taking French), and biology. For non-science students, the subjects are Arabic, English, history, geography, Islam (for Muslims), math, and economics—I think.

As soon as we get our averages, we fill out forms that go to the Ministry of Higher Education. In these forms, you list the colleges and universities you would like to end up in, the first being the one you want most. I recall nothing on the form asking me if I was a Ba'athist or loyalist, but maybe I filled out the wrong form . . .

Anyway, according to the student's average, and the averages of the people applying to other colleges, the student is "placed." You don't even meet the dean or department head until after classes have begun. Ironically, the illiterate females Shatha mentions have higher averages than the males. A guy can get into an engineering college with a 92%, while for females the average is around 96% because the competition between females is so high.

What Shatha doesn't mention is that in engineering, science, and medical colleges over half of the students in various departments are females—illiterate females, by the way. Our male and female graduates are some of the best in the region and many public universities arrange for scholarships and fellowships in Europe and America. But Shatha wouldn't know that . . . or I must be wrong. Either way, excuse me please, I am after all, illiterate and unlearned.

Iman Abdul Jabar brought up a good point—she said that during the examinations in June and July, the people who were working in the mosques were protecting many of the local schools in Baghdad—which is very true. She doesn't, however, mention that those people aren't likely interested in running for president or any other political position in the country—the people currently mixing religion and politics are Al-Hakim and SCIRI, who were terrorizing girls, and Al-Sadr and his thugs (who met with [Colin] Powell this time around and was promised a marvelous political career).

Yanar was outraged during the whole conference. She is currently in Baghdad and they say that there have been attempts made on her life. She read my mind when she said that the story of police in Baghdad was a farce—they weren't nearly enough and the Americans were doing nothing about the security of the people. She said that the theory of females contributing to post-war Iraq politically or socially was a joke. How are females supposed to be out there helping to build society or even make a decent contribution when they suddenly seem to be a #1 target? She talked about a "Women's Conference" arranged by the CPA where she wasn't allowed to enter because the "women representatives of Iraqi females" were all selected by the feminist extraordinaire L. Paul Bremer.

More and more females are being made to quit work or school or college. I spent last month trying to talk a neighbor's mother into letting her 19-year-old daughter take her retests in a leading pharmaceutical college. Her mother was adamant and demanded to know what she was supposed to do with her daughter's college degree if anything happened to her daughter, "Hang it on her tombstone with the consolation that my daughter died for a pharmaceutical degree??? She can sit this year out."

The worst part of the whole show was when they showed a mortician in Baghdad claiming he hardly ever saw any rape victims! What rape victim is going to go, in our current situation, file a complaint? Who do you complain to? Besides that, women are too ashamed to make rape public, and why bother when you just *know* the person will never be caught—when no one is going to bother to look for the aggressor?

They showed a girl who was around 15 talking about how she was abducted. She went out one morning to buy groceries with a brother who looked around 5 or 6. Suddenly, a red Volkswagen screeched to a stop in front of her. She was pulled inside of the car and the headscarf on her head was used to tie up her mouth. They took her and her little brother to a mud hut far away from A'adhamiya (the area she lives in). She was kept in the hut for 4 days and systematically beaten and questioned—how much money do your parents have? Do you have any valuables in your home? She wasn't allowed to sleep . . . the only sleep anyone got was her little brother while she held him in her arms. They gave them no food for four days.

Finally, one of the abductors took pity on her. He told her that the rest of the tattooed gang were going to leave somewhere and he would leave the door of the hut open. She should meet him behind a little "kushuk," or shop, made of straw, down the street. She left the hut with her little brother as soon as the coast was clear. She left the door unlocked because inside the same hut were 15 other girls abducted from a secondary school in Zayoona [Zayunah]—a nice residential area in Baghdad where many Christians choose to settle. The man dropped her and her brother off near a hospital far away from her house.

The interview with the girl ended when the reporter asked her if she was still scared . . . the girl looked incredulous at the question and said, "Of course I'm still scared." The reporter then asked if she was going to go back to school that year . . . the girl shook her head "no" as her eyes welled up with tears and the screen faded back to the show.

I spent last night tossing, turning and wondering if they ever found the 15 girls from Zayoona and praying for the sanity of their families . . . **posted by river @ 6:25 PM**

Thursday, September 18, 2003

BUSHMAIL

Feeling much better today . . . but the thing that cheered me up the most was some "fanmail" from George W. "hisself" so I thought I would share it with y'all . . . (Thank you Bob Fredrick—you know how to make a girl smile)

***

Dear Iraqi Person,

Could y'all please stop killin' each other? The folks over here are startin' to git madder than a feller in a canoe what done forgot his paddle! Wuts worse, the more y'all keep tellin' folks on that com-putter thing-a-ma-bob wuts goin' on down there, the more they don't pay no attention to my TV reporter guys on Fox to tell 'em wut they need to know! Next thing ya know, I'll be out on my butt come next eleckshun an' Daddy'll hafta start me another oil company so Ican look like I'm an important guy who is reely smart!

At the last meetin' I got to go to with Daddy & all his friends, Mr. Ashcroft said wut we need to do is git Iraq some of them "Patriot Act" freedoms so we can start lockin' more people up, but Mr. Powell told him to "keep it in his pants" wut ever that means. Daddy & Mr. Cheney wuz laughin' an' havin a good ole time cuz they just read some kind of profit paper fer Mr. Cheney's company that he ain't sposed to work for anymore . uh, Halyberton or sumptin like that . . . Then they wuz about to go inta whut we're gonna do in Iraq, but Mr. Cheney reminded Daddy that it was my bed time, so I had to leave.

So, if ya'll could do me a favor, please stop all that killin' and when ya see camera or reporter guys, just smile and tell'em just how much yer lives have gotten better since us 'mericans came and liverated ya'll! Keep it up and Daddy tells me after I'm re-elektid, we can liverate Iran & Syria next! Ain't that cool!

Yer Bestest Buddy,
George W. Bush,
Pres. Of Texas & 'Merica

(Note: All spelling errors are original to the soon-to-be-unemployed chimp that wrote them.) **posted by river @ 12:10 AM**

Friday, September 19, 2003

TERRORISTS . . .

The weather has "broken" these last few days. It's still intolerably hot, but there's a wind. It's a heavy, dusty wind more reminiscent of a gust from a blow-dryer than an actual breeze. But it is none-the-less a wind, and we are properly grateful.

The electrical situation is bizarre. For every 6 hours of electricity, three hours of darkness. I wish they would give us electricity all night and cut it off during the day. During the day it's hotter, but at least you can keep busy with something like housework or a book. At night the darkness brings along all the fears, the doubts, and . . . the mosquitoes. All the sounds are amplified. It's strange how when you can see, you can't hear so many things . . . or maybe you just stop listening.

Everyone is worried about raids lately. We hear about them from friends and relatives, we watch them on tv, outraged, and try to guess where the next set of raids are going to occur.

Anything can happen. Some raids are no more than seemingly standard weapons checks. Three or four troops knock on the door and march in. One of them keeps an eye of the "family" while the rest take a look around the house. They check bedrooms, kitchens, bathrooms and gardens. They look under beds, behind curtains, inside closets and cupboards. All you have to do is stifle your feelings of humiliation, anger, and resentment at having foreign troops from an occupying army search your home.

Some raids are, quite simply, raids. The door is broken down in the middle of the night, troops swarm in by the dozens. Families are marched outside, hands behind their backs and bags upon their heads. Fathers and sons are pushed down on to the ground, a booted foot on their head or back.

Other raids go horribly wrong. We constantly hear about families who are raided in the small hours of the morning. The father, or son, picks up a weapon—thinking they are being attacked by looters—and all hell breaks loose. Family members are shot, others are detained, and often women and children are left behind wailing.

I first witnessed a raid back in May. The heat was just starting to become unbearable and we were spending the whole night without electricity. I remember lying in my bed, falling in and out of a light sleep. We still weren't sleeping on the roof because the whole night you could hear gunshots and machine-gun fire not very far away—the looters still hadn't organized themselves into gangs and mafias.

At around 3 am, I distinctly heard the sound of helicopters hovering not far above the area. I ran out of the room and into the kitchen and found E. pressing his face to the kitchen window, trying to get a glimpse of the black sky.

"What's going on?!" I asked, running to stand next to him.

"I don't know . . . a raid? But it's not an ordinary raid . . . there are helicopters and cars, I think . . ."

I stopped focusing on the helicopters long enough to listen to the cars. No, not cars—big, heavy vehicles that made a humming, whining sound. E. and I looked at one another, speechless—tanks?! E. turned on his heel and ran upstairs, taking the steps two at a time. I followed him clumsily, feeling for the banister all the way up, my mind a jumble of thoughts and conjectures.

Out on the roof, the sky was black streaked with light. Helicopters were hovering above, circling the area. E. was leaning over the railing, trying to see into the street below. I approached tentatively and he turned back to me, "It's a raid . . . on Abu A.'s house!" He pointed three houses down the road.

Abu A. was an old, respected army general who had retired in the mid '80s. He lived a quiet life in his two-storey house on our street. All I knew about him was that he had four kids—two daughters and two sons. The daughters were both married. One of them was living in London with her husband and the other one was somewhere in Baghdad. The one in Baghdad had a 3-year-old son we'll call L. I know this because, without fail, ever since L. was six months old, Abu A. would proudly parade him up and down our street in a blue and white striped stroller.

It was a scene I came to expect every Friday evening: the tall, worn, old man pushing the small blue stroller holding the round, pink, drooling L.

I had never talked to Abu A. until last year. I was watering the little patch of grass in front of the wall around our garden and trying not to stare at the tall old man walking alongside the tottering toddler. Everything my mother had taught me about how impolite it was to ogle people ran around in my brain. I turned my back to the twosome as they came down the street and casually drowned the flowers growing on the edge of the plot of grass.

Suddenly, a voice asked, "Can we wash ourselves?" I turned around, stupefied. Abu A. and L. stood there, smeared with enough chocolate to qualify for a detergent commercial. I handed over the hose, almost drenching them in the process, and watched as the old man washed L.'s sticky, little fingers and wiped clean the pursed lips while saying, "His mother can't see him like this!"

And after handing back the hose, they were off on their way, once again . . . I watched them go down the remainder of the street to Abu A.'s home—stopping every few steps so L. could look down at some insect that had caught his attention.

That was last year . . . or maybe 9 months ago . . . or maybe 100 years ago. Tonight, the armored cars were pulling up to Abu A.'s house, the helicopters were circling above, and the whole area was suddenly a mess of noise and lights.

E. and I went back downstairs. My mother stood anxiously by the open kitchen door, looking out at my father who was standing at the gate. E. and I ran outside to join him and watch the scene unfolding only 3 houses away. There was shouting and screaming—the deep, angry tones of the troops mixed with the shriller voices of the family and neighbors—the whole symphony boding of calamity and fear.

"What are they doing? Who are they taking?!" I asked no one in particular, gripping the warm, iron gate and searching the street for some clue. The area was awash with the glaring white of headlights and spotlights and dozens of troops stood in front of the house, weapons pointed—tense and ready. It wasn't long before they started coming out: first it was his son, the 20-year-old translation student. His hands were behind his back and he was gripped by two troops, one on either side. His head kept twisting back anxiously as they marched him out of the house, barefoot. Next, Umm A., Abu A.'s wife, was brought out, sobbing, begging them not to hurt anyone, pleading for an answer . . . I couldn't hear what she was saying, but I saw her looking left and right in confusion and I said the words instead of her, "What's going on? Why are they doing this?! Who are they here for?"

Abu A. was out next. He stood tall and erect, looking around him in anger. His voice resonated in the street, above all the other sounds. He was barking out questions—demanding answers from the troops, and the bystanders. His oldest son A. followed behind with some more escorts. The last family member out of the house was Reem, A.'s wife of only 4 months. She was being led firmly out into the street by two troops, one gripping each thin arm.

I'll never forget that scene. She stood, 22 years old, shivering in the warm, black night. The sleeveless nightgown that hung just below her knees exposed trembling limbs—you got the sense that the troops were holding her by the arms because if they let go for just a moment, she would fall senseless to the ground. I couldn't see her face because her head was bent and her hair fell down around it. It was the first time I had seen her hair . . . under normal circumstances, she wore a hijab.

That moment I wanted to cry . . . to scream . . . to throw something at the chaos down the street. I could feel Reem's humiliation as she stood there, head hanging with shame—exposed to the world, in the middle of the night.

One of the neighbors, closer to the scene, moved forward timidly and tried to communicate with one of the soldiers. The soldier immediately pointed his gun at the man and yelled at him to keep back. The man held up an "abaya," a black cloak-like garment some females choose to wear, and pointed at the shivering girl. The soldier nodded curtly and told him to, "Move back!." "Please," came the tentative reply, "Cover her . . ." He gently put the abaya on the ground and went back to stand at his gate. The soldier, looking unsure, walked over, picked it up, and awkwardly put it on the girl's shoulders.

I gripped at the gate as my knees weakened, crying . . . trying to make sense of the mess. I could see many of the neighbors, standing around, looking on in dismay. Abu A.'s neighbor, Abu Ali, was trying to communicate with one of the troops. He was waving his arm at Umm A. and Reem, and pointing to his own house, obviously trying to allow them to take the women inside his home. The troop waved over another soldier who, apparently, was a translator. During raids, a translator hovers in the background inconspicuously—they don't bring him forward right away to communicate with terrified people because they are hoping someone will accidentally say something vital, in Arabic, thinking the troops won't understand, like, "Honey, did you bury the nuclear bomb in the garden like I told you?!"

Finally, Umm A. and Reem were allowed inside of Abu Ali's house, escorted by troops. Reem walked automatically, as if dazed, while Umm A. was hectic. She stood her ground, begging to know what was going to happen . . . wondering where they were taking her husband and boys . . . Abu Ali urged her inside.

The house was ransacked . . . searched thoroughly for no one knows what—vases were broken, tables overturned, clothes emptied from closets . . .

By 6 am the last cars had pulled out. The area was once more calm and quiet. I didn't sleep that night, that day, or the night after. Every time I closed my eyes, I saw Abu A. and his grandson L. and Reem . . . I saw Umm A., crying with terror, begging for an explanation.

Abu A. hasn't come back yet. The Red Cross facilitates communication between him and his family . . . L. no longer walks down our street on Fridays, covered in chocolate, and I'm wondering how old he will be before he ever sees his grandfather again . . . **posted by river @ 2:09 AM**

Sunday, September 21, 2003

AKILA . . .

There was an attempt yesterday on Akila Al-Hashimi's life. We heard about [it] yesterday morning and have been listening for news ever since. She lives in Jihad Quarter and was leaving for work yesterday when two pick-up trucks with armed men cut off her car and opened fire on her and her "bodyguards"—her brothers. Neighbors heard the commotion, armed themselves, and went out to see what it was. The neighbors and the gang began shooting at each other.

Akila was taken to Al-Yarmuk hospita,l where her stomach was operated upon, and [she was] then shipped off in an American army ambulance to no one knows where, but people say it was probably the hospital they have set up in Baghdad Airport. They say she was wounded in the foot, the shoulder, and the stomach—her condition is critical, but stable.

It's depressing because she was actually one of the decent members on the council. She was living in Iraq and worked extensively in foreign affairs in the past. It's also depressing because of what it signifies—that no female is safe, no matter how high up she is . . .

Everyone has their own conjectures on who it could have been. Ahmad Al-Chalabi, of course, right off, before they even started investigations said, "It was Saddam and his loyalists!"—he's beginning to sound like a broken record . . . but no one listens to him anyway. The FBI in Iraq who examined the site said they had no idea yet who it could be. Why would it be Ba'athists if Akila herself was once a Ba'athist and handled relations with international organizations in the Ministry of Foreign Affairs before the occupation? Choosing her was one of the smartest thing the CPA did since they got here. It was through her contacts and extensive knowledge of current Iraqi foreign affairs that Al-Chalabi and Al-Pachichi were received at the UN as "representatives" of the Iraqi people. She was recently chosen as one of three from the Governing Council, along with Al-Pachichi, to work as a sort of political buffer between the Governing Council and the new cabinet of ministers.

But there has been bitterness towards her by some of the more extreme members of the Governing Council—not only is she female, wears no hijab, and was the first actual "foreign representative" of the new government, but she was also a prominent part of the former government. The technique used sounds like the same used with those school principals who were killed and the same used with that brilliant female electrician who was assassinated . . . I wonder if Akila got a "warning letter." She should have had better protection. If they are not going to protect one of only 3 female members of the Governing Council, then who are they going to protect? Who is deemed worthy of protection?

Yeah, Baghdad is real safe when armed men can ride around in SUVs and pick-ups throwing grenades and opening fire on the Governing Council, of all people.

I really hope they find whoever did this, and I hope the punishment is severe. **posted by river @ 2:07 PM**

W e d n e s d a y , S e p t e m b e r 2 4 , 2 0 0 3

FOR SALE: IRAQ

For Sale: A fertile, wealthy country with a population of around 25 million . . . plus around 150,000 foreign troops, and a handful of puppets. Conditions of sale: should be either an American or British corporation (forget it if you're French) . . . preferably affiliated with Halliburton. Please contact one of the members of the Governing Council in Baghdad, Iraq for more information.

To hear of the first of the economic reforms announced by Kamil Al-Gaylani, the new Iraqi Finance Minister, you'd think Iraq was a Utopia and the economy was perfect only lacking in . . . foreign investment. As the BBC so wonderfully summarized it: the sale of all state industries except for oil and other natural resources. Basically, that means the privatization of water, electricity, communications, transportation, health . . . The BBC calls it a "surprise" . . . why were we not surprised?

After all, the Puppets have been bought—why not buy the stage too? Iraq is being sold—piece by piece. People are outraged. The companies are going to start buying chunks of Iraq. Or, rather, they're going to start buying the chunks the Governing Council and CPA don't award to the "Supporters of Freedom."

The irony of the situation is that the oil industry, the one industry that is *not* going to be sold out, is actually being run by foreigners anyway.

The whole neighborhood knows about S., who lives exactly two streets away. He's what is called a "merchant" or "tajir." He likes to call himself a "businessman." For the last six years, S. has worked with the Ministry of Oil, importing spare parts for oil tankers under the surveillance and guidelines of the "Food for Oil Program." In early March, all contracts were put "on hold" in expectation of the war. Thousands of contracts with international companies were either cancelled or postponed.

S. was in a frenzy: he had a shipment of engines coming in from a certain country and they were "waiting on the border." Everywhere he went, he chain-smoked one cigarette after another and talked of "letters of credit," "comm. numbers," and nasty truck drivers who were getting impatient.

After the war, the CPA decided that certain contracts would be approved. The contracts that had priority over the rest were the contracts that were going to get the oil pumping again. S. was lucky—his engines were going to find their way through . . . hopefully.

Unfortunately, every time he tried to get the go-ahead to bring in the engines, he was sent from person to person until he found himself, and his engines, tangled up in a bureaucratic mess in-between the CPA, the Ministry of Oil, and the UNOPS [UN Office for Project

Services]. By the time things were somewhat sorted out, and he was communicating directly with the Ministry of Oil, he was given a "tip." He was told that he shouldn't bother doing anything if he wasn't known to KBR. If KBR didn't approve of him, or recommend him, he needn't bother with anything.

For a week, the whole neighborhood was discussing the KBR. Who were they? What did they do? We all had our own speculations . . . E. said it was probably some sort of committee like the CPA, but in charge of the contracts or reconstruction of the oil infrastructure. I expected it was probably another company—but where was it from? Was it Russian? Was it French? It didn't matter so long as it wasn't Halliburton or Bechtel. It was a fresh new name or, at least, a fresh new set of initials. Well, it was "fresh" for a whole half-hour until curiosity got the better of me and I looked it up on the internet.

KBR stands for Kellogg, Brown and Root, a subsidiary of . . . guess who?! . . . Halliburton. They handle "construction and engineering services for the energy community," amongst other things. Apparently, KBR is famous for more than just its reconstruction efforts. In 1997, KBR was sued $6 million dollars for overcharging the American army on sheets of plywood! You can read something about the whole sordid affair here.

"Halliburton: Not just the Oil," The Institute for Southern Studies, http://www.southernstudies.org/reports/halliburton.pdf

---

Company History
* *Dallas-based Halliburton was founded in 1919 and is the second largest provider of products and services to the oil and gas industries.*
* *Halliburton purchased the Houston-based Brown & Root in 1962 and Dresser Industries in 1998, which had brought the petroleum technology company M.W. Kellogg in 1988. From these companies emerged Kellogg, Brown & Root (KBR), now a subsidiary of Halliburton that handles construction and engineering services to the energy community and the government and civil infrastructure customers.*

Political Connections
* *Vice President Dick Cheney served as the CEO until 2000 when*

---

he left the position to run for office. He is reported to have received company stock worth over $33 million, but ultimately sold it under public pressure for $30 million. Still, he exited with an early retirement package and remains eligible for up to $1 million a year in deferred compensation.
- From 1999-2000 Halliburton gave $709,320 in political contributions and 95% of the money went to Republicans and $17,677 directly to George Bush.

Scandals—At Home and Abroad
- In July, a federal bankruptcy court granted Halliburton more time to review 300,000 pending asbestos claims. This is the third extension since Halliburton agreed to a settlement in December worth about $4 billion in cash and stocks. Halliburton inherited these claims four years ago when it acquired Dresser Industries. According to the Seattle Post Intelligencer, the company and its former chief executive gave $157,500 in political donations to 49 co-sponsors of the asbestos bill in the House and to 14 co-sponsors of a similar measure in the Senate. A spokesperson for Halliburton claims that these contributions were "purely coincidental."
- KBR's record includes claims of overcharging taxpayers. In 1997, the GAO found that the Army was "unable to ensure that the contractor adequately controlled costs," such that KBR was charging the Army $86 each for $14 sheets of plywood. KBR was sued for $6 million of alleged overcharges between 1995 and 1997.

Contracts in Iraq
- A 2-year, $7 billion contract (awarded through a non-competitive bidding process) to fight oil fires in Iraq and to pump and distribute Iraqi oil.
- Since March 2002, U.S. Army has issued 24 task orders to KBR totaling $425 million under a contract for work related to Operation Iraqi Freedom.
- A $30 million contract awarded from the Defense Threat Reduction Agency to dismantle and neutralize any chemical or biological weapons in the region.
- $62 million contract to feed and house U.S. Troops in Iraq.

Additional Resources
"The world according to Halliburton" on the Mother Jones site:
http://www.motherjones.com/news/features/2003/28/we_455_01.html

...

They [KBR] are currently located in the "Conference Palace." The Conference Palace is a series of large conference rooms, located in front of the Rashid Hotel, and was reserved in the past for major international conferences. It is now the headquarters of KBR, or so they say. So foreign companies can't completely own the oil industry, but they can run it . . . just like they'll never own Iraq, but they can run the Governing Council.

Someone sent me an email a couple of weeks back praising Halliburton and Bechtel to the skies. The argument was that we should consider ourselves "lucky" to have such prestigious corporations running the oil industry and heading the reconstruction efforts because a. they are efficient, and b. they employ the "locals."

Ok. Fine. I'll pretend I never read that article that said it would take at least two years to get the electricity back to pre-war levels. I'll pretend that it hasn't been 5 months since the "end of the war" and the very efficient companies are terrified of beginning work because the security situation is so messed up.

As for employing the locals . . . things are becoming a little bit clearer. Major reconstruction contracts are being given to the huge companies, like Bechtel and Halliburton, for millions of dollars. These companies, in turn, employ the Iraqis in the following way: they first ask for bids on specific projects. The Iraqi company with the lowest bid is selected to do the work. The Iraqi company gets *exactly* what it bid from the huge conglomerate, which is usually only a fraction of the original contract price. Hence, projects that should cost $1,000,000 end up costing $50,000,000.

Now, call me naïve, or daft, or whatever you want, but wouldn't it be a. more economical and b. more profitable to the Iraqis to hand the work over directly to experienced Iraqi companies? Why not work directly with one of the 87 companies and factories that once worked under the "Iraqi Military Council" and made everything from missiles to electrical components? Why not work directly with one of the 158 factories and companies under the former Ministry of Industry and Minerals that produced everything from candy to steel girders? Why not work with the bridge, housing, and building companies under the Ministry of Housing that have been heading the reconstruction efforts ever since 1991?

Some of the best engineers, scientists, architects, and technicians are currently out of work because their companies have nothing to do and there are no funds to keep them functioning. The employees get together a couple of days a week and spend several hours brooding over "istikans" of lukewarm tea and "finjans" of Turkish coffee. Instead of spending the endless billions on multinational companies, why not spend only millions on importing spare parts and renovating factories and plants?

My father has a friend with a wife and 3 children who is currently working for an Italian internet company. He communicates online with his "boss" who sits thousands of kilometers away, in Rome, safe and sure that there are people who need to feed their families doing the work in Baghdad. This friend, and a crew of male techies, work 10 hours a day, 6 days a week. They travel all over Baghdad, setting up networks. They travel in a beat-up SUV armed with cables, wires, pliers, network cards, installation CDs, and a Klashnikov for . . . you know . . . technical emergencies.

Each of the 20 guys who work with this company get $100/month. A hundred dollars for 260 hours a month comes to . . . $0.38/hour. My 16-year-old babysitter used to get more. The Italian company, like many other foreign companies, seems to think that $100 is appropriate for the present situation. One wonders the price of the original contract the Italian company got . . . how many countless millions are being spent so 20 guys can make $100/month to set up networks?

John Snow, US Treasury Secretary, claimed that the reforms were the "proposals, ideas, and concepts of the Governing Council" with no pressure from the American administration. If that's true, then Bush can pull out the troops any time he wants because he'll be leaving behind a Governing Council that is obviously more solicitous of Halliburton and Co. than he and Cheney can ever hope to be . . . **posted by river @ 3:41 AM**

Saturday, September 27, 2003

FREEDOM OF THE PRESS

Apparently our leader of the moment, Al-Chalabi, isn't pleased with the two leading news networks in the region. I can't really blame him . . . he has had some of his worst interviews on Al-Arabia and Al-Jazeera. He always ends up looking smug like he's just done something evil, or conniving like he's planning something evil. When is he going to learn that there is no network in this wide world that has the technology or capacity to make him look good?

A few days ago, Intifadh Qambar, Ahmad Al-Chalabi's sidekick, was on-screen, shifty-eyed and stuttering, claiming that the two major Arab news networks, Al-Arabia and Al-Jazeera, were "encouraging terrorism." It gives me chills to hear someone like Qambar talk about terrorism. He sits behind the microphones looking like a would-be mafia king in his pin-striped suits, slicked-back hair, and arrogant smile. He seems to have forgotten that the INC, a few months back, were a constant source of terror on the streets of Baghdad while they were "confiscating" cars at gunpoint.

The allegations are purportedly based on the fact that the two news networks have been showing "masked men in black" as resistors to occupation. This, apparently, promotes terrorism. The truth is that Al-Jazeera and Al-Arabia have been black-listed since May, when the first attacks against the troops started getting some real publicity. They were also covering some of the not-so-successful raids that had been carried out by the troops, and the indignant families or victims who suffered them.

Back in May, though, there was no Governing Council and the CPA evidently realized that expelling, or banning, the two major Arabic news networks would look less than diplomatic. They were "warned." Their reporters were yelled at, detained, barred from press conferences, expelled from news sites, and sometimes beaten. The Governing Council have fewer scruples about looking good.

Our media frenzy began in April. Almost immediately after the occupation, political parties began sprouting up everywhere. There were the standard parties that everyone knew—Al-Da'awa, SCIRI,

INC, and PUK—and there were the not-so-famous ones that suddenly found the political vacuum too tempting to pass up. Suddenly, they were all over Baghdad. They scoped out the best areas and took over schools, shops, mosques, recreational clubs, houses, and bureaus. The ones who were ahead of the game got to the printing presses, set up headquarters, and instantly began churning out semi-political newspapers that discussed everything from the "liberation" to Jennifer Lopez's engagement ring.

We would purchase several papers at a time, awed by the sudden torrent of newsprint. Some of them were silly, some of them were amusing, and some of them were serious, polished, and constructive; all of them were pushing a specific political agenda. It was confusing and difficult, at first, to decide which newspapers could be taken seriously and which ones were vying for the coveted position of the best scandal paper in Iraq. Regardless of their productivity, their crossword puzzle, or their horoscopes, they all ended up either on the floor or on the coffee table, under platters of hot rice, flat bread and "marga."

I don't know if it's done in other parts of the Arab world, but when Iraqis don't feel like gathering around a dinner table, they have a cozier meal on the coffee table in the living room or gathered in a circle on the floor. The table, or ground, is spread with newspapers to keep it clean and the food is set up sort of like an open buffet.

During July and August, when it was particularly hot, we ate on the floor. Houses and apartments in Iraq are rarely ever carpeted during the summer. At the first signs of heat, people roll up their Persian rugs and carpeting and store them away in mothballs for at least 5 months. So before lunch or dinner, we mop the tile floor in the living room with cold, clean water, let it dry, and set up the newspapers on the ground. The floor is hard but cool, and somehow the food tastes better and the conversation is lighter.

As plates and forks clash and arms cross to pass a particular food, I keep my eye on the papers. It has become a habit to scan the bold headings under the platters for something interesting. I remember reading the details of UN resolution 1483 for the first time while absently serving rice and "bamia"—an okra dish loved by all Iraqis irrespective of religion or ethnicity. It's funny how although we get most of our information from the internet, the television, or the radio, I still associate the smell of a newspaper with . . . news. When all is said and done, there are just some things you're not going to get anywhere but an Iraqi newspaper (like the fact that SARS came from a comet that hit Earth a couple of years ago—I'll wager no one has read *that*).

This media free-for-all lasted for about two months. Then, some newspapers were "warned" that some of their political content was unacceptable—especially when discussing occupation forces. One or two papers were actually shut down, while others were made to retract some of what they had written. The news channels followed suit. The CPA came out with a list of things that weren't to be discussed— including the number of casualties, the number of attacks on the Coalition, and other specifics. And we all began giving each other knowing looks—it's only "freedom of the press" when you have good things to say . . . Iraqis know all about *that*.

Then the Governing Council came along and they weren't at all comfortable with the media. They have their own channel where we hear long-winded descriptions of the wonderful things they are doing for us and how appropriately grateful we should be, but that apparently isn't enough.

So now, Al-Jazeera and Al-Arabia are suspended for two weeks from covering the official press conferences held by the CPA and the Puppet Council . . . which is really no loss—they are becoming predictable. The real news is happening around us.   **posted by river @ 2:58 AM**

WORRIED IN BAGHDAD . . .

Aqila Al-Hashimi was buried today in the holy city of Najaf, in the south. Her funeral procession was astounding. Rumor has it that she was supposed to be made Iraq's ambassadress to the UN. There are still no leads to her attackers' identities . . . somehow people seem to think that Al-Chalabi and gang are behind this attack just like they suspect he might have been behind the Jordanian Embassy attack. Al-Chalabi claims it's Saddam, which is the easy thing to do—pretend that the only figures vying for power are the Governing Council, currently headed by Al-Chalabi, and Saddam and ignore the fundamentalists and any intra-Council hostilities, rivalries, and bitterness between members.

What is particularly disturbing is that the UN is pulling out some of its staff for security reasons . . . they pulled out a third tonight and others will be leaving in the next few days. Things are getting more and more frightening. My heart sinks every time the UN pulls out because that was how we used to gauge the political situation in the past: the UN is pulling out—we're getting bombed.

Someone brought this to my attention . . . it's an interesting piece on some of the companies facilitating the whole shady contract affair in Iraq. The original piece is published by The Guardian Unlimited and discusses contracts, the Bush administration, and how Salem Al-Chalabi, Ahmad Al-Chalabi's nephew, fits into the whole situation— Friends of the Family.

"Friends of the Family," Guardian Unlimited, September 24, 2003
http://www.guardian.co.uk/elsewhere/journalist/story/0,7792,104820
4,00.html

IILG (Iraqi International Law Group) says it was established in the wake of the "recent coalition victory" in Iraq and is proud to be the first international law firm based inside the country . . .

IILG is surprisingly modest about the family connections of its founder, Salem Chalabi. The website doesn't mention that he is a nephew of Ahmed Chalabi, who just happens to be the leader of the US-backed Iraqi National Congress (INC) . . .

Interestingly, the firm's website is not registered in Salem Chalabi's name but in the name of Marc Zell, whose address is given as Suite 716, 1800 K Street, Washington. That is the address of the Washington office of Zell, Goldberg &Co . . . and the related FANDZ International Law Group . . .

The unusual name "FANDZ" was concocted from "F and Z," the Z being Marc Zell and the F being Douglas Feith. The two men were law partners until 2001, when Feith took up his Pentagon post as undersecretary of defence for policy . . .

This ties in with a recent announcement by Zell, Goldberg & Co that it has set up a "task force" dealing with issues and opportunities relating to the "recently ended" war in Iraq . . .

There's a shorter, equally good version of the same on Joshua Marshall's site that is worth reading—Talking Points Memo (http://www.talkingpointsmemo.com). **posted by river @ 3:00 AM**

Monday, September 29, 2003

SHEIKHS AND TRIBES . . .

A few people pointed out an article to me titled "Iraqi Family Ties Complicate American Efforts for Change," by John Tierney.

> *"Iraqi Family Ties Complicate American Efforts for Change,"*
> *New York Times, September 28, 2003*
> *http://query.nytimes.com/gst/abstract.html?res=F70A16FB3B590C7B8*
> *EDDA00894DB404482*

Iqbal Muhammad does not recall her first glimpse of her future husband, because they were both newborns at the time, but she remembers precisely when she knew he was the one. It was the afternoon her uncle walked over from his house next door and proposed that she marry his son Muhammad.

"I was a little surprised, but I knew right away it was a wise choice," she said, recalling that afternoon nine years ago, when she and Muhammad were 22. "It is safer to marry a cousin than a stranger."

Her reaction was typical in a country where nearly half of marriages are between first or second cousins, a statistic that is one of the more important and least understood differences between Iraq and America. The extraordinarily strong family bonds complicate virtually everything Americans are trying to do here, from finding Saddam Hussein to changing women's status to creating a liberal democracy.

"Americans just don't understand what a different world Iraq is because of these highly unusual cousin marriages," said Robin Fox of Rutgers University, the author of "Kinship and Marriage," a widely used anthropology textbook. "Liberal democracy is based on the Western idea of autonomous individuals committed to a public good, but that's not how members of these tight and bounded kin groups see the world. Their world is divided into two groups: kin and strangers" . . .

The families resulting from these marriages have made nation-building a frustrating process in the Middle East, as King Faisal and

> *T.E. Lawrence both complained after efforts to unite Arab tribes . . .*
> *That dichotomy remains today, said Ihsan M. al-Hassan, a sociol-*
> *ogist at the University of Baghdad. At the local level, the clan tra-*
> *ditions provide more support and stability than Western institutions,*
> *he said, noting that the divorce rate among married cousins is only*
> *2 percent in Iraq, versus 30 percent for other Iraqi couples. But the*
> *local ties create national complications.*
> *"The traditional Iraqis who marry their cousins are very suspicious*
> *of outsiders," Dr. Hassan said. "In a modern state a citizen's allegiance*
> *is to the state, but theirs is to their clan and their tribe. If one person*
> *in your clan does something wrong, you favor him anyway, and you*
> *expect others to treat their relatives the same way" . . .*

You need to be registered in [the] New York Times to read it, but since registration is free, the articles are sometimes worth the hassle. I could comment for days on the article but I'll have to make it as brief as possible, and I'll also have to make it in two parts. Today I'll blog about tribes and sheikhs and tomorrow I'll blog about cousins and veils.

Iraqi family ties are complicating things for Americans—true. But not for the reasons Tierney states. He simplifies the whole situation incredibly by stating that because Iraqis tend to marry cousins, they'll be less likely to turn each other in to American forces for all sorts of reasons that all lead back to nepotism.

First and foremost, in Baghdad, Mosul, Basrah, Kirkuk, and various other large cities in Iraq, marrying cousins is out of style, and not very popular, when you have other choices. Most people who get into college end up marrying someone from college or someone they meet at work.

In other areas, cousins marry each other for the simple reason that many smaller cities and provinces are dominated by 4 or 5 huge "tribes" or "clans." So, naturally, everyone who isn't a parent, grandparent, brother, sister, aunt, or uncle is a "cousin." These tribes are led by one or more sheikhs.

When people hear the word "tribe" or "sheikh," they instantly imagine, I'm sure, Bedouins on camels and scenes from Lawrence of Arabia. Many modern-day sheikhs in Iraq have college degrees. Many have lived abroad and own property in London, Beirut, and various other glamorous capitals . . . they ride around in Mercedes and live in sprawling villas fully furnished with Victorian furniture, Persian carpets, oil paintings, and air conditioners. Some of them have British, German, or American wives. A sheikh is respected highly both by his clan members and by the members of other clans or tribes. He is usually considered the wisest or most influential member of the family. He is often also the wealthiest.

Sheikhs also have many duties. The modern sheikh acts as a sort of family judge for the larger family disputes. He may have to give verdicts on anything from a land dispute to a marital spat. His word isn't necessarily law, but any family member who decides to go against it is considered on his own, i.e., without the support and influence of the tribe. They are also responsible for the well-being of many of the poorer members of the tribe who come to them for help. We had relatively few orphans in orphanages in Iraq because the tribe takes in children without parents and they are often under the care of the sheikh's direct family. The sheikh's wife is sort of the "First Lady" of the family and has a lot of influence with family members.

Shortly after the occupation, Jay Garner began meeting with the prominent members of Iraqi society—businessmen, religious leaders, academicians, and sheikhs. The sheikhs were important because each sheikh basically had influence over hundreds, if not thousands, of "family." The prominent sheikhs from all over Iraq were brought together in a huge conference of sorts. They sat gathered, staring at the representative of the occupation forces who, I think, was British and sat speaking in broken, awkward Arabic. He told the sheikhs that Garner and friends really needed their help to build a democratic Iraq. They were powerful, influential people—they could contribute a lot to society.

A few of the sheikhs were bitter. One of the most prominent had lost 18 family members with one blow when the American forces dropped a cluster bomb on his home, outside of Baghdad, and killed women, children, and grandchildren all gathered together in fear. The only survivor of that massacre was a two-year-old boy who had to have his foot amputated.

Another sheikh was the head of a family in Basrah who lost 8 people to a missile that fell on their home, while they slept. The scenes of the house were beyond horrid—a mess of broken furniture, crumbling walls, and severed arms and legs.

Almost every single sheikh had his own woeful story to tell. They were angry and annoyed. And these weren't people who loved Saddam. Many of them hated the former regime because in a fit of socialism, during the eighties, a law was established that allowed thousands of acres of land to be confiscated from wealthy landowners and sheikhs and divided out between poor farmers. They resented the fact that land they had owned for several generations was being given out to nobody farmers who would no longer be willing to harvest their fields.

So they came to the meeting, wary but willing to listen. Many of them rose to speak. They told the representative right away that the Americans and British were occupiers—that was undeniable, but they were willing to help if it would move the country forward. Their one stipulation was the following: that they be given a timetable that gave a general idea of when the occupation forces would pull out of Iraq.

They told the representative that they couldn't go back to their "3shayir," or tribes, asking them to "please cooperate with the Americans although they killed your families, raided your homes, and detained your sons" without some promise that, should security prevail, there would be prompt elections and a withdrawal of occupation forces.

Some of them also wanted to contribute politically. They had influence, power, and connections . . . they wanted to be useful in some way. The representative frowned, fumbled, and told them that there was no way he was going to promise a withdrawal of occupation forces. They would be in Iraq "as long as they were needed" . . . that might be two years, that might be five years, and it might be ten years. There were going to be no promises . . . there certainly was no "timetable" and the sheikhs had no say in what was going on—they could simply consent.

The whole group, in a storm of indignation and helplessness, rose to leave the meeting. They left the representative looking frustrated and foolish, frowning at the diminishing mass in front of him. When asked to comment on how the meeting went, he smiled, waved a hand, and replied, "No comment." When one of the prominent sheikhs was asked how the meeting went, he angrily said that it wasn't a conference—they had gathered up the sheikhs to "give them orders" without a willingness to listen to the other side of the story or even to compromise . . . the representative thought he was talking to his own private army—not the pillars of tribal society in Iraq.

Apparently, the sheikhs were blacklisted because, of late, their houses are being targeted. They are raided in the middle of the night with armored cars, troops, and helicopters. The sheikh and his immediate family members are pushed to the ground with a booted foot and held there at gunpoint. The house is searched and often looted and the sheikh and his sons are dragged off with hands behind their backs and bags covering their heads. The whole family is left outraged and incredulous: the most respected member of the tribe is being imprisoned for no particular reason except that they may need him for questioning. In many cases, the sheikh is returned a few days later with an "apology," only to be raided and detained once more!

I would think that publicly humiliating and detaining respected members of society like sheikhs and religious leaders would contribute more to throttling democracy than "cousins marrying cousins." Many of the attacks against the occupying forces are acts of revenge for assaulted family members, or people who were killed during raids, demonstrations, or checkpoints. But the author fails to mention that, of course.

He also fails to mention that because many of the provinces are in fact governed by the sheikhs of large tribes, they are much safer than Baghdad and parts of the south. Baghdad is an eclectic mix of Iraqis from all over the country and sheikhs have little influence over members outside of their family. In smaller provinces or towns, on the other hand, looting and abduction are rare because the criminal will have a virtual army to answer to—not a confused, and often careless, occupying army and some frightened Iraqi police.

Iraq is not some backward country overrun by ignorant land sheikhs or oil princes. People have a deep respect for wisdom and "origin." People can trace their families back for hundreds of years and the need to "belong" to a specific family or tribe and have a sheikh doesn't hinder education, modernization, democracy, or culture. Arabs and Kurds in the region have strong tribal ties and it is considered an honor to have a strong family backing—even if you don't care about tribal law or have strayed far from family influence.

I'm an example of a modern-day, Iraqi female who is a part of a tribe—I've never met our sheikh—I've never needed to . . . I have a university degree, I had a job, and I have a family who would sacrifice a lot to protect me . . . and none of this hinders me from having ambition or a sense of obligation towards law and order. I also want democracy, security, and a civil, healthy society . . . right along with the strong family bonds I'm accustomed to as an Iraqi.

Who knows? Maybe I'll start a tribal blog and become a virtual sheikh myself . . . **posted by river @ 11:36 PM**

Wednesday, October 01, 2003

CURRENT READING . . .

I'm reading a great book by Danny Schechter called "Embedded: Weapons of Mass Deception" which can be found on MediaChannel.org (http://www.mediachannel.org/giving/embedded/download.html). The book is fantastic . . . it discusses the media deception that went on before the war and is still occurring today. Some chapters leave me awed with thoughts like, "Were they actually doing that?! How could they have done that?!" Other chapters leave me angry, "Didn't the world know *that*?!" . . . the whole book leaves me relieved: the world is finally waking up.

Another site I'm checking out lately is a site by "Malcom Lagauche," a journalist/author who writes about Iraq, amongst other things. His site is called Lagauche is Right (http://www.malcomlagauche.com). One post that got my attention was his September 25 post about that atrocious toy that was being sold in America—the "Forward Command Post," which shows an Iraqi home, complete with bloodstains, crumbling walls, no family members (they were probably detained), and a triumphant American soldier . . .

I can imagine a child receiving the huge package for Christmas or a Birthday and opening it up with glee . . . seeing the chaos, the havoc, the destruction and feeling . . . what? Pride? Victory? Elation? And they say it's Al-Jazeera that promotes violence. Sure. **posted by river @ 11:03 PM**

COUSINS AND VEILS . . .

This is some further commentary on John Tierney's article "Iraq Family Ties Complicate American Efforts for Change," printed in the New York Times.

"A key purpose of veiling is to prevent outsiders from competing with a woman's cousins for marriage," Dr. Kurtz said. "Attack veiling, and you are attacking the core of the Middle Eastern social system." ("Iraqi Family Ties Complicate American Efforts for Change," NY Times, September 28, 2003, http://query.nytimes.com/gst/abstract. html?res=F70A16FB3B 590C7B8EDDA00894DB404482)

Thank you Stanley Kurtz, anthropologist at the Hoover Institution.

He took hundreds of years of wearing the veil for religious reasons and relegated it all to the oppression of females by their male cousins. Wow—human nature is that simple.

I can see the image now—my cousins roaming the opening of our cave, holding clubs and keeping a wary eye on the female members of their clan . . . and us cowed, frightened females all gathered in groups, murmuring behind our veils . . .

I have a question: why is Dr. Kurtz using the word "veil" in relation to Iraq? Very, very few females wore veils or burqas prior to the occupation. Note that I say "veil" or "burqa." If Dr. Kurtz meant the general "hijab" or headscarf worn on the hair by millions of Muslim females instead of an actual "veil," then he should have been more specific. While a "veil" in Saudi Arabia or Afghanistan is quite common, in Iraq it speaks of extremism. It is uncommon because the majority of moderate Muslim clerics believe it is unnecessary.

A "veil" is a piece of cloth that covers the whole face and head. It is called a "veil" in English and called a "burgu3" (burqa), "khimar," or "pushi" in Iraq. The khimar or burqa either covers the whole face, or covers it all with the exception of the eyes.

The standard "hijab" or "rabta" is a simple headscarf that covers the hair and neck, and can be worn in a variety of ways. The majority of "covered" females in Iraq wear a simple hijab. Some fashionable females wear a turban-like head cover and something with a high collar that generally serves the same purpose. The hijab can be any color. Some women prefer white, others black and I have friends who own every color and design imaginable and look so good, it almost seems more like a fashion statement than a religious one.

The "abaya," on the other hand, is a long, cloak-like garment and is more traditional than it is religious. Although designs vary, the abaya is similar in style to the standard graduation robe—long, wide, and flowing. Some abayas are designed to cover the head, and others are made only to wear on the shoulders. Men, as well as women, wear abayas. The feminine abayas are often black and may have some sort of design on them. Male abayas are plain, with perhaps some simple embroidery along the edges, and are brown, black, gray, beige, or khaki. Abayas are often worn in Iraq, although the younger generations don't like them—I haven't worn one yet.

The hijab can be worn with ordinary clothing—skirts, shirts and pants as long as they are "appropriate." The skirt should be somewhat long, the shirt a little bit loose, and the sleeves should be below the elbows and, if worn with pants, a bit long. The purpose of the hijab is to protect females from sexual harassment. It acts as a sort of safe-guard against ogling and uninvited attention.

Muslim females do not wear a hijab or veil because their male cousins *make* them wear it. They wear it for religious reasons. I personally don't wear a hijab or headscarf, but I know many females who do—in Baghdad, in Mosul, in Najaf, in Kerbela, in Falloojeh . . . in Jordan, in Syria, in Lebanon, in Saudi Arabia . . . and *none* of these females wear a headscarf because their *cousins* make them wear it. They wear the headscarf out of a conviction that it is the correct thing to do and out of the comfort and security it gives them. Cousins have nothing to do with it and Dr. Kurtz's very simplistic explanation is an insult.

Dr. Kurtz would have better said, "Attack the headscarf or the hijab and you are attacking the core of the Middle Eastern social system because the majority of the Middle East is Muslim and the headscarf is considered a required part of Islam by a huge number of Muslims." Attacking the hijab would be the equivalent of attacking a Christian's right to wear a cross, or a Jew's right to wear a yarmulke . . . **posted by river @ 11:04 PM**

Sunday, October 05, 2003

RIOTS . . .

There were riots in Baghdad today . . . the group was a combination of expelled soldiers and jobless people. They say the mob started getting loud and moving forward, crowding the troops standing in front of the building they receive wages from so one of the American troops started firing into the air . . . a few people started throwing rocks . . . all hell broke loose. They say two people were killed—one was shot by the troops in the head and another was beaten on the head with a nightstick and was unconscious for several hours before he died. The riots were near Al-Muthana airport near Mansur—an upscale area in the center of Baghdad . . .

About "Forward Command Post" . . . for those of you who claim that it doesn't exist—there's plenty of information if you Google it. For those of you who corrected me—thank you—apparently, it doesn't represent an "Iraqi home," it just represents some war-torn home anywhere in the world . . . **posted by river @ 1:07 AM**

FIRST DAY OF SCHOOL . . .

Today was the first day of the new academic year. Well, it was actually on October 1, but most students didn't bother going on Wednesday. University students have decided they are not going to start classes until next week.

Yesterday, I went with my cousin, his wife, and my brother, E., to shop for school supplies for his two daughters—a pretty 10-year-old and a loud 7-year-old. Every year his wife, S., takes the girls to pick out their own pencils, notebooks, and backpacks but ever since the war, she hasn't let them step outside of the house—unless it is to go visit a relative.

So we packed into the car and headed off for a shopping area in the middle of Baghdad. We don't have shopping malls or huge shopping centers in Iraq. We have shops, big and small, up and down commercial streets and located on corners of residential blocks. School supplies are sold at "makatib" or stationary shops that sell everything from toys to desk sets.

We pulled up in front of a little stationary shop and all got down. It felt a bit ridiculous—four grown people all out shopping for Barbie notebooks and strawberry-scented erasers . . . but I knew it was necessary. E. and the cousin loitered outside of the shop while we went inside to make our purchases.

I have missed stationary shops . . . the row upon row of colored copybooks, the assorted cans of pencils, pens, and markers are the best part of any school year. I used to anticipate shopping for school supplies well before the start of the school year. The long, unsharpened pencils with no bite marks, multi-colored pens, and clean erasers somehow held the promise of achievements to come . . .

My cousin's wife, S., was in a hurry. She had left her daughters at our house with my parents and was sure that the little one was going to talk them to death. She went to pick out the pencils and crayons while I got to choose the copybooks. In the end, I went with a few Senafir (Smurfs) copybooks, some Barbie notebooks for the older one, and was hard-pressed to choose between Winnie the Pooh and Lion King for the younger. I went with Winnie the Pooh in the end.

The erasers were all in a big, clear fishbowl. S. wanted to go with some generic pink ones that looked like pieces of gum and smelled like tires, but I argued that kids don't take care of their school supplies if they're ugly and she should just let me choose—they all cost the same anyway. I rummaged around in the fishbowl, pulled out one colored eraser after the other, and tried to decide which ones would look the best with the copybooks I had chosen.

The shop assistant looked exasperated when I started smelling them and S. hissed that they all smelled the same anyway. No, they DON'T all smell the same—they all *taste* the same (and don't shake your head—we've all tasted an eraser at some point or another). In the end, we went with some strawberry-shaped erasers that, oddly enough, smelled like peaches . . . S. said I was confusing the kids but I reminded her that they had never tasted strawberries anyway (they only grow in the northern region in Iraq and rarely reach Baghdad) . . . her kids wouldn't know the difference.

At home, we found the girls waiting impatiently. There were mixed feelings—their summer vacation had started at the end of

June this year and since they had been cooped up at home the whole summer, the last couple of months didn't count as a summer vacation to them. On the other hand, they were going to get to see their friends, and leave the confines of their house on a daily basis . . . I would gladly trade places.

They greeted us at the door, reaching for the bags their mother was carrying. The older one was appropriately pleased with everything I had chosen . . . the younger one was another story. Apparently, she had outgrown Winnie Dabdoob (Winnie the Pooh, in Arabic) and wanted a Barbie copybook instead . . . I tried to divert her with the "pretty horse with a plait and a bow . . ." but she loudly proclaimed that he was a "7mar benefseji" (purple donkey) and if I liked donkeys so much, I could keep the copybook . . . so from now on I'm going to jot things down for my blog in a little notebook with a purple donkey and a bear gracing its cover.

My cousin and S. made arrangements on how the kids would get to school and back. They agreed that my cousin would walk them to school (which was two blocks away) and wait around to see when school would be out and what sort of security arrangements the administration had made.

This morning, at 8:30, they headed out to the school, the girls dressed in their uniforms, new pencils and deceptive erasers ready for use . . . my cousin, pistol at his waist, clutching each girl firmly by the hand, reached the school just as other parents and kids were getting there—school normally starts no later than 8 am, but today was an exception.

The school was full of people . . . but many of the classrooms were practically empty—the desks were gone . . . the chairs were gone . . . but, the blackboards were still there and they would have to do. The good news was that the windows that had shattered when a site behind the school was bombed, had been replaced. The parents agreed that any child who could would bring two pieces of chalk a week until the school could sort out the situation with the Ministry of Education. An architect with 3 kids in the school volunteered to provide white paint for walls at a reasonably low price.

We've heard of a few schools that are being renovated in Baghdad by the UNICEF and the UNESCO, but it's a slow process and there's a lot of damage. Some schools suffered from the bombing, others from the looting and quite a few from the "political parties" that set up camp at various schools all over Baghdad.

The curriculums aren't going to be changed drastically and the students will be using the same books but teachers have been asked not to teach specific topics in the history and geography books.

My cousin met with the teachers and with other fathers and everyone decided that the best option would be to have the kids bring in small chairs or stools to sit on while the teachers gave classes. The fathers were agreeing amongst themselves to take shifts "guarding" the school during the day . . . lucky for my cousin, the school is in a residential area and the majority of the students' parents live nearby—the whole area keeps an eye on the kids. Very few of them will be walking to and from school, at this point.

I remember watching them every year—I'd be off to my university or work just as the kids started leaving for school. The majority were on foot, early morning, wearing their uniforms. The uniforms are usually a navy-blue smock and white shirt for the girls, and navy-blue or gray pants and a white shirt for the boys. Many parents prefer uniforms because they are more economical and the financial backgrounds of the children are far less conspicuous when everyone is in navy-blue and white.

They always looked crisp and clean in the morning—shirts pressed, hair tidy, faces clean and backpacks where they should be—on the back. By 2 o'clock, the majority of them are straggling home after school in little groups, backpacks being dragged on the sidewalks, shirts half yanked out of pants, sweaters tied around their waists or around their heads and white socks a dingy gray and bunching around little ankles.

This year will be different . . . S. says she doesn't know how she's going to spend the day without the girls "in front of her eyes" . . . "It felt like they took my lungs with them—I couldn't breathe until they got home..." **posted by river @ 1:09 AM**

Thursday, October 09, 2003

Check out Justin Alexander's blog from Baghdad. Justin works for a nonprofit organization called Jubilee Iraq, which is dedicated to cancelling Iraqi debt. My favorite post is "Have You Seen the Planning Minister?"

Iraqi Wannabe, http://www.justinalexander.net, October 6, 2003

Have you seen the planning minister?

He's in his 50s, about 5 foot 10, classic Iraqi looks with moustache and probably somewhere in Northern Europe. But we're not sure, and nor is his ministry. They haven't heard from him in a week, don't know if he'll be back in Baghdad before November and have no email or phone number to contact him on. I'm really not kidding you, and it's not just the Planning Ministry, this is a familiar senario in Iraq today. Apart from being incredibly frustrating for someone whose traveled 5000 miles to try and consult with Iraqis, I think it says something about the resources and responsibilities being allotted to Iraaqis by the CPA—pretty much nil. I've visited 5 ministries today, and only one had working phones and email, indeed only one (the Ministry of Oil) had a contactable Minister (who I'm meeting next Monday, inshallah). The really frightening thing is that in November the UN Oil-for-Food program ends and somehow the CPA and the Ministries (most squatting in temporary building since their offices were largely looted and burnt) are going to have to manage food distribution for the 16 million people who are dependent on the ration for survival.

Oh, here's today's cute detail: the windows in the reception room for the Ministry of Trade were covered with —you guessed it —Pokemon stickers! I tried to find a cinema for a bit of relaxation this evening, but it seems that everywhere I showing either Egyptian movies or pornography, so that was a dead end. Ended up in a 9asiir (juice) bar as usual. Got an invite to go play dominos with some Iraqi students one evening soon, which should be fun. One of them is making his first film and said I can have a cameo role . . . Cannes here we come!

Some good news—It seems like I've wrangled my way onto a trip down to Najaf and Karbala to meet the major Shia clerics like

---

Ayatollah Sistani in a few days time. Tisbah al-khayr (good night). Justin

POSTSCRIPT: I went out onto my hotel balcony (overlooking the Palestine hotel next door where a Salsa class, of all things, was happening) last night, and began chatting to the American film crew on the next door balcony. They told me with great glee how much fun they'd had earlier that evening lobbing bananas at the homeless kids on the street seven floors below . . . I had to dig my nails into my palms to prevent sending one of them sailing after the fruit . (7:59 PM)

posted by river @ 9:04 PM

JEWELRY AND RAIDS . . .

Yesterday afternoon we went to visit a relative who had recently come home from London. He wasn't a political refugee there, nor was he a double-agent . . . or anything glamorous . . . just a man who had decided to live his life in England. He came to visit every year, usually during December. He was in a state of . . . shock at what he saw around him. Every few minutes he would get up in disbelief, trailing off in mid-sentence, to stand in the window—looking out at the garden like he could perhaps see beyond the garden wall and into the streets of Baghdad.

"We watch it on television over there . . . but it's nothing like *this* . . . " And I knew what he meant. Seeing it on the various networks covering the war is nothing like living in its midst. Watching the 7 o'clock news and hearing about "a car bomb in Baghdad" is nothing like standing in the street, wary of the moving vehicles, wondering if one of them is going to burst into a flying ball of flames and shrapnel. Seeing the checkpoints on Al-Jazeera, CNN, or BBC is nothing like driving solemnly up to them, easing the car to a stop and praying that the soldier on the other side doesn't think you look decidedly suspicious . . . or that his gun doesn't accidentally go off.

The relative had some interesting gossip on a few of our new "elite": "Oh *him*?! He had shares in a club in London . . . didn't know he was into politics." And, "Oh hiiiiiiiiiiiiiim . . . his house *was* a club—smashing parties!" When we asked him why in the world he had moved up his trip to October when it would have been better to wait a couple of months for security reasons, he dismissed us with a wave of the hand: "I saw the nine-member presidential council . . . maybe I'll run for president."

We took my aunt and her daughter home with us, after the brief family gathering. E. was in a big hurry to get us home before it darkened. Luckily, our relative's house wasn't all that far from our own and we made it to our area just as the sun was setting over some distant palms. The tension during the brief journey eased up somewhat as we turned into the main road that led to our street, and then we all tensed up again.

There, pulled up to the side of the road, with one armored car in front and one behind, was a huge, beige-green tank. My aunt moaned and clutched at her handbag possessivel. "Is this a checkpoint? What are they searching for? Are they going to check us?" She was carrying all of her gold jewelry in the black, leather bag which, every time she reached inside to rummage for something, I imagined would swallow her up into its depths.

Iraqi people don't own gold because they are either spectacularly wealthy, or they have recently been on a looting spree . . . Gold is a part of our culture and the roll it plays in "family savings" has increased since 1990 when the Iraqi Dinar (which was $3) began fluctuating crazily. People began converting their money to gold—earrings, bracelets, necklaces—because the value of gold didn't change. People pulled their money out of banks before the war, and bought gold instead. Women here call gold "zeeneh ou 7*azeeneh (khazeeneh)," which means "ornaments and savings." Gold can be shown off and worn, but in times of economical trouble, a few pieces can be sold to tide the family over.

Many troops claimed that they took gold from houses because they couldn't believe people like *that* could own gold . . . what they don't know is that when two Iraqis get married—regardless of religion—the man often gives the woman a "mahar" or dowry, composed of gold jewelry. When a couple has a child, the gifts are often little gold trinkets that the parents can sell or keep . . . this was especially popular before the blockade.

"They might be checking houses . . ." E. said. We traveled the last kilometer home in a thoughtful silence, each lost in their own worries. I was worried about the computer. In areas where they claimed to have gotten a "tip," the computers were often confiscated for checking, never to be seen again. I practiced various phrases in my head: "Take the money, gold, and gun, leave the computer . . ."

At home, my mother was anxiously clearing up the kitchen. We told her about the tank "parked" on the main road. "I know," she said, rubbing at a stubborn stain on the counter, "It's been there for the last hour . . . they might check the area tonight." My aunt went into a tirade against raids, troops, and looting, then calmed down and decided that she wouldn't hide her gold tonight· her daughter and I would wear it. I stood there with my mouth hanging open—who is to stop anyone from taking it off of us? Was she crazy? No, she wasn't crazy. We would wear the necklaces, tucking them in under our shirts and the rest would go into our pockets. There would be "abayas" or robes on standby—if they decided to check the house, we would throw on the abayas and leave the house calmly, waiting for the raid to end.

My mother had hidden our not-particularly-impressive valuables in a few ingenious places. It was a game for days, during May, when the raids began and we started hearing tales of the "confiscation" of valuables like gold and dollars during the raids. Everyone started thinking up creative hiding places to hide the money and jewelry. Neighbors and relatives would trade tips on the best hiding places and the ones that were checked right away . . . the guns were a little bit more difficult. They were necessary for protection against gangs and armed militias. People were allowed to have one pistol and one rifle. If the troops walk into your home, armed to the eyeballs, guns pointed and tense with fear, and find an extra rifle or gun, it is considered "terrorism" and the family may find itself on the evening news as a potential terrorist cell.

We went on with our usual evening activities—well, almost. My aunt wanted to bathe, but was worried they'd suddenly decide to raid us while she was in the bathroom. In the end, she decided that she would bathe, but that E. would have to stand on the roof, diligently watching the road, and the moment an armored car or tank found itself on our street, he'd have to give the warning so my aunt would have time to dress. My cousin and I joined him on the roof and debated the degree of "fun" it would be to run downstairs screaming "Raid! Raid!," and pound on the bathroom door. After a few minutes, we regretfully decided we were all too mature for that.

The electricity went out during dinner, which was composed of not-too-sweet watermelon, salty cheese, khubz, cucumber and yoghurt salad and tomatoes. In the pitch dark, while waiting for a candle, I accidentally poked a finger in the cucumber and yoghurt salad (well, ok, a few fingers). I held up my hand, waiting for the light so I could find some tissues. E. walked in with a kerosene lamp and as my eyes adjusted to the light, I saw the box of tissues next [to] my cousin. I pointed to them and as she reached out to hand me a few, the picture of us suddenly made me want to laugh and cry all at once.

Here we were, 10 p.m., no electricity and all fully clothed because no one wanted to be caught in a raid in their pajamas. I haven't worn pajamas for the last . . . 6 months. Tonight though, my cousin and I looked particularly funny. She was reaching out to hand me tissues and her fingers flashed . . . the gold ring on her thumb was glittering under the rays of kerosene light. Her hair was piled up in a falling mass on top of her head and the necklaces glinted as she moved on the faded blue t-shirt with the words "Smile at ME!" in purple.

I didn't look much better—I sat in cargo pants and an old shirt, feet bare on the cool tiles, with three necklaces, two rings, and a bracelet that kept getting caught on my shirt and in my hair. I told everyone that we looked like maids who were playing dress-up with the mistress's jewelry . . . E. said we actually looked like gypsies ready to make off with the mistress's jewelry. The "mistress" called out that we could laugh all we wanted but since the jewelry was everything she had saved since 1965, we had better be careful.

We went to sleep early . . . except no one slept. E. kept checking for cars or tanks and I sat listening to the night and trying to sleep around the jewelry, thinking of all the pictures I had seen of Elizabeth Taylor and Marilyn Monroe sleeping in diamonds and emeralds. At 3 am, I decided I wasn't Elizabeth Taylor, took off the rings and bracelet ,and stuffed them in my pillowcase.

The morning eventually came, with no tanks—only some distant shots in the background and something that sounded vaguely like an explosion. E. said that they weren't even on the main road anymore

. . . apparently they had left during the night. I returned the jewelry, relieved, but my cousin kept it on, deciding she had grown accustomed to seeing a "wealthy-looking reflection" in the mirror. **posted by river @ 9:07 PM**

Monday, October 13, 2003

PALMS AND PUNISHMENT . . .

Everyone has been wondering about the trees being cut down in Dhuluaya area ("US Soldiers Bulldoze Farmers' Crops," by Patrick Cockburn, Independent, October 12, 2003, http://news.independent.co.uk/world/middle_east/story.jsp?story=452375). Dhuluaya is an area near Sammara, north of Baghdad. It's an area popular for its wonderful date palms, citrus trees, and grape vines. The majority of the people who live in the area are simple landowners who have been making a living off of the orchards they've been cultivating for decades.

Orchards in many areas in Iraq—especially central Iraq—are almost like oases in the desert. From kilometers away, you can see the vivid green of proud date palms shimmering through the waves of heat and smoke, reaching for a sky rarely overcast. Just seeing the orchards brings a sort of peace.

There are over 500 different kinds of palm trees in Iraq. They vary in type from short, stocky trees with a shock of haphazard, green fronds . . . to long, slim trees with a collection of leaves that seem almost symmetrical in their perfection. A palm tree is known as a "nakhla" and never fails to bring a sense of satisfaction and admiration. They are the pride and joy of Iraqi farmers and landowners. A garden isn't complete if there isn't a palm tree gracing it. We locate houses by giving the area, the street and then, "Well, it's the fourth—no, wait . . . the fifth house on the left . . . or was it the right? Oh never mind— it's the house on the street, with the tallest palm tree."

The palm trees, besides being lovely, are highly useful. In the winter months, they act as "resorts" for the exotic birds that flock to Iraq. We often see various species of birds roosting between the leaves, picking on the sweet dates and taunting the small boys below who can't reach the nests. In the summer months, the "female

. . .

palms" provide hundreds of dates for immediate consumption, storage, or processing.

In Iraq, there are over 300 different types of dates—each with its own name, texture, and flavor. Some are dark brown, and soft, while others are bright yellow, crunchy, and have a certain "tang" that is particular to dates. It's very difficult to hate dates—if you don't like one type, you are bound to like another. Dates are also used to produce "dibiss," a dark, smooth, date syrup. This dibiss is eaten in some areas with rice, and in others it is used as a syrup with bread and butter. Often it is used as a main source of sugar in Iraqi sweets.

Iraqi "khal" or vinegar is also produced from dates . . . it is dark and tangy and mixed with olive oil, makes the perfect seasoning to a fresh cucumber and tomato salad. Iraqi "areg," a drink with very high alcoholic content, is often made with dates. In the summer, families trade baskets and trays of dates—allowing neighbors and friends to sample the fruit growing on their palms with the enthusiasm of proud parents showing off a child's latest accomplishment . . .

Every bit of a palm is an investment. The fronds and leaves are dried and used to make beautiful, pale-yellow baskets, brooms, mats, bags, hats, wall hangings and even used for roofing. The fronds are often composed of thick, heavy wood at their ends and are used to make lovely, seemingly-delicate furniture—similar to the bamboo chairs and tables of the Far East. The low-quality dates and the date pits are used as animal feed for cows and sheep. Some of the date pits are the source of a sort of "date oil" that can be used for cooking. The palm itself, should it be cut down, is used as firewood, or for building.

My favorite use for date pits is . . . beads. Each pit is smoothed and polished by hand, pierced in its center and made into necklaces, belts, and rosaries. The finished product is rough, yet graceful, and wholly unique.

Palm trees are often planted alongside citrus trees in orchards for more than just decoration or economy. Palm trees tower above all other trees and provide shade for citrus trees, which wither [sic] under the Iraqi sun. Depending on the type, it takes some palm trees an average of 5 – 10 years to reach their final height (some never actually stop growing), and it takes an average of 5 -7 years for most palms to bear fruit.

The death of a palm tree is taken very seriously. Farmers consider it devastating and take the loss very personally. Each tree is so unique, it feels like a member of the family . . . I remember watching scenes from the war a couple of days after the bombing began— one image that stuck in my mind was that of a palm tree broken in half, the majestic fronds wilting and dragging on the ground. The sight affected me almost as much as the corpses.

Historically, palm trees have represented the rugged, stoic beauty of Iraq and its people. They are a reminder that no matter how difficult the circumstances, there is hope for life and productivity. The palm trees in the orchards have always stood lofty and resolute—oblivious of heat, political strife, or war . . . until today.

One of the most famous streets in Baghdad is "shari3 il mattar" or "The Airport Street." It is actually two streets—one leading to Baghdad Airport and the other leading from it, into Baghdad. The streets are very simple and plain. Their magnificence lay in the palm trees growing on either side, and in the isle separating them. Entering Baghdad from the airport, and seeing the palm trees enclosing you from both sides, is a reminder that you have entered the country of 30 million palms.

Soon after the occupation, many of the palms on these streets were hacked down by troops for "security reasons." We watched, horrified, as they were chopped down and dragged away to be laid side by side in mass graves overflowing with brown and wilting green. Although these trees were beautiful, no one considered them their livelihood. Unlike the trees Patrick Cockburn describes in Dhuluaya.

Several orchards in Dhuluaya are being cut down . . . except it's not only Dhuluaya . . . it's also Ba'aquba, the outskirts of Baghdad and several other areas. The trees are bulldozed and trampled beneath heavy machinery. We see the residents and keepers of these orchards begging the troops to spare the trees, holding up crushed branches, leaves, and fruit—not yet ripe—from the ground littered with a green massacre. The faces of the farmers are crushed and amazed at the atrocity. I remember one wrinkled face holding up 4 oranges from the ground, still green (our citrus fruit ripens in the winter), and screaming at the camera—"Is this freedom? Is this democracy?!" And his son, who was about 10, stood there with tears of rage streaming down his cheeks and quietly said, "We want 5 troops dead for each tree they cut down . . . five troops." A "terrorist," perhaps? Or a terrorized child who had to watch his family's future hacked down in the name of democracy and freedom?

Patrick Cockburn says that Dhuluaya is a Sunni area—which is true. Sunnis dominate Dhuluaya. What he doesn't mention is that the Khazraji tribe, whose orchards were assaulted, are a prominent Shi'a tribe in Iraq.

For those not interested in reading the article, the first line summarizes it perfectly: "US soldiers driving bulldozers, with jazz blaring from loudspeakers, have uprooted ancient groves of date palms as well as orange and lemon trees in central Iraq as part of a new policy of collective punishment of farmers who do not give information about guerrillas attacking US troops."

. . . which reminds me of another line from an article brought to my attention yesterday . . .

"A dozen years after Saddam Hussein ordered the vast marshes of southeastern Iraq drained, transforming idyllic wetlands into a barren moonscape to eliminate a hiding place for Shiite Muslim political opponents . . ." ("'A Gift From God" Renews a Village," the Washington Post, October 11, 2003) http://www.washingtonpost.com/wp-dyn/articles/A10572-2003Oct10.html)

Déjà vu, perhaps? Or maybe the orchards differ from the marshlands in that Saddam wasn't playing jazz when he dried up the marshlands . . . **posted by river @ 1:40 AM**

BAGHDAD HOTEL . . .

Baghdad Hotel was bombed today on Al-Sa'adun street, which is a mercantile area in Baghdad. Al-Sa'adun area is one of the oldest areas in Baghdad. The street is lined with pharmacies, optometrists, photographers, old hotels, doctors, labs, restaurants, etc.

The Baghdad Hotel is known to be "home" [to] the CIA and some prominent members from the Governing Council. No one is sure about the number of casualties yet—some say it's in the range of 15 dead, and 40 wounded . . . while other reports say 8 dead and 40 wounded.

There were other bombings in Baghdad—one in Salhiya, one in Karrada (near the two-storey bridge). **posted by river @ 1:47 AM**

Tuesday, October 14, 2003

"SHADOW GOVERNMENT"

Why is no one covering this: Parallel Government Finds Support?! I don't read about it anywhere except on Al-Jazeera—we only hear about on our Arab media networks . . . It's a big deal because Moqtada Al-Sadr has A LOT of support with fundamentalist Shi'a Muslims.

"Parallel "Government" Finds Suport," Aljazeera, October 12, 2003
http://english.aljazeera.net

Hundreds of Iraqis have taken to the streets in support of the parallel government that Shia cleric Moqtada al-Sadr has announced for the country.

A day after al-Sadr announced the formation of his "Iraqi Government" in defiance of the US-led occupation, a large crowd gathered in the city of Najaf, pledging their whole-hearted support.

"We are ready to sacrifice our souls for you, Sadr," chanted the demonstrators as they roamed the streets of the city.

A firebrand cleric, al-Sadr had announced the formation of the government during his weekly sermon in the town of Kufa . . .

Moqtada Al-Sadr is one of the more powerful Shi'a clerics currently in the south. He has a huge backing and his followers are very angry that he wasn't included in the power grab. For the last few months he has been building an armed militia known as the "Imam Mahdi's Army." The majority of this militia are young, and very angry. I think they were meant to be a sort of antidote to "Badr's Brigade"—SCIRI's armed militia.

We've been hearing all sorts of strange things about the happenings in Najaf. One report said that Al-Sadr's followers have been abducting some prominent Shi'a sheikhs that aren't supporting him. One thing is certain—a couple of nights ago, the Spanish troops in Najaf went to detain Al-Sadr and disarm his militia (many were guarding his house)

. . .

and hundreds of supporters flocked about his house, pushing the troops back and threatening that things would get very ugly if Al-Sadr was detained . . . the Spanish troops had to pull out of the area.

Very recently, Al-Sadr announced a "hikoomet dhill" or "shadow government" as a parallel government to the one selected in Baghdad by Bremer. The Shadow Government includes 13 different ministries (including an information ministry) . . .

Al-Sadr announced the following:

" . . . I have formed a government made up of several ministries, including ministries of justice, finance, information, interior, foreign affairs, endowments and the promotion of virtue and prevention of vice" ("Parallel "Government" Finds Support," Aljazeera, October 12, 2003, http://english.aljazeera.net/NR/exeres/62D93B71-232E-414F-B111-D8BF9511A34E.htm)

So what if this new "shadow government" has orders or laws that differ with the Governing Council? What happens when the hundreds of thousands (some say millions) of Sadr supporters decide that Al-Sadr's word is law?   **posted by river @ 12:03 PM**

Saturday, October 18, 2003

EVENING TEA AND TURKISH TROOPS . . .

In the evening, most Iraqi families gather together for "evening tea." It's hardly as formal as it sounds . . . No matter how busy the day, everyone sits around in the living room, waiting for tea.

Iraqi tea isn't a simple matter of teacups and teabags. If you serve "teabag tea" to an Iraqi, you risk scorn and disdain—a teabag is an insult to tea connoisseurs. It speaks of a complete lack of appreciation for the valuable beverage.

The exact process of making tea differs from family to family, but, in general, it is a three-stage process. First, a kettle of water is put on the burner to boil. Next, the boiling water and a certain amount of tealeaves are combined in a separate teapot and put on a low burner just until the tealeaves rise to the top and threaten to "boil over."

Finally, the teapot is set on top of the tea kettle on a low burner and allowed to "yihder" or settle.

There are hundreds of different types of tea available on the market. The best types are from Ceylon. Tea is so important in Iraq, that it makes up a substantial part of the rations we've been getting ever since the sanctions were imposed upon the country. People drink tea with breakfast, they drink tea at midday, they drink tea in the evening and often drink tea with dinner.

Our tea in Iraq is special because it is flavored with cardamom and served in "istikans." Istikans are little glasses shaped like the number "8," but open at the top, and flat at the bottom. They are made of thin glass and sit in little glass saucers—or porcelain saucers with intricate designs drawn on them. The color of the tea has to be just right—clear, yet strong—preferably a deep reddish-brown color.

So we sit, during the evenings, gathered around the small coffee table which has seen conversations on blockade, war strategies, bombings, and politics, with a tray of tea and something simple to eat—like biscuits or bread and cheese. One of us pours the tea, adding the sugar—2 spoons for dad and I, 3 for E., and one for mom.

Before the conversation officially begins, you can hear the gentle music of small, steel teaspoons clinking against the istikan, or teacup, as the tea is stirred. Unlike the typical family conversation around the world, "How was your day, dear?" doesn't get a typical answer in Iraq. Depending on who is being asked, the answer varies from stories of abductions and hijackings, to demonstrations, to empty gas cylinders and burned out water pumps.

The topic of the moment is "Turkish troops." We discuss Turkish troops at breakfast, we discuss them as we get ready for lunch, we discuss them with neighbors as we communicate over the walls separating our homes. E. says it's the same topic at gas stations, shops, and street corners.

The discussion isn't actually about Turkish troops, per se: it revolves more around the Puppets and their ability, or lack thereof, to convince the CPA what a bad idea introducing Turkish troops into Iraq would be. Iraqis of different ethnicities all have different opinions of late, but this is one thing we all seem to be agreeing upon—Turkish troops will only make the situation worse.

There are all sorts of reasons why people don't like the idea of Turkish troops in the region. First, there's a lot of animosity between the Kurds and Turks; thousands of Kurds faced constant persecution while on Turkish territory—many of them were driven into Iraq. Ever since the beginning of the war, there have been several clashes between Kurdish militias and Turkish troops in northern Iraq.

Second, everyone knows that Turkey has certain interests in the region—namely, Kirkuk and Mosul. Turkey has been overly eager to send in troops ever since the "end" of the war in April.

Third, Shi'a are adamant about not allowing Turkish troops into Iraq because Turks are predominantly Sunni and the thought of an aggressive Sunni army makes the majority of Shi'a nervous.

One faction of Christian society in Iraq, Armenian-Iraqis, are dead set against having Turkish troops in Iraq. They speak of Turkish occupation, bloodshed, executions, and being driven into Iraq. Armenian-Iraqis are horrified with the thought of having Turkish troops inside of Iraq.

Then there are all of the historical reasons. For almost 400 years, Iraq was ruled by the Ottoman Empire. . . . The Ottoman Rule in Iraq ended in 1918, with the start of the British occupation. Iraqis haven't forgotten that during World War I, hundreds of thousands of Iraqis were forced to fight and die for the Ottoman Empire.

Then there's the little issue of all the problems between Iraq and Turkey. Iraqis still haven't forgotten the infamous Ataturk Dam on the Furat (Euphrates), the fourth largest dam in the world. We had to watch the Euphrates diminish in front of our very eyes year after year, until in many areas, it seemed like nothing more than a stream. In a country that is largely composed of desert land, ebbing the flow of a river that many people depend on for survival is an atrocity.

People here don't understand why there's so much insistence to bring in a Turkish army anyway. What good can it possibly do? America is emphasizing how important it will be to have "Muslim troops" in the region—but what difference will it make? If Turkish troops enter under the supervision of an occupation army, they will be occupation troops—religion isn't going to make a difference.

It's like this: imagine America being invaded and occupied by, say, North Korea. (Note: I only say "North Korea" because of the cultural differences between the US and North Korea, and the animosity . . . I, unlike Chalabi, am not privileged to information on WMD, etc.) Imagine Korean troops invading homes, detaining people, and filling the streets with tanks and guns. Then imagine North Korea deciding it "needed help" and bringing in? Mexico. And you ask, "But why Mexico?!" and the answer is, "Well, Mexicans will understand you better because the majority of Americans are Christian, and the majority of Mexicans are Christian—you'll all get along famously."

The Puppet Council is completely opposed to a Turkish presence inside of the country; America is insistent that there should be one . . . we're all just watching from the sidelines, waiting to see just how much real respect the CPA has for the Puppet Council. **posted by river @ 2:49 AM**

NEW LINKS

I've updated my links on the right. I've added MediaChannel.org, which is the site Danny Schechter blogs on (he's the executive editor of the site). The site tackles some fantastic media issues—especially related to the war and occupation.

The other site is Juan Cole's *Informed Comment* (www.juancole.com). Juan Cole is a professor of history at the University of Michigan, author, and translator. His site has some great commentary on Iraq. He tackles political, social, and religious issues in the region with style and objectivity. His latest post is on the fighting between the troops and some followers of a Shi'a cleric in the south . . . things are looking frightening in Karbala and Najaf—people all over are worried. **posted by river @ 2:49 AM**

Tuesday. October 21. 2003

CIVILIZATION . . .

I heard some more details about the demonstration today . . . The whole situation was outrageous and people are still talking about it.

Ever since the occupation, employees of the Ministry of Oil are being searched by troops—and lately, dogs. The employees have

...

been fed up . . . the ministry itself is a virtual fortress now with concrete, barbed wire, and troops. The employees stand around for hours at a time, waiting to be checked and let inside. Iraqis have gotten accustomed to the "security checks." The checks are worse on the females than they are on the males because we have to watch our handbags rummaged through and sometimes personal items pulled out and examined while dozens of people stand by, watching.

Today, one of the women who work at the ministry, Amal, objected when the troops brought forward a dog to sniff her bag. She was carrying a Quran inside of it and, to even handle a Quran, a Muslim has to be "clean" or under "widhu." "Widhu" is the process of cleansing oneself for prayer or to read from the Quran. We simply wash the face, neck, arms up to the elbows and feet with clean water and say a few brief "prayers." Muslims carry around small Qurans for protection and we've been doing it more often since the war—it gives many people a sense of security. It doesn't mean the person is a "fundamentalist" or "extremist."

As soon as Amal protested about letting the dog sniff her bag because of the Quran inside, the soldier grabbed the Quran, threw it out of the bag, and proceeded to check it. The lady was horrified and the dozens of employees who were waiting to be checked moved forward in a rage at having the Quran thrown to the ground. Amal was put in hand-cuffs and taken away and the raging mob was greeted with the butts of rifles.

The Iraqi Police arrived to try to intervene, and found the mob had increased in number because it had turned from a security check into a demonstration. One of the stations showed police officers tearing off their "IP" badge—a black arm badge to identify them as Iraqi Police and shouting at the camera, "We don't want the badge—we signed up to help the people, not see our Quran thrown to the ground . . ."

Some journalists say that journalists' cameras were confiscated by the troops . . .

This is horrible. It made my blood boil just hearing about it—I can't imagine what the people who were witnessing it felt. You do not touch the Quran. Why is it so hard to understand that some things are sacred to people?!

How would the troops feel if Iraqis began flinging around Holy

Bibles or Torahs and burning crosses?! They would be horrified and angry because you do not touch a person's faith . . .

But that's where the difference is: the majority of Iraqis have a deep respect for other cultures and religions . . . and that's what civilization is. It's not mobile phones, computers, skyscrapers, and McDonalds; It's having enough security in your own faith and culture to allow people the sanctity of theirs . . . **posted by river @ 3:05 PM**

DEMONSTRATIONS IN BAGHDAD . . .

Thousands were demonstrating today—I think near the Ministry of Oil (though someone said it was somewhere else). There were even women demonstrating because a female has been detained for refusing to have her bag checked by the troops . . . The troops began firing into the air and fighting suddenly broke out between the mob and some troops . . . we still don't know what's happening. **posted by river @ 3:05 PM**

Saturday, October 25, 2003

MADRID CONFERENCE . . .

So the Madrid Conference is over. Half of the people here weren't really aware it was going on anyway. No one seems to bother with stuff like that anymore because we have more pressing affairs to attend to. I, personally, spent the last 4 days cleaning out the pantry in preparation for Ramadhan. I'd pop into the living room every once in a while to catch a glimpse of the conference and what was going on in it.

Always, there was Aznar's big teeth and Palacio's big hair. What struck me in particular was how lavish the whole conference looked. I wonder how much was spent on it . . . how many schools it could have renovated . . . how many clinics it could have provided with medication . . . But that's not reconstruction, of course—clinics and schools are luxuries what's really important is making sure the CPA, Governing Council, and ministerial cabinet are all housed comfortably in the palaces and hotels they call home.

The most embarrassing part of the conference was watching Muwafaq Al-Ruba'i grovel for international funds for the reconstruction effort. He batted his lashes, spoke softly, and kept dragging "the Iraqi people" into his speeches—as if the Iraqi people would actually ever see the uncountable billions that somehow enter the country and are spent before you can say "reconstruction."

I must be sounding ungrateful, what with the $33 billion dollars being agreed upon, but the idea of being financially indebted to America, the IMF and the World Bank somehow has the appeal of selling one's soul to the devil. It sounds like, in conclusion, more debt upon debt. It's not that I want everything to be donated to the country, but I think that our oil revenues should be able to cover a substantial part of rebuilding Iraq. I also think that many of the countries have every right to ask for their money "back" at some point in the future . . . I'm sure the Japanese could use their $5 billion for something useful at home. One good thing is that the money is going to be under UN supervision.

Christian Aid have done a fascinating report on some "missing billions." Apparently, there are $4 billion that have gone up in smoke and Bremer & Co. can only account for $1 billion. The report does some explaining on how the CPA spends the money and what committees are gone through. The PDF report asks the CPA to give a "transparent account" of how the billions were spent. But that's ridiculous—I mean, who can keep track of $4 billion dollars . . . I'm sure Ahmad Al-Chalabi can tell you first-hand that all those zeros are difficult to manage.

**Iraq: The Missing Billions, Christian Aid,
www.christianaid.org.uk/indepth/310iraqoil/iraqoil.pdf**

> . . . In May, Christian Aid published a major report that revealed how oil revenues can fuel poverty, war, and corruption in developing countries. The toppling of Saddam Hussein's regime, it was suggested, was a unique opportunity to show that this did not have to be the future for Iraq . . .
>
> Initial indications, however, are not optimistic—with billions of dollars of unaccounted for money now in the hands of unelected

> foreign officials. This combination of pre-war oil sales, post-war oil sales, and seized invested assets from Saddam Hussein's regime already tops US $5 billion, of which only around US $1 billion can be accounted for. By the end of this year, that total figure will top US $9 billion . . .
>
> Action needs to be taken now to ensure that the CPA reveals where this money has gone. The structure agreed upon at the UN must be implemented urgently, so that this Iraqi money is used in the best interests of Iraq's people and with their cooperation and involvement. Oil revenues should benefit those who need help most—the country's poor, not just those with power and influence . . .

And what is $4 billion anyway?! First off, there are all those snazzy suits being worn by our Governing Council—I haven't yet seen Al-Chalabi in the same suit twice . . . the silk ties, Rolex watches, and leather shoes. (I can tell you that canary yellow ties are the rage in men's fashion because just about every minister/council member has worn one by now).

There are rumors that each new minister makes around $40,000 a month. For $40,000, you can build a large house in an elegant area in Baghdad. For $40,000, you can build, and fully furnish, a school. For $40,000, you can stock up a storage room in a hospital. For $40 K, you can feed 80 Iraqi families for a month *lavishly*. (Or you could buy 400 used Sony Play Stations—as my younger cousin calculated.)

And then you have the extra expenses of the Governing Council—meals and abode, of course. The majority don't live in houses because they have homes and families abroad. They live in various hotels like Baghdad Hotel, Al-Rashid, and Palestine Hotel . . . some of them reside in palaces. One minister, they say, even sends for his staff to meet at the hotel because he refuses to visit the ministry itself. Employees at the ministry know him as "il shabah" or "the phantom" because no one beyond his deputy ministers has ever seen him in the flesh.

There's also the little matter of the Interim Government jetting about, all over the world . . . traveling from one place to the next. Every time one of the Puppets is rotated, they make it their immediate business to leave the country. It's ironic how the Iraqi people hear about the majority of the major decisions (like selling off the country) through foreign media networks and sometimes through a voice-over, translating to Arabic. To see them shaking hands and kissing feet, you'd think our immediate concerns are Iraq's diplomatic affairs outside of the country and not the mess *inside* of it.

Then you have the food and beverages necessary to keep our interim government alive. There used to be $5,000 lunches (which the International Herald Tribune claim were reduced). Now $5,000 lunches may seem like no big deal for 25 people in New York or Paris . . . but $200 per person is . . . beyond belief in Baghdad. Pre-war, the best meal in Iraq wouldn't cost you more than $30 per person (and there were only a handful of people who could afford a meal like that). Even now, restaurant food is quite cheap, albeit a bit risky.

A friend of an uncle, who is privy to certain purchases made by the CPA and Governing Council, says that millions each month are spent on . . . water. Yes. Apparently our Iraqi Council and interim government deems the water we drink not worthy of their thirst. I can understand worries about the quality of the water, but even the troops drink and eat off of vendors in the streets.

So when people here heard about the Madrid Conference . . . well, it's hardly going to make a difference to the average Iraqi. People are very worried about the fact that the Food-for-Oil program ends next month. Some say that the "husseh" or ration that makes up a substantial part of the average Iraqi diet will probably be continued until January. People will literally starve without rations. Already the ration has been reduced and the quality of what remains of it is just terrible.

I wanted to write up a paper and send it off to Madrid suggesting a "Ransom Fund." I'd like to suggest opening up a special fund for the families who have people abducted. It is becoming incredibly common to hear about a man, woman, or child being abducted and ransom as high as $250,000 being asked. The standard price is $25,000, but for wealthy families, $250,000 is not uncommon. Wealthy Christian families have been particularly vulnerable to abductions of late. One man had to sell his home and car to pay his son's ransom because his money was all tied up in various projects.

And who are behind these abductions . . . common criminals, sometimes . . . other times they are Al-Sadr's goons or SCIRI's thugs.

The SCIRIs are often politically motivated in their abductions and the money is said to go to supporting "Badr's Brigade," the SCIRI militia. More and more lately, the CPA has been complaining of the militia—but what did they expect? Giving them power in the first place was wrong, wrong, wrong. It's safe to say that no matter HOW much they promise otherwise, an armed extremist is going to mean trouble. A militia of armed extremists is going to mean chaos—especially when you allow them to enforce "security" in volatile areas.

Al-Sadr has been making waves in the south and Baghdad. He is frightening and I don't think his influence should be underestimated. He easily has over a million followers (some say it's up to 4 million) and they practically revere him. It's not him personally that makes him so important with his followers, it's the fact that he is the son of a famous Shi'a cleric who was assassinated in 1999. While the majority of the middle and upper class Iraqis want a secular government, Al-Sadr seems to resonate with the impoverished, currently jobless men in the south and in some of Baghdad's slums.

Currently, the CPA believe he was responsible for Al-Kho'i's assassination back in April. Others suspect that he might have been responsible for Al-Hakim's death a couple of months ago . . . detaining him is going to be a major problem because his followers will make sure to wreak havoc . . . judging from the last few months, they'll just strike up a deal with him.   **posted by river @ 9:45 PM**

Monday, October 27, 2003

RED CROSS BOMBING . . .

Horrible news. There was an explosion in front of the Red Cross this morning . . . just terrible. Some say it was an ambulance but others who saw the scene claim that the ambulance had a car right behind it that stopped suddenly for "car trouble" and then exploded. Nada Domani, the head of the Red Cross in Iraq, said that they might have to reduce their staff even further at this point . . . There were a series of other explosions all over Baghdad this morning and a couple last night . . . we still don't know everything that has been attacked. I'll post more later . . .   **posted by river @ 1:45 PM**

Wednesday, October 29, 2003

RIVERBEND AND MULTIPLE PERSONALITIES . . .

No, I do not have Multiple Personality Disorder. Many of you have pointed out a fake "Baghdad Burning" site at riverSbend.blogspot.com (notice the "S"). It is not being run by me in parallel to my own site—I knew it existed for some time now (a friend pointed it out to me in late September). Apparently, someone was so angry at my site, they decided to make an identical site named "Baghdad Burning" being written by, supposedly, me. The contents are almost completely opposite to what I write—and most of the posts are just copied and pasted from different sources (mostly USA government sources).

When I first noticed it, the first post was on September 11, I think. It was about American troops and Iraqi women falling in love with each other, etc. etc. Apparently, someone pointed out the fact that while the fake BB site began in September, my site began in August. Sooooooooo, our fraud backdated his posts and created some hollow, silly archives dating back to July. Anyone who uses Blogger knows how easy that is.

I wrote to Blogger, telling them about the site and how the person was pretending to be me, they said that if I wanted to make an official complaint, I had to mail in (by snail-mail) a letter complaining that someone was stealing the contents of my site. Besides my identity, the only thing the fraud has stolen is the line I use, "I'll meet you 'round the bend my friend, where hearts can heal and souls can mend." And yes, this is MY line—it's a line from a poem I wrote for a friend. Perhaps one day I'll post the complete poem.

A great guy named Brian has been following this fraud carefully. Check out the site http://suzerainty.blogspot.com for details.

http://suzerainty.blogspot.com, October 22, 2003

> *Wednesday, October 22, 2003*
>
> *. . . A foreign—probably American—citizen has produced a similar blog, almost stealing her name, but writing at riverSbendblog. blogspot.com—note the extra S. This blog is a shabby, poorly cob-*

bled together collection of material plagiarised from various foreign sources. It is not a blog by any true defintion . . .

In all likelihood, this is the work of an embittered American who does not like what Riverbend writes. But who is too cowardly to debate it honestly. Instead this individual preferred to set up this spoiler site, and try to deliberately lead people to believe that Riverbend's message has changed by deceivingly misleading them to it . . .

At this point this blog is intended to shame the fake riverSbend blogger into giving up the game. And to provide some amusement for those with a passing interest in just how desperate some are to silence a message that does not correspond to their own worldview . . .

Another blogger has more information on the culprit, check out: http://www.gorenfeld.net/john/blog.html

http://www.gorenfeld.net, October 27, 2003

Team Leader

A lot of people over at Atrios's blog—including me—have been wondering what's up with a blog called Riversbend that supposedly posts from Iraq. There was already a very similar site called Riverbend, run by a woman in Iraq, but it didn't have the "S" in the middle, and it tended to attack Halliburton bidding practices rather than copy optimistic passages from Thomas Friedman.

So when some guy on Usenet going under the names "Troy" and "Diego Gastor" began promoting it in several message groups, those who hadn't read it in a while were confused. They blinked, and meanwhile Riverbend had become really psyched about the war. "I can honestly say now that I'm proud to be an Iraqi. Because of what has happened, because there is freedom here like I have not known before. Now I can talk-to you, to people I could never talk to before. I am a simple woman. I am just a worker. But even these simple things—talking—give me hope." Was Donald Rumsfeld posting this stuff? . . .

Thank you both of you.

Now, while I am very flattered there are people out there taking so much trouble to prove me wrong, I am rather annoyed that it wasn't all done with better style. I mean, the guy who runs the fake site is retired, for God's sake—he has all the time in the world to make me look bad. I think it only fair to demand he should have put in a little more effort. Furthermore, I don't like the way many words are misspelled and that the grammar is just atrocious in an apparent attempt to make it look more "Iraqi"—or maybe that's just the way this person actually writes.

My favorite post is the first one, supposedly written on July 6:

Time to Blog!

We finally returned to my Baghdad. The evening walks along the river are much refreshing. We were living with relatives near Erbul for the better part of five months. al-Jazeera kept us informed regarding the war. I gasped and held my breath not believing as we watched Baghdad burning.

The Real Riverbend's Comment: Huh? Erbul? Where is that? Somewhere between Kirkuk and Erbil?! Give me a break. Another part I loved was one of the posts describing how the dear "girl" got a tour of Baghdad Airport (which no one is allowed near): please don't miss that one—the blogger might change it. I can't decide which is worse—the dry stuff copied and pasted directly from governmental sites, or when Troy gets lyrical and writes how "walks along the river are much refreshing."

The writer of the fake riverSbend site is someone named Troy who is ex-military, retired, and a GOP Team Leader (?):

El Solerito Troy, Artist, HAM, Korean War, Reg. Army & USAF Retired, MOPH L38342 Unit 1849, Phi Theta Kappa, RNC 146441197-D186, GOP Team Leader, NRA 040959746

One thing our friend Troy didn't take into consideration while writing the blog was the following: even if you backdate your archives, the month you originally started with won't contain the faked archives. If you check out the September archives for the fake riverSbend blog, you'll see that the list of archives on the left only dates back to September—which is when the blog originally started!!

Finally, thank you, dear Troy—the fake riverSbend—for trying to imitate Baghdad Burning—I am flattered. However, 1. You make a horrible 24-year-old girl from "Erbul," 2. When you copy and paste stuff from articles and sites, try to make sure the date *you* post them on isn't before the original date the material was posted, and 3. Find a hobby—get a cat, grow a garden, play chess, golf—i.e. Get a life.

Drop Troy a line—he obviously has lots of time to correspond—he has several email addresses, this is one of them: buleria@enesaca. net. Brian over at suzerainty.blogspot.com has several more. **posted by river @ 9:31 PM**

THE RED CROSS AND TERRORISM

The Red Cross have started pulling out their personnel. A friend of mine who works with the Red Crescent said that they were going to try to pull out most of their personnel, while trying to continue with what they're doing—humanitarian assistance. When I heard Nada Domani, the head of the ICRC [International Committee of the Red Cross] in Iraq, say that they'd begin pulling out their personnel on Tuesday, I wished I could yell out, "Don't abandon us Nada!" But I realize that their first priority is to ensure the safety of their employees.

The Red Cross is especially important at this point because they are the "link" that is connecting the families of the detainees and the military. When someone suddenly disappears, people go to the Red Cross and after a few grueling days, the missing person can often be tracked down at one of the prison camps or prisons.

The easy and naïve thing to do would be to blame the whole situation on fundamentalists/extremists/terrorists/loyalists/ba'athists/foreigners which many people, apparently, think are one and the same. Another trend in western media is to blame the whole of them on the "Sunni triangle" and "neighboring countries."

There are *several* groups orchestrating the attacks against the various targets. The first and most obvious indicator is the method of attack, while the second indicator is the variety of the targets.

. . .

The techniques being used in the attacks range from primitive, to professional. We hear that some of the explosive devices being used are home-made and uncomplicated, obviously made by amateurs. We know for a fact that there are high-tech attacks against Coalition headquarters—like at the Baghdad International Airport and some of the palaces where high-ranking army personnel are located. On some of these places, like the airport, missiles are being used which is an indicator that the source of the attack is a highly trained group.

One of my uncles lives in one of the areas closer to the airport, which is on the outskirts of Baghdad. During June, we spent a couple of weeks with him. Almost every night, we would wake up to a colossal explosion that seems to be coming from the direction of the airport and less than a minute later, the helicopters would begin hovering overhead. Another example of a high-tech attack, was the attack on Rasheed Hotel a few days ago, where Wolfowitz was shocked and awed out of a meeting. (I don't understand why the CPA is trying very hard to pretend the attack had nothing to do with his presence there).

The majority associate such attacks with resistance and many people believe that they are being carried out by people with access and knowledge of advanced military equipment—perhaps Iraqis who were a part of the Guard or former members of the Iraqi army. Now, while some may certainly be labeled as Ba'athists, or loyalists, they aren't fundamentalists. We do, after all, have hundreds of thousands of disgruntled former military personnel and soldiers who were made to sit at home without retirement, a pension or any form of compensation. The relatively few who were promised a monthly "retirement wage," complain that they aren't getting the money. (I can never emphasize enough the mistake of dissolving the army; was anyone thinking when they came up with that decision?!)

New resistance groups are popping up every day. The techniques are becoming more sophisticated and we even hear of "menshoorat" being passed around. Menshoorat are underground "fliers."

The suicide bombings, on the other hand, are more often attributed to fundamentalist groups. To say that these groups are fighting to bring back the former regime is ridiculous: people chose to ignore the fact that the majority of fundamentalists were completely against the former regime because members of Al-Qaeda, Ansar Al-Islam, Al-

Da'awa and other political fundamentalist groups were prone to detention, exile and in some cases, execution.

These groups are both Sunni and Shi'a fundamentalist groups (as the attacks on the British and Polish troops in the southern region have proven). Al-Qaeda claimed responsibility for the attack on Baghdad Hotel a couple of weeks ago, while in the south, people swear that one of Al-Hakim's personal bodyguards helped to conspire with his assassination (which would explain how a car full of explosives made it through his personal army of bodyguards and into the parking area where his own car was).

The irony is hearing about the "War on Terrorism" on CNN and then tuning in to the CPA channel to see the Al-Da'awa people sitting there, polished and suited, Puppet Knights of the Round Table. To see Al-Jaffari, you almost forget that they had a reputation for terrorism over the decades, here in Iraq. They were one of the first political/religious groups to use bombings in Iraq to get their political message across to the people.

Their most famous debacle was one that occurred in 1980. One of the most prominent universities in Iraq, Mustansiriya University, was hosting a major, international conference on economics for various international youth groups. Tariq Aziz, who was then the Minister of Foreign Affairs in Iraq, was visiting the conference during the opening. Suddenly, in the middle of thousands of students from over 70 international and Iraqi youth organizations, two bombs exploded, killing 2 students and injuring dozens. The next day, while a demonstration of outraged students was following the funeral procession to a local graveyard, two more bombs were thrown in their midst, killing two high school students. Al-Da'awa later claimed responsibility.

Later that same year, in an attempt to assassinate the president of the University of Technology in Baghdad, they instead killed one of the university custodians who stood in their way.

In the '70s, members of Al Da'awa used to throw "acid" in the faces of "safirat" or females who don't wear the "hijab," both in certain parts of Baghdad, and in certain areas in the south of Iraq. Shi'a clerics who didn't agree with their violent message, were often assassinated or assaulted.

The fact that they are currently one of the leading political parties involved with the "New Iraq" sends a wonderful message to "terrorist organizations": Bombing works, terror works. People here are terrified we'll end up another Afghanistan . . . that these fundamentalist groups the CPA is currently flirting with are Iraq's Taliban.

Finally, there are all those strange, mystery attacks that no one understands and even the most extreme members of society can't condone or legitimatize. One such attack includes the attack on the UN headquarters. No one claimed responsibility for that. Another such attack was the bombing of the Jordanian Embassy in Baghdad, the Red Cross, the police stations . . . Many people believe that Al-Chalabi and his party are responsible for such incidents. Some of his guards are trained terrorists . . .

Al Chalabi arrived in April with a militia of Free Iraqi Fighters who, after several weeks of car hijacking, a few abductions, and some even say assassinations, suddenly disappeared; his 600+ thugs were supposedly "interpreters." I have very limited information on them, but someone said they were trained in Hungary? Today, people think they are acting as a sort of secret militia responsible for many of the assassinations and explosions all over Baghdad.

I'll blog about Ramadhan tomorrow; there's so much to tell.
posted by river @ 9:31 PM

Friday, October 31, 2003

RAMADHAN . . .

Ramadhan is the 9th month in the Islamic year (which also has 12 months, but only has around 358 days). Ramadhan is considered one of the holiest months of the Islamic year—in my opinion, it is the most interesting. We spend the whole of Ramadhan fasting, every day, from the first rays of light at dawn, until the sun sets. In other words, we can neither eat, nor drink, nor smoke, nor chew gum until it is time to "break the fast" during the evening.

Ramadhan is the month during which the angel Gabriel first visited our Prophet, with the message of Islam and the Quran. That is why it is celebrated by Muslims all over the world. The exact date of the momentous occasion can't be calculated exactly, but it is believed that "Laylet il Qadir" (the night the Prophet was first visited by Gabriel) is towards the end of Ramadhan (many believe that it falls on the 27th night).

Ramadhan is a festive month, in many ways. It's like the last two weeks of December—a little bit hectic, but important, all the same. It's that month where you get to see all the family you never you knew you had—the intolerable cousins, the favorite aunt, the grandparents, nieces, nephews, uncles and even the great-uncle you thought had died last year. The whole month is sort of a "family month."

The fasting works like this: at the break of dawn, we simply stop eating and drinking. This lasts through the whole day until "al maghrib" or dusk. Fasting is considered one of the "arkan" of Islam, which means it is required of all Muslims. There are certain exceptions—people who are ill aren't required to fast during Ramadhan, and people who are traveling. If the fasting affects a person's health in any way (i.e. if the person is diabetic, or pregnant, etc.), they are excused from fasting.

Of course, the "moral fasting" comes with the physical fasting. In other words, a person can break their fast without using food. Gossiping, fighting, lying, cheating, angry words and more have to be avoided during Ramadhan, otherwise your fast, or "siyam" is considered useless. Prayer and Quran reading are also stepped-up during the whole of the month because it is believed to be a "blessed month."

Someone might ask, but why fast? What is the point of denying yourself food and drink for over half a day? Fasting is supposed to teach tolerance, patience, and hunger. Yes, hunger. The average person forgets what it's like to be hungry . . . and I don't mean the wow-I-could-really-use-a-burger-and-some-fries type of hunger. I mean the hunger you feel when you haven't had anything to eat or drink for over 12 hours and your stomach feels ready to cave in and your head feels like exploding because you didn't get that zap of caffeine you need to function.

The point of being hungry is to help you appreciate food more. It helps you realize that food and water shouldn't be taken for granted, especially when there are people who feel like this every day regardless of it being a holy month or otherwise. Many doctors also believe fasting is healthy, as it often lowers blood pressure and keeps people from smoking or drinking. I currently have an uncle who swears he's

. . .

going to give up smoking this Ramadhan (like he gave it up last Ramadhan—and the one before).

We begin preparing for the "futoor," or the meal with which we break our fast, over an hour before its time. Traditionally, most people break their fast on a date, and then proceed to whatever is on the menu. Often, people begin the meal with some sort of soup because it warms the stomach without shocking it after all those hours without food. The most popular Ramadhan soup is lentil soup, or "addess." It is a pale, yellow soup that is both light and flavorful. There are dozens of different ways to make it, but I enjoy it with a squeeze of lime and "khubz."

After the soup comes a whole procession of often traditional foods . . . maybe I should post the recipes. There's so much food because the "futoor" is more of a daily celebration than it is an ordinary meal. During previous years, we would spend almost every day breaking our fast with various family or friends. This year is different because the security situation doesn't allow for traipsing around Baghdad or other provinces on a daily basis. It's also not the same because, under normal circumstances, our "futoor" gatherings often last well into the night, sometimes past 12 am, before the group breaks up to go home.

The neighbors are often a big part of the month. If they're not dropping by to sample futoor, then they're sending over a plate of something for you to sample. We also get together to agree who will be sending food over to the local mosque to feed the mosque keepers and the Imam, and to arrange who will be sending what to the more destitute families in the neighborhood. Ramadhan is the time of year when we put aside neighborhood differences (like the fact that Abu K.'s dog howls at anyone who goes down the street) and combine culinary skills and a general feeling of empathy.

The most active part of the whole day is the quarter of an hour directly before breaking the fast . . . the whole family is often in a flurry of action, with someone setting the table, someone carrying the food, someone giving orders about where to put everything . . . and everyone impatient with hunger. The last five minutes before you hear the call for prayer signifying the end of the fast are always the most difficult.

Every second of those last five minutes passes with the heaviness of an hour . . . you can literally see every one strain to hear the sound of the call for prayer echoing through the Baghdad streets. And then it is finally time for futtoor . . . and we begin to eat with relish. The platter of rice that seemed ridiculously small 15 minutes ago is now "too much" and no one eats as much as they had hoped they were going to eat—everyone is exhausted with simply contemplating the food, the choices and the possibilities.

After futtoor, the smokers fall upon their cigarettes with an enthusiasm only other smokers can appreciate. We watch them taking puff after puff with a contentment that even screaming kids and loud televisions cannot taint.

The rest of the night is spent in eating snacks and sweets, like baqlawa saturated in syrup, and warm kunaffa (a cheese sweet). Everyone moves somewhat slower and the general mood is one of contentment and joviality (no one can get up the energy to be angry after a large meal) . . . the only thing that can thoroughly ruin a futtoor is an air strike (like in 1998) or an electricity cut.

Tomorrow we're expecting to break our fast with an uncle's family and one of our neighbors (who are Christian). Christians don't fast during Ramadhan, but they do often join us while breaking the fast and many refuse to eat and drink in places like college and school (where eating is allowed) out of solidarity and respect.

And now you'll excuse me . . . they've just warmed the kunaffa drenched in a sugar syrup and if I don't hurry, there'll be nothing left for Riverbend . . . **posted by river @ 12:20 AM**

LINK . . .

Remember "Malcom Lagauche" . . . the author whose site was shut down after he got too many hits? You can now find him here: Lagauche is Right (http://www.malcomlagauche.com) **posted by river @ 12:25 AM**

BETWEEN A HAMMER AND AN ANVIL . . .

I haven't written these last few days for several reasons. I could barely get an internet connection and when I did connect, it was very slow. I gave up yesterday. I've also been a bit tired with Ramadhan. It's not the fasting that makes me tired, but the preparing for breaking the fast in the evening. There's always so much to do. After we've eaten, I'm just too exhausted to do anything besides sit around with the family, drinking tea, abusing the smokers and discussing the usual topics families discuss while gathered together these days—the occupation and politics.

Even the kids are involved with the news and current situation, but in a smaller way. My cousin's younger daughter is infatuated with one of the anchors on Al-Arabia. Every time he's on tv, the usually loud 7-year-old stands, bedazzled, in front of the television, absorbing every word of the dry, detached commentary. Her mother, who can be impressively conniving, is tricking the poor kid into being good simply by saying things like, "But what would that nice man on Al-Arabia say if he saw you didn't eat your potatoes?!"

So many things have been happening this last week. The various UN organizations began pulling out their volunteers and employees. The Red Cross is currently doing the same. Someone asked me why Iraqis seemed to have so much faith in UN organizations. It's not that we have unrealistic views about the capabilities of the UN or humanitarian organizations; it's simply that when organizations begin to pull out their people, you know things are going downhill. While being threatened with war, we used to watch the UN people very carefully and when they'd start packing up and leaving in helicopters, we'd know things are going to get difficult.

People started going back to work today. Saturday, Sunday and Monday everyone was basically stuck at home because of the fliers going around talking about 3 days of resistance. Some say the fliers have no definite threat—just a vague order for people to stay at home for three days in protest of the occupation, others claim that there's an underlying "warning" in the words.

Baghdad was eerily quiet, besides the occasional explosion (yesterday near the CPA headquarters and tonight within the "Green Zone"). Everything seemed to be at a stand-still—relatively few cars in the streets, hardly any children in the schools and even government employees deciding to remain safe in their homes. Colleges were also practically empty, although the students started going back today. There are troops just about every where—check points, road blocks and soldiers waving the cars back, back, back, "Take another road . . . "

My cousin and his wife spent the last two days with us. They had kept the girls home from school just to be on the safe side. My cousin's wife was more relieved than I had seen her since the academic year began. She'd just as soon have the girls under her watchful eye than at school and this is a perfect excuse for her. The other day she was debating the sanity of keeping them at home the whole year and tutoring them. We told her she was crazy because our educational system doesn't allow for that in elementary school. Unless there's a great reason, the child is required to actually be at the school. I told her they would lose a year, and considering her older daughter is an excellent student, it would be a shame. She doesn't seem to care— all she wants is to sense that they are safe. I think many parents had to have that debate this year. Young girls, especially, have been prone to kidnappings and abductions.

I don't envy parents during this crisis.

Unviersities are facing their own set of problems. We heard there was some sort of student demonstration because the situation in the universities isn't much better than on the street. Students complain of being made to miss classes because of the long lines while cars and people are being checked before being allowed to enter the university. There are also complaints that the deans and presidents of certain universities are so concerned with their physical safety, they refuse to see students, hear complaints or tour the facilities to find out about certain problems. University faculty complain of everything from receiving death threats from students for giving bad grades to bad attendance by students due to the security situation.

The latest today is that missiles were fired inside of the Green Zone (the press says it could be mortar). We heard the explosions

. . .

which were LOUD, but I think the majority have gotten used to hearing them. Even the kids hardly flinch any more. The moment we hear explosions, there's a rush to get to the roof and try to determine the general direction of the smoke (there is usually smoke). Then there's a rush to check the news, if there's electricity. If it's in a residential area, we immediately think of all our relatives and acquaintances in the area and wonder if everyone is alright, how close it was to a specific home/person/shop/school. Almost everyone has relatives living all over Baghdad—there's always someone to worry about. We then try to contact someone from the bombed area and if there's no telephone, we try to contact someone who might have extra information. The process has become too familiar.

There have also been a number of assassinations these last few days. The ones that are making headlines are the judges. Yesterday, a judge was kidnapped and killed in Najaf. Today, a judge was killed outside of his home in Mosul and another judge was shot twice in the head in his car in Kirkuk. It seems, these days, that judges in Iraq are caught "bayn il mattraqa wil sindan," as one Arab reporter said, which means "between a hammer and an anvil." This is because while the judge in Najaf was killed by loyalists, it seems, the one in Kirkuk was killed by American troops who said he got caught in "cross fire." The one in Mosul is still a mystery.

These last few days have been particularly difficult. There's a strain on everybody. People are tense and worried. They're worried about their children, worried about their jobs or lack of employment, worried about the security situation, worried about jumpy troops. The attacks are becoming more sophisticated and the troops are becoming more brutal in some areas . . . It's like we graduate from one phase to another. Everyone is so tired.   **posted by river @ 2:15 AM**

IS SOMETHING BURNING?!

Due to the overwhelming number of requests that I post some Iraqi Ramadhan recipes, I'm going to start posting recipes on this page: Is Something Burning?! (http://iraqrecipes.blogspot.com/). I'm still trying it out and I think I'll change the links to link to recipe pages (especially Middle Eastern food). We'll see how it goes. I'd love to hear some feedback if anyone tries the recipes. **posted by river @ 2:19 AM**

Sunday, November 09, 2003

GALUB MEMDESHEN . . .

These last few days have been a bit tiring—a few visitors (relatives) and a couple of friends who we haven't seen since July. It's ridiculous—we live in the same city but it feels like we're all worlds apart. Everyone is so consumed with their own set of trials and tribulations these days—the son that lost a job, the daughter that lost a husband . . . the problems feel endless and everyone has their own story to tell. As my mother constantly says, "Kul wahid yihtajleh galub memdeshen," or "every person [you listen to] requires a brand new heart." This is usually said when anticipating a sad, frustrating story. Every story begins with a deep *sigh* and ends with an "Allah kareem."

Our latest visitor has left us more than perturbed. A friend of E. passed by, a junior in the electrical engineering department at Baghdad University. He sat, for an hour, describing an incident that occurred last week at the university which we had heard about, but didn't know the details. It has been the biggest problem yet in Baghdad University.

Just some information on Baghdad University: Baghdad University was established in the '30s, I think. It is Iraq's oldest contemporary university and its most famous. It started out small and kept on expanding until it became one of the largest universities in the region. There are 6 different campuses spread all over Baghdad and I'm not sure just how many colleges there are. The main campus is the one located in the leafy, elegant area of Jadriya, in the center of Baghdad. The colleges of engineering, science, political science, physical education, and women's education are all located on the Jadriya campus, as is the university president's office.

The Jadriya campus was designed in 1961 by Walter Adolph Gropius, a German who emigrated to America in 1937. The campus is huge, and beautiful. The buildings are sprawling and punctuated with little gardens planted with palms and other trees and grass. There are also several dormitories that provide living quarters for out-of-town students, and in the physical education college, there are football fields, basketball courts and a pool.

My favorite feature on the Jadriya campus is the arc framing the entrance. The arcs, which look like a pale, elongated rainbow that doesn't quite meet in the middle, symbolize Arabic architecture. The opening in the middle of the arcs symbolizes open minds, allowing for the entrance of knowledge. Or that's what they say it symbolizes. The whole campus is a wonderful contrast of green trees, and beige buildings swarming with busy students. Even during difficult times, it was an oasis.

Up until the early 1990s, the majority of the teaching staff had gotten their post-graduate degrees from abroad. The College of Medicine leaned towards an English curriculum because most of the doctors were graduates of British medical schools, the College of Engineering leaned towards an American curriculum because the majority of the professors and teachers were graduates of American colleges. The College of Science was a combination of American/British-taught teachers and professors, and most of the syllabuses were in English.

After 1991, the university began deteriorating, like all other universities. Chemicals weren't purchased for the science labs because many of the basic experimental materials were "banned" according to the sanctions resolution. The physics labs suffered the same fate. Engineering departments complained of a lack of equipment and books. Because curriculums were American or British, the books also originated from these countries. Major publishing houses refused to sell books to Iraqi universities because their governments considered it illegal (apparently, you can make WMD using a calculus book . . .). We had to wait until someone brought a copy of the necessary book in, by chance, and make dozens of photocopies of it, which would be sold in little "makatib" or bookshops all over Baghdad.

Many of the professors started emigrating after 1991 because the economic situation was so bad, they could barely afford to support themselves, let alone their families. They started leaving to places like Jordan, Yemen, Libya, Syria and the Emirates, hoping to find a decent position in a university or research center. The ones who remained were highly appreciated . . . we still talk of the mathematician from MIT, or the programmer from Berkeley.

In spite of all this, Baghdad University remained one of the best universities in the region. It was well-known throughout the Arab world and its graduates were welcome almost anywhere. Its reputation, more or less, remained intact About 90% of the college applicants always put Baghdad University at the top of their application form. It accepts the highest grades because, as a total, it accepts only around 10,000 students a year and every year, 75,000 students graduate from Iraqi high schools and apply for college. So, in addition to some of the best teachers in Iraq, they also get the smartest students.

The University was looted heavily during the days immediately after April 9. Some campuses were worse off than others. The Jadriya campus was looted the first few days, but because American troops were posted nearby, the looting was lighter than in other places. Many professors quit working after the occupation, while others were fired. The ones remaining in the university got together and had a "democratic" vote, choosing specific staff to head the departments, colleges and they even chose a university president.

The problem was that many of the professors were former Ba'athists . . . some of the best teachers were Ba'athists (we had over 6 million). Sami Mudhafar, who was chosen as university president, was respected, competent and . . . anti-Ba'athist. A few weeks into the occupation, Chalabi started insisting on the implementation of his "de-Ba"athification plan. The first place it began in was the universities. Any Ba'athists, with administrative positions, were asked to step down and hand over the reins. The next step the CPA insisted upon was that any Ba'athists professors should be made to quit. That was too much. Sami Mudhafar realized that making all the ex-Ba'athist teachers and employees quit would mean that he'd have too big a shortage of academicians to continue classes. Things were already tough before the war, this would make things impossible. So, he refused. He told the representative for the Ministry of Higher Education that it was a mistake and he couldn't be responsible for the result of an action like that . . .

Sami Mudhafar was promptly changed. He was asked to resign his post and the Minister of Higher Education, appointed by the Governing Council, chose someone else to fill his post. The Jadriya campus was in an uproar. Students and teachers protested, holding signs that said things like, "The Minister of Higher Education was appointed— Sami was elected." And it was a good point: one of the first buds of democracy was promptly squelched by a minister appointed by the CPA and the Puppet Council.

The problems started after that. It seemed like every day brought a new story of some minor dissent or some major disagreement between the staff, the students and the new administration—and sometimes, even the American troops at the university got involved.

Before the troops pulled out of the Jadriya campus, they assigned "campus security," which some say were trained by the soldiers. The campus security are a bunch of men between the ages of 20 and 40 (the majority, they say, are in their twenties). Students have been annoyed because the campus security seem to be there not so much to ensure safety, but to watch the students. Almost every day, there has been a new skirmish with the campus security, and any time someone tried to take the matter to higher authorities, they had to go through even more security to make an official complaint.

A few days ago, one of the students got into an argument with one of the security members over a parking space. The student apparently pulled in to a "reserved" parking spot and was rushing off to class when one of the security members asked him to remove his car. The computer engineering student argued, the campus security guy yelled, angry words were spoken, another security guard joined in—and suddenly the three were fighting. Friends of the student joined in the scuffle, and the security people suddenly pulled out knives . . . more students joined in—everyone was enraged—and the security people asked for back up. The back up came in the form of several security guys in two pick-up truck. They pulled up to the road leading to the department of computer and electrical engineering, pulled out their Klashnikovs and opened fire on the department building!

Students began dropping to the ground, windows were broken, chunks of beige plaster were dropping from the balconies and teachers rushed to herd students out of classes and into the corridors (to avoid windows). One of the students got into his car and went to get the dean of the college and some Iraqi Police. A few minutes later, the police pulled up and yelled at the security people to stop shooting. The security people then turned and began shooting in the direction of the police. The police pulled out their guns and began firing threatening shots to get the campus security to stop. The dean came along—a small, earnest man, pale and bewildered, wondering what the problem was and was instantly greeted by terrified students, angry security guards and the IP.

The students went home that day, enraged and disoriented, unable to continue classes. Luckily, injuries were minor. A few scrapes from the knives, a few bruises, and some mental scars, probably, but nothing else. Since that day, they have been on a strike—demanding an official apology from the campus security and a limit to their power, i.e. they shouldn't get to fire at a bunch of students over a parking space . . .

Today (well, yesterday, technically—it's almost dawn here) there were some more explosions in the city center . . . not sure where it's coming from but someone said it was near the Green Zone again. Nothing on the internet about it.

But, other than irate security guards, explosions in the capital, bombing in Tikrit, strikes in Nassriya over the security situation, a few assassinations, some abductions, car bombs, frightened humanitarian organizations, and exhausted people—everything is just rosy . . . *sigh* . . . Allah Kareem. **posted by river @ 5:06 AM**

FOOD . . .

I updated the Is Something Burning?! (http://iraqrecipes.blogspot.com/) page and have added it to my sidebar. **posted by river @ 5:27 AM**

Thursday, November 13, 2003

IRAQI GOVERNING COUNCIL . . .

I have to post this fast. The electrical situation has been hellish today. There's no schedule . . . in our area the electricity is on 30 minutes for every two hours of no electricity. People suspect it's a sort of punishment for what happened in Nassiryah this morning and the bombings in Baghdad this last week. There were also some huge explosions today—the troops got hit by mortars, I think, and retaliated by bombing something.

Also, Mohammed Bahr Ul-Iloom was shot at today. Bahr Ul-Iloom is one of the Sh'ia clerics (a "rotating president") and the father of the Minister of Oil. He was unharmed, it seems, but his driver is wounded. While I'm sure Bahr Ul-Iloom would love to blame it on loyalists, Ba'athists and Al-Qaeda, the shots actually came from American troops—it was a "mistake." Oops.

Bremer is currently in Washington, explaining why the Governing Council are completely useless. The Washington Post article on the diminishing popularity of the Governing Council came as no surprise:

The United States is deeply frustrated with its hand-picked council members because they have spent more time on their own political or economic interests than in planning for Iraq's political future, especially selecting a committee to write a new constitution, the officials added. ("Alternatives to Iraqi Council Eyed," Washington Post, November 9, 2003 http://www.washingtonpost.com/ac2/wp-dyn? pagename=article&contentId=A17199-2003Nov8&notFound=true)

I think it's safe to say that when you put a bunch of power-hungry people together on a single council (some who have been at war with each other), they're going to try to promote their own interests. They are going to push forward their party members, militias and relatives in an attempt to root themselves in Iraq's future.

Bremer noted that at least half the council is out of the country at any given time and that at some meetings, only four or five members showed up ("Alternatives to Iraqi Council Eyed," Washington Post, November 9, 2003 http://www.washingtonpost.com/ac2/wp-dyn? pagename=article&contentId=A17199-2003Nov8&not Found=true).

Of course they're outside of the country—many of them don't have ties in it. They have to visit their families and businesses in Europe and North America. For some of them, it sometimes seems like the

"Governing Council" is something of an interesting hobby—a nice little diversion in the monthly routine: golf on Saturdays, a movie with the family in London on Fridays, a massage at the spa on Tuesdays, and, oh yes—nation-building for 5 minutes with Bremer on the Xth of each month.

People here never see them. Most live in guarded compounds and one never knows what country they are currently in. For example, Chalabi is presently missing. I haven't seen him on the news for . . . I don't know how long. If anyone has seen him, please send an email—I'm dying to know what he's up to.

I can imagine Bremer preparing for a meeting with the pioneers of Iraqi democracy, the pillars of liberty . . . the Iraqi Puppet Council. He strides in with his chic suit, flowing hair and polished shoes (the yellow nation-building boots are only for press conferences and photo shoots in Iraqi provinces). He is all anticipation and eagerness: today will be the day. *This* meeting will be the productive meeting which will make headlines.

He strides into the lavish room, Italian heels clicking on the marble floor—there will be 25 faces today. Twenty-five pairs of adoring eyes will follow him around the room. Twenty-five pairs of eager ears will strain to hear his words of wisdom. Twenty-five faces will light up with . . . but where are the 25? He stops in the middle of the room, heart sinking, ire rising in leaps and bounds. Why are there only 5 unsure faces? Did he have the schedule wrong? Was this the wrong conference room?!

And Bremer roars and rages—where are the Puppets? Where are the marionettes?! How dare they miss yet another meeting! But they all have their reasons, Mr. Bremer: Talbani is suffering from indigestion after an ample meal last night; Iyad Allawi is scheduled for a pedicure in Switzerland this afternoon; Al-Hakim is jetting around making covert threats to the Gulf countries, and Chalabi says he's not attending meetings anymore, he's left the country and will be back when it's time for the elections . . .

People have been expecting this for some time now. There's a complete and total lack of communication between the Council members and the people—they are as inaccessible as Bremer or Bush. Their speeches are often in English and hardly ever to the Iraqi public. We hear about new decisions and political and economical maneuverings through the voice-overs of translators while the Council members are simpering at some meeting thousands of miles away.

We need *real* Iraqis—and while many may argue that the Council members are actually real Iraqis, it is important to keep in mind that fine, old adage: not everyone born in a stable is a horse. We need people who aren't just tied to Iraq by some hazy, political ambition. We need people who have histories inside of the country that the population can relate to. People who don't have to be hidden behind cement barriers, barbed wire and an army.

Their failure has nothing to do with attacks on troops or terrorism. It has to do with the fact that many of them are only recommendable because they were apparently very good at running away from a difficult situation—and running into the right arms. Another problem is the fact that decent, intelligent people with political ambition refuse to be a part of this fiasco because everyone senses that the Governing Council cannot do anything on its own. Bremer is the head and he's only the tip of the iceberg—he represents Washington.

A national conference is a good idea, but it will fail as miserably as the Puppet Council, unless . . . there's a timetable. The occupation forces need to set a definite date saying, "We're going to begin pulling out on *this* month, next year—let's get organized before that." A timetable is vital to any progress, if any is going to be made. Only then will things begin to move forward.

Prominent, popular politicians and public figures don't want to be tied to American apron strings—this includes lawyers, political scientists, writers, and other well-known people. Not because they are American apron-strings per se, but because this is an occupation (by American admission, no less). No matter how much CNN and the rest try to dress it up as a liberation, the tanks, the troops, the raids, the shootings (accidental or otherwise), and the Puppet Council all scream occupation. If it were French, it'd get the same resistance . . . just as if it were a Saudi, Egyptian or Iranian occupation.

It is also vital that all interested political parties be allowed to be a part of the national conference. Any political conferences in the past have been limited to American-approved political and religious parties which have left a large number of political groups outside of the circle—groups that have more popular support. Furthermore, the conference can't be run and organized by occupation forces (troops and the CPA). If there's one thing Iraqis are good at—it's organizing conferences. Why should vital political decisions critical to Iraq's independence be made under the watchful eyeball of an American Lieutenant or General? Everyone wants a democratic Iraq, but that just isn't going to happen if people constantly associate the government with occupation.

Why should any Iraqi government have to be christened and blessed by Bremer? He wasn't Iraqi, last time I checked . . .

Juan Cole and Joshua Marshall both have some interesting things to say on the subject (they both give some good links too).

Informed Comment, November 12, 2003, http://www.juancole.com

> US civil administrator Paul Bremer's sudden, rushed trip to Washington earlier this week signalled that the White House is considering a radical rethinking of Iraq policy. As Josh Marshall notes, rumors are flying that he himself may resign or be fired.
>
> He and his colleagues in Washington are also clearly thinking of abolishing the Interim Governing Council and resorting to an Afghanistan model. This step would require some sort of Iraqi selection process for a Karzai-like president, who could appoint a cabinet and establish a legitimate government while the new constitution is being written. Az-Zaman newspaper, which is close to IGC member Adnan Pachachi, describes the plan as a "purge of the Interim government" . . .

Talking Points Memo, November 11, 2003
http://www.talkingpointsmemo.com/archives/week_2003_11_09.php

> IS BREMER OUT? Is he being promoted? Suspended? Two weeks ago the rumor was that he was trying to resign.
>
> I've heard every rumor under the sun today. And all that seems really clear is that something major is about to happen on the ground in the US occupation . . .
> Almost two weeks ago now, Bremer had consultations with senior Pen-

> *tagon officials. And the chatter out of those meetings said that Bremer had grown deeply pessimistic about his job in Iraq and that John Abizaid, chief of the US Central Command, was advocating some sort of decisive move back toward actual war-fighting to arrest the rapidly deteriorating security situation . . .*

posted by river @ 2:35 AM

S u n d a y , N o v e m b e r 1 6 , 2 0 0 3

UPDATE . . .

These last few days have been tense—gunshots, helicopters, and explosions. A couple of days ago, we counted around 23 explosions. My cousin, his wife and their two daughters were at our house when the commotion began. A few explosions were so loud, the windows began to rattle with each impact and I had flashbacks of March and April.

The kids reacted differently—the older one ran to sit beside her mother, as far away from the living-room window as possible. She once confided to me that the glass terrified her; four of the windows at her grandparents' home cracked during the "shock and awe" phase of the bombing and she still remembers the incident. The younger one was silent and stoic. You can hardly tell she's scared except that if you sit particularly close, you can hear her grinding her little teeth, which is what she does when she's frightened. It drives my cousin crazy because the kid loses herself in a sort of trance when she does that and it's all we can do to keep her mind off of whatever she's brooding about. At one point she asked, "Is it war again?" No, it isn't war, dear . . . the helicopters, tanks, missiles, rattling windows and explosions aren't war—they are "protection": they are Operation Iron Hammer, not to be confused with war.

When it got particularly heavy, and the helicopters began hovering above, E. wanted to go out to the roof and see what was happening and what exactly was being bombed. My mother declared NO ONE would go up to the roof—the helicopters were flying low and the troops haven't been too discriminating lately when it came to civilians—especially the ones in helicopters and tanks.

At one point, the helicopters got so loud, it felt like they were going to land on the roof. E. was restless, pacing between the house and garden, trying to catch a glimpse of the commotion. We found out later an old Republican Guard facility had been bombed—though no one understands why: who would use *that* as a meeting place?! Other areas were bombed and one of the areas was evacuated—although some people preferred staying in their homes.

The 14th of July Bridge was closed again. The 14th of July Bridge is also known as the "Mu'alaq Bridge," or the suspended bridge. It's the bridge I described in one of my earlier posts. The bridge was closed to civilians during the war (after the 9th of April, I think) and was re-opened about two weeks ago. I haven't been on the bridge since late March. I dread having to cross it again because it was the scene of many horrible deaths—many civilian cars were burned on that bridge. A friend of ours lost his wife and dog on that bridge when a tank fired at his SUV in April. It was 5 days before he was allowed to remove her corpse from the burnt vehicle and give her a proper burial.

I heard about the new "acceleration to transfer power" to the GC. I'm not sure how it's going to work. Chalabi gave his speech in English today with Talbani on his right and Pachachi peering over his shoulder on the left. I read Juan Cole's blog and he describes a report given by ABC, which didn't sound like the speech.

Informed Comment, http://www.juancole.com, November 15, 2003

... ABC News (http://abcnews.go.com/sections/wnt/World/iraq_bremer_031114.html) seems to have been the first to get the details Friday of the plan presented by Paul Bremer to the Interim Governing Council. My concise paraphrase is as follows:

1. The Interim Governing Council will craft a Basic Law allowing a transitional government to be elected and operate.

2. By the spring, each of Iraq's 18 provinces will hold conventions made up of notables, elders and tribal chieftains. These conventions will elect altogether 200-300 members of the interim parliament, based on proportional representation. This interim parliament would in turn elect a prime minister. This process would be complete by June, 2004.

> 3. Mr. Bremer's Coalition Provisional Authority would hand over power to the new government and close up shop. The US and UK military would remain in Iraq, however, and the new government could invite other international contributors of troops and other help.
>
> 4. The Interim government would hold elections for delegates to a constitutional convention to draft the new constitution, in accordance with the fatwa or legal ruling of Grand Ayatollah Ali Sistani.
>
> 5. Formal elections on the basis of one person, one vote, will be held to install a new government, to which the interim government will hand power . . .

From the speech, I gathered that by June, the GC would nominate and elect a "sovereign government." But, again, who elected the GC? Someone asked Talabani, I think, whether the same GC members would actually be in the "elected" government, the answer was "Yes, if our parties still want us as their representatives." I'll have to look into it more. I'm still not sure what this means. There's still some confusion here as to how this whole new government will be chosen by June . . . **posted by river @ 5:21 AM**

SOME LINKS . . .

People have been asking about the casualties in Iraq. Check out this report: Continuing Collateral Damage: The health and environmental costs of war on Iraq.

Continuing Collateral Damage: The health and environmental costs of war on Iraq. http://www.medact.org/content/wmd_and_conflict/final %20final%20report%20proof.pdf

> . . . This report assesses the impact of the 2003 war on the environment and on the physical and mental health of civilians and combatants. It describes the war and some of the weapons used; its impact on health and the environment; and health-related issues in postwar reconstruction. The health of civilians and combatants has suffered greatly and continues to suffer. Its conclusions may help to determine whether waging war on Iraq was more or less damag-

> ing than alternative courses of action; how best to conduct postwar affairs to minimise further loss of life and maximise health gain; and how to approach such issues in debates about other conflicts. The report ends with recommendations relating both to Iraq and prevention of war . . .

As for the deaths of troops in Iraq, the best page that summarizes these is Today in Iraq—I know nothing about the page beyond the fact that it gives a daily summary of the main newsworthy events and gives links, brief commentary and occasional rants. It is worth checking daily.

Today in Iraq, http://dailywarnews.blogspot.com

War News for October 31, 2003

Bring 'em on: Grenade attack in Baghdad wounds two US soldiers.

Bring 'em on: Troops clash with demonstrators in Baghdad. Two more US soldiers wounded, one Iraqi policeman killed, three Iraqi civilians wounded.

Bring 'em on: Clashes in Baghdad escalate into urban firefight.

Bring 'em on: Bomb causes fire in Baghdad. Two Iraqis killed.

Bring 'em on: Grenade attack on Iraqi police station in Baghdad's Green Zone.

Bring 'em on: Polish army convoy mortared near Karbala.

Bring 'em on: Mayor's office attacked in Fallujah. One Iraqi reported killed.

Bring 'em on: Mayor's office attacked in Mosul, US base shelled.
Bring 'em on: Two Iraqi civilians killed by land mine near Baquba.

posted by yankeedoodle : 1:45 AM

I updated the recipes page (iraqrecipes.blogspot.com).

Danny Schechter has a new page called "Dissectorville" (www. newsdissector.org/dissectorville). **posted by river @ 5:50 AM**

DIFFICULT DAYS . . .

They've been bombing houses in Tikrit and other areas! Unbelievable . . . I'm so angry it makes me want to break something!!!! What the hell is going on?! What do the Americans think Tikrit is?! Some sort of city of monsters or beasts? The people there are simple people. Most of them make a living off of their land and their livestock—the rest are teachers, professors and merchants—they have lives and families . . . Tikrit is nothing more than a bunch of low buildings and a palace that was as inaccessible to the Tikritis as it was to everyone else!

People in Al Awja suffered as much as anyone, if not more—they weren't all related to Saddam and even those who were suffered under his direct relatives. Granted, his bodyguards and others close to him were from Tikrit, but they aren't currently in Tikrit—the majority have struck up deals with the CPA and are bargaining for their safety and the safety of their families with information. The people currently in Tikrit are just ordinary people whose homes and children are as precious to them as American homes and children are precious to Americans! This is contemptible and everyone thinks so—Sunnis and Shi'a alike are shaking their heads incredulously.

And NO—I'm not Tikriti—I'm not even from the "triangle"—but I know simple, decent people who ARE from there and just the thought that this is being done is so outrageous it makes me want to scream. How can that ass of a president say things are getting better in Iraq when his troops have stooped to destroying homes?! Is that a sign that things are getting better? When you destroy someone's home and detain their family, why would they want to go on with life? Why wouldn't they want to lob a bomb at some 19-year-old soldier from Missouri?!

The troops were pushing women and children shivering with fear out the door in the middle of the night. What do you think these children think to themselves—being dragged out of their homes, having their possessions and houses damaged and burned?! Who do you think is creating the "terrorists?!!" Do you think these kids think to themselves, "Oh well—we learned our lesson. That's that. Yay troops!" It's like a vicious, moronic circle and people are outraged . . .

The troops are claiming that the attacks originate from these areas—the people in the areas claim the attacks are coming from somewhere else . . . I really am frightened of what this is going to turn into. People seem to think that Iraq is broken into zones and areas— ethnically and religiously divided. That's just not true—the majority of people have relatives all over Iraq. My relatives extend from Mosul all the way down to Basrah—we all feel for each other and it makes decent people crazy to see this happening.

There have also been a string of raids all over Baghdad, but especially in Al-A'adhamiya. They've detained dozens of people with the excuse that they own more than one weapon. Who owns less than two weapons? Everyone has at least one Klashnikov and a couple of guns. Every male in the house is usually armed and sometimes the females are too. It's not because we love turning our homes into arsenals, but because the situation was so dangerous (and in some areas still is) that no one wants to take any risks. Imagine the scene: a blue mini-van pulls up . . . 10 dirty, long-haired men clamber out with Klashnikovs, pistols and grenades and demand all the gold and the kids (for ransom). Now imagine trying to face them all with a single handgun . . . if Baghdad were SECURE people would give up their weapons. I hate having weapons in the house.

I'm so tired. These last few days have been a strain on every single nerve in my body. The electricity has been out for the last three days and while the weather is pleasant, it really is depressing.

No one knows why the electricity is out—there are murmurings of storms and damage to generators and sabotage and punishment . . . no one knows exactly what's going on. There are explosions everywhere. Yesterday it was especially heavy. Today there was a huge explosion that felt like it was nearby but we can't really tell. How do you define a war? This sure as hell feels like war to me . . . no electricity, water at a trickle, planes, helicopters and explosions.

We didn't send the kids to school today. My cousin's wife spent last night talking about horrible premonitions and it didn't take much to convince my cousin that they would be better off at home.

It's hard for adults without electricity, but it's a torment for the kids. They refuse to leave the little pool of light provided by the kerosene lamps. We watch them nervously as they flit from candle-light to lamplight, trying to avoid the dark as much as possible. I have flashes of the children knocking down a candle, hot, burning wax, flames . . . I asked the 7-year-old the other night if she was afraid of "monsters" when she shied away from a dark room. She looked at me like I was crazy—monsters are for losers who don't need to fear war, abductions and explosions.

We (5 houses in the neighborhood) all chipped in and bought a generator immediately after the war. What we do now is 2 houses get enough electricity for some neon lights, a television, a refrigerator and a freezer. We asked them to "save our electricity up" and give us a couple of hours after futtoor and that's how I'm typing now. But my time is almost up and I'm afraid if the electricity goes off suddenly, it'll damage my computer.

E. and I hang out on the roof after futtoor and only duck inside when the helicopters begin hovering above. We watch the main street from the roof. One of the merchants has a little generator and he sets up chairs outside of his shop, in front of a small black and white tv. The guys in the neighborhood all stream towards the lights like ants towards a sticky spot. They sit around drinking tea and chatting.

You really can't appreciate light until you look down upon a blackened city and your eyes are automatically drawn to the pinpoints of brightness provided by generators . . . it looks like the heavens have fallen and the stars are wandering the streets of Baghdad, lost and alone.

I have to go now. Hope the electricity is back tomorrow, at least.
posted by river @ 10:52 PM

Saturday, November 22, 2003

THANK YOU . . .

A very special thanks to three people. The first is Frank Tobin (http://www.neverending.org/~ftobin/) who got Blogger (www.blogger. com) to upgrade my blog so that the advertisements are gone and I can do a lot of things I couldn't do before. The second person is Jeff Reed who has registered riverbendblog.com – Riverbend is a dot com now! The third person is Diana over at Letter from Gotham (http://letterfromgotham.blogspot.com) for . . . well, she knows why!

BTW, I've updated Is Something Burning (iraqrecipes.blogspot. com/) . . . **posted by river @ 12:50 AM**

DONKEYS AND GUERILLAS . . .

Today's blog is going to look like something straight out of The Onion.

Could Donkeys Could Be the Missing Link?

Baghdad, Iraq—At around a quarter past 7 this morning, residents in downtown Baghdad awoke to the sound of explosions. Many inhabitants claimed that they assumed the sounds were the result of Operation Iron Hammer—the latest military tactic designed to send a message to Iraqi insurgents.

Upon turning on their televisions, Baghdadis realized that two prominent hotels and the Ministry of Oil had recently been attacked. The two hotels assailed with missiles were the Sheraton and Palestine Hotel, both situated in a busy, commercial locale in the Iraqi capital. The hotels are home to the reporters and journalists of many major news networks, including the CNN, as well as foreign contractors. While there seem to be no casualties in either of the hotels, or the Ministry, witnesses confirmed there were injuries.

The assailants? Donkeys. Yes, donkeys were found in various locations in Baghdad, leading colorful carts with missile launchers and missiles camouflaged with hay. The donkeys, looking guilty and morose, were promptly taken into custody for questioning and were not available for a statement.

"He looks just like the purple donkey in Winnie Dab-Doob!"
gasped one young Baghdad resident, related to the reporter, in refer-
ence to one of the terrorists.

The First Real Link
Could this be the first real tie to Al-Qaeda? After months of trying to
connect Iraq to terrorist activities, this latest attack could prove to be
the Pentagon's "missing link." After all, donkeys and mules are very
widely used in Afghanistan to travel through the rocky, mountainous
region—their presence in Baghdad is highly suspicious. It is, as yet,
unclear whether the donkeys are foreign guerillas who crossed into Iraq
from one of the neighboring countries, or are actually a part of a local
Al-Qaeda cell.

Baghdad residents are wondering: could these culprits be the first
donkeys sent to Guantanamo?

By Riverbend, Baghdad Burning

It's true . . . it's all we've been talking about all day.   **posted by river**
@ 12:56 AM

Tuesday, November 25, 2003

EID MUBAREK . . .

The last few days I've had to give up the keyboard and blog for something less glamorous—the bucket and mop.

It started about 3 days ago. I was out on the driveway, struggling
with the garden hose and trying to cunningly arrange it to give a maximum trickle of water. My mother was standing at the door, chatting
lightly with Umm Maha, from across the street—a stocky, healthy
woman in her late forties.

Umm Maha had made us "kilaycha"—a special Eid desert (and
the recipe is a bit too complicated to post). Kilaycha are like . . . not
exactly cookies or bars but something like dry, sweet dumplings. They
are, basically, a sort of baked dough filled with either nuts, sesame
seeds and sugar, dates or just flat and plain, almost like Christmas cook-

ies—but less brittle and sweet. Every house either makes them or buys them for Eid—they are almost as necessary as lentil soup.

I was vaguely listening to the conversation. They were discussing the blackouts and how they were affecting the water flow in some areas (like ours). My mother was mentioning how she was thawing out the freezer because the intermittent electricity was turning everything to mush and Umm Maha suddenly looked awed, "But isn't your freezer clean? Haven't you began with the Eid cleaning?!" I froze as I heard the words and peered around at my mother. She was looking uncomfortable—no we hadn't started with the "Eid cleaning," but how do you say that to the Martha Stewart of Baghdad?

Yes, Umm Maha is the Martha Stewart of Baghdad—I defy anyone who can show me a neighbor with a cleaner driveway. Her whole house is spotless . . . rain, shine or cluster bombs. Her kids are always groomed and ironed. Their car, while old and dented, is spotless. She's always the first one to make the Eid kilaycha. She's the first one who is out of the door and washing down the house, the car, the driveway and the TREES after an infamous Iraqi dust storm. She's the neighbor who will know the latest cleaning fads (like using talcum powder to get out oil stains), and the one who'll be chasing the stray cats away from the garbage bins with (what else?) a broom.

My mother smiled wanly—we all knew Eid was coming up, but no one had the energy or initiative to begin the huge job of making the house spotless before Eid. Eid Il Futtir, as it is called, is the 3 day holiday that comes directly after Ramadhan. In Iraq, we celebrate it by visiting family and friends, and, generally, eating. It's a celebration of the end of fasting (especially if you were able to fast all month).

Preparations for Eid often begin a week ahead of the holiday. Kids have to have new clothes, pajamas and haircuts. The kitchen has to be stocked with good things to eat for visiting family, friends and neighbors. The family has to be prepared to have guests every minute of the 3 days of Eid. The house has to be spotlessly clean.

It's traditional for households to begin "tandheef il eid" a few days before Ramadhan ends. On Arafat, or the eve of Eid, many people stay at home to get things organized. It is believed that Eid isn't complete and the holiday "spirit" won't enter the home if the house is unclean or messy.

So Martha Stewart, aka Umm Maha, reminded my mother of the coming event a few days ago. That moment, I tried to subtly drop the hose and disappear behind a shrub, knowing my involvement in the cleaning process was going to be extensive. It didn't help. As soon as Umm Maha left the house, clucking disapprovingly, my mother got into "cleaning mode" and began "Operation Spotless Eid."

Major General "Riverbend's Mother" instantly gathered her army of cleaners together and began giving orders. Riverbend would get to do the closets, father would have to attack that pile of "valuable" junk in the driveway, and E. would move around heavy furniture to wipe beneath—dust bunnies must be abolished and dirt must be demolished.

That's what I've been doing the last few days—scrubbing, folding, polishing and flushing. It has been difficult because of the constant blackouts. Vacuuming is next to impossible and most of the clothes have to be washed by hand because the water tank on top of the roof is never full enough.

For some Sunnis, Eid began yesterday (as it did in Jordan and Egypt). For the rest, Eid is tomorrow. For families like mine, with a combination of Sunnis and Shi'a, we follow Saudi Arabia and they have declared Eid to be today—the 25th of November. It bothers me that we didn't begin Eid "together" this year because that's what Eid is really about—togetherness.

Mosques are being watched carefully and most people are safely in their homes by 8 pm. We're not quite sure how our families are going to meet—who will go where? Not everyone has telephone access and many people, in certain areas, are somewhat hesitant to gather together in large groups for fear of being mistaken for "terrorists." It's a strange sort of Eid this year—with helicopters and tanks . . . and possibly raids.

To those who began Eid yesterday, and to those who begin it today—Happy Eid, or Eid Mubarek . . . **posted by river @ 3:12 PM**

S a t u r d a y , N o v e m b e r 2 9 , 2 0 0 3

EID RECAP . . .

And so Eid Al Fittur has come and gone once again. This year was, of course, different from every year. It was more quiet and solemn than usual. The first day we spent at home, welcoming relatives and neighbors who came to say "Eid Mubarek" and having some tea and kilaycha.

On the second day, we went to visit a couple of family friends and a relative who are in mourning. It seems like so many people are in mourning this Eid. When you visit someone during the holidays who is in mourning, you can't say "Eid Mubarek" to them because it, in a way, is an insult to wish them joy during their difficult time. Instead, we say "Akhir il ahzan" which basically means, "May this be the last of your sorrows . . ." The person will often simply nod their head, fight back the tears and attempt to be civil. I hate making these visits because it really seems like a terrible intrusion.

One of our Eid visits was to a close friend of my mother who lives in Al-A'adhamiya. In April, she lost her husband, son and young daughter when a tank fired at their car as they were trying to evacuate their house. We went to visit her on the second day of Eid. I was dreading the visit because the last time I had seen her, she was only this fragment of a person. It was like she was only a whole person with her husband and kids and now she is only 1/4 of a whole. For the first month after their death, she couldn't eat, sleep or speak. When we saw her in May, she couldn't or wouldn't recognize us.

We went to see her at her sister's house in the same area. She doesn't live in her old house anymore—she can't stand how suddenly empty it is. She was speaking and moving around this time, but she isn't the same person—not even close to the same person. She speaks politely and tries to follow with the conversation but you can tell that her mind is somewhere else and it's a huge effort to stay focused on what is being said or done.

A part of me knew that being there, sharing Eid with her, was the right thing to do—the proper thing to do. Another part of me felt like we were committing some sort of terrible sin and that it was just unforgivable to be sitting there, talking about rain and explosions when this woman's life had fallen apart on a black day in April. I couldn't decide which was worse—to see the agonized look in her eyes during moments of remembrance, or to see the vague, void look of indifference she'd sometimes wear when she disappeared inside of herself.

As we were leaving, I leaned down and hugged her, whispering "Akhir il ahzan . . . " and as I pulled away, she simply looked at me, shook her head and said, "Of course it'll be the last of my sorrows— there's nothing else to mourn because nothing else matters . . . "

And then there was the last day of Eid . . .

Bush was in Iraq on the 27th. He made a fleeting visit to Baghdad International Airport. Don't let the name fool you—Baghdad Airport is about 20 minutes outside of Baghdad. It's in this empty, desert-like area that no one is allowed to go near. No one knew about it until he was gone and then we were all saying, "Huh? What was that about?!"

Everyone here sees it for what it is—just a lame attempt to try to look good. We actually expected him in Iraq during his Asia tour—he was bound to stop by for a good gloat. I just think the whole thing could have been a little bit less transparent (and I expected it would occur closer to elections).

Seeing him on tv was amusing—so why did he have to sneak into and out of Iraq with such secrecy? Why didn't he walk the streets of the country he helped "liberate?" Why didn't he at least *hover* above the country he "liberated?" He constantly claims the situation is much better now than pre-war, so why isn't he taking advantage of our excellent security situation?! We all sat there, watching him garble out the usual stream of words and shook our heads . . . he's just as much of an ass in Baghdad as he is in Washington.

I am curious about how the troops felt about his presence though . . . I'm sure the hand-picked group in the airport were elated, but I can't help but wonder about the troops stuck in Tikrit, Najaf, Falloojeh or Mosul . . . I imagine they'd much rather be at home.

The most amusing thing about his visit was watching Chalabi and Talabani jumping up and down at the airport, cheering and clapping as Bush made the rounds. Muwafaq Al-Rubai'i, also a member of the Governing Council, was just embarrassing—he was standing on tiptoe and clapping like a 5-year-old watching a circus clown. Later, he gushed about how happy the Iraqis were and how delighted the whole country was going to be, like he would know, almost as inaccessible to Iraqis as Bush himself is.

Bush must be proud today—two more "insurgents" were shot

dead in Ba'aquba: two terrorist sisters, one 12 years old and the other 15. They were shot by troops while gathering wood from a field . . . but nobody bothers to cover that. They are only two Iraqi girls in their teens who were brutally killed by occupation troops—so what? Bush's covert two-hour visit to Baghdad International Airport is infinitely more important . . .

Note: To all of you who sent me Eid greetings—thank you. The number of emails was unbelievable. I'll try to respond soon—be patient—the electrical situation has been a nightmare. **posted by river @ 5:08 AM**

Sunday, November 30, 2003

TWO SIDES TO THE STORY . . .

It has been brought to my attention that there are two different sides of the incident I mentioned in my previous blog—about the 12 and 15 year old girls who were shot in a field while gathering wood. The CPA announced the girls were actually *found* in the field, dead, and were handed over to Iraqi police. Their brother, though, claims that US troops shot them. The first to come out with the story were the AFP (France Press) and Al-Jazeera and several others picked it up afterwards.

This is the modified story on Al-Jazeera.

"Two Iraqi Sisters Found Dead," Aljazeera, November 29, 2003
http://english.aljazeera.net/NR/exeres/F9EAD9BE-BC2D-47B3-9C24-
4276D6C99B4B.htm

Bodies of two young Iraqi sisters have been discovered by US troops near
Baquba, some 60km (35 miles) north of Baghdad, according to the
occupation force.

A US military source said on Friday that they informed Iraqi police
and handed over the bodies. The source said both deaths appear to
be civil murder cases . . .

> However, the brother of the girls had earlier said that US troops at
> Ibn Firnas airport, 7km (4 miles) from Baquba, shot Fatima and Azra,
> 15 and 12, on Thursday at midday as they were collecting wood from
> a field some 30m away . . .
>
> "Azra died on the spot and my other sister later died from her
> wounds," said 18-year-old Qusay . . .
>
> Policeman Hussein Ali said US forces handed one of the girls'
> bodies over to the police "arguing that she had a gun in her posses-
> sion" . . .
>
> Police searched the girls' home, "without finding anything illegal,"
> Ali added . . .

And a confirmation at News Interactive.

**"US army denies killing sisters," News Interactive, http://www.news.
com.au/common/story_page/0,4057,8012117%255E1702,00.html**

> THE US-led coalition ruling Iraq today strongly denied a report that
> American troops had killed two young Iraqi sisters near Baqubah,
> 60km north of Baghdad.
>
> "US forces had nothing to do with the death of either of the young
> women. Both incidents appear to be murder. Iraqi police in the area
> are investigating," said a Coalition Provisional Authority spokesman.
>
> The girls were found dead by the US army and Iraqi police, he said.
>
> "US forces, in pursuit of two men who had been digging a hole in a
> field north of Baqubah, found a young girl, already dead. The men
> may have been preparing to bury the girl. Later the same day, Iraqi
> police and US forces found the remains of a second young girl . . .

I hope whoever did this is caught and punished *severely.*
posted by river @ 11:48 PM

IRAQ'S NUCLEAR MIRAGE . . .

I can't believe it—just today I was planning on blogging about Imad Khadduri's book "Iraq's Nuclear Mirage" (www.iraqsnuclearmirage. com/) when I found this article:

Iraqi Scientists: Lied About Nuke Weapons

"Iraqi Scientists: Lied About Nuke Weapons," by Charles J. Hanley,
The Associated Press, November 30, 2003
http://www.phillyburbs.com/pb-dyn/news/93-11302003-204751.html

> . . . Before that first Gulf War, the chief of the weapons program resorted to "blatant exaggeration" in telling Iraq's president how much bomb material was being produced, key scientist Imad Khadduri writes in a new book . . .
>
> Iraqi scientists never revived their long-dead nuclear bomb program, and in fact lied to Saddam Hussein about how much progress they were making before U.S.-led attacks shut the operation down for good in 1991, Iraqi physicists say . . .

Imad Khadduri was one of Iraq's leading nuclear scientists. He's a cultured, super-smart man who was born into a Catholic family dedicated to the education of its children. His father was a prominent doctor who practiced in Baghdad and was well-known for his medical abilities, as well as his compassion and dedication.

Imad Khadduri studied physics at the University of Michigan, and then continued to study nuclear reactor technology at the University of Birmingham. He later returned to Iraq and became one of the key scientists working on Iraq's nuclear program.

His book is fantastic. The book takes you through growing up in Baghdad, during the '50s and '60s, to the first experiences of studying abroad and adjusting to a foreign culture, to becoming one of the leading weapons scientists in the country, during the '80s.

On a brisk autumn evening in 1968, Basil al-Qaisi, a dear friend from high school, sat down next to me while I was playing Backgammon in an open-air café meters away from the Tigris. He had heard that I had returned from the US, where I was studying physics since 1961, via a sojourn in Jordan. Sipping his tea, he dropped a suggestion that changed the course of my life. In his gentle, shyly provocative manner, he asked,"Why don't you join us at the Nuclear Research Centre? Our friends are already working there, Jafar Dhia Jafar, Nazar Al-Quraishi and others."

I was thoroughly taken aback. I was not aware that the Russians had built a two Megawatt research reactor at Tuwaitha, 20 kilometers east of Baghdad that went critical a year earlier during November 1967. (http://www.iraqsnuclearmirage.com)

The book gives details of the varying nuclear and "secret" sites that were open to inspections and discusses how the program fell apart after the war in 1991 and what happened to the documents and information gathered by the scientists for over a decade. It also discusses the fakes and the flakes, like Chalabi and Khidhir Hamza, the "bomb-maker" who helped build the WMD case against Iraq with the help of Chalabi and a very vivid imagination.

Imad Khadduri writes about Khidhir Hamza:

In the mid-nineties, an Iraqi physicist, Khidhir Hamza, managed to escape from Iraq and seek tutelage of the CIA. At the end of 1999, he published a book titled "Saddam's Bomb Maker." It is worth mentioning that at no point in time did Khidhir Hamza get involved in any research work related to the nuclear bomb or the effects of a radioactive accident when we dabbled with such research . . . (http://www.iraqsnuclearmirage.com)

I found the book particularly fascinating, I guess, because Imad Khadduri is a *real* person. He's not one of those exiles who have been outside of Iraq for decades (he left in late 1998) and his words are painfully familiar—especially when he discusses family bonds and life in Iraq during the sanctions. He's very real, and very well-known and respected in Iraq. The author also played a prominent role in rebuilding Iraq after the 1991 war. He was one of the people who helped in restoring the electricity after.

The power stations' electrical grids were covered with air dropped special nets embedded with graphite pea-sized pellets that caused extensive electrical shorts bringing the whole electrical distribution over Iraq to a halt and hurling the whole country into darkness . . . [during the Gulf War] (http://www.iraqsnuclearmirage.com)

The book doesn't read like a dry, scientific journal . . . it is an education in nuclear weapons, reactors and Iraqi culture, all at once.

If you want to know all about Iraq's nuclear program, and its sudden halt in 1991, read the book. If you just want a fascinating, yet true, story—read the book . . .

Some articles by Imad Khadduri:

"The Mirage of Iraq's Weapons of Mass Destruction," yellowtimes.org,
http://www.scoop.co.nz/mason/ stories/HL0305/S00198.htm

There are no weapons of mass destruction in Iraq. This apparently became the case a few months after the end of the 1991 war when Hussain Kamel, the man in charge of the nuclear, chemical and biological weapons programs, ordered the destruction of the chemical and biological materials and their warheads. The nuclear weapons program had already come to a halt on the first night of bombing in January 1991. The weapons were destroyed secretly, in order to hide their existence from inspectors, in the hopes of someday resuming production after inspections had finished. Hussain Kamel even disclosed the location of the hidden documents relating to the remnants of the chemical and biological programs during his futile escape to Jordan in 1995.

Yet Bush, Blair and their senior cohorts kept brandishing their "intelligence sources" in order to whip up a fervor over the danger of Iraq's supposed weapons of mass destruction up until the last day before the invasion of Iraq. Once they were in Iraq, with their hundreds of "specialists," they promised to uncover the hidden weapons of mass destruction . . .

"Mobile Lies," yellowtimes.org
http://www.scoop.co.nz/mason/stories/HL0306/S00075.htm

> As the swelter of anger bubbles from the machination of misinforma-
> tion that led to the faltering WMD casus belli for invading Iraq, the
> retreat and half-baked excuses of Bush, Blair, Cheney, Wolfowitz and
> Powell further expose the sharp edge of their deceit. Whether it was
> "intelligence" failure or "flailing" the intelligence, time will soon tell.
> In the meantime, the fig leaves keep falling.
>
> During CNN's Late Edition with Colin Powell, reported by the Toron-
> to Star on June 9, 2003, Powell claimed that "the two alleged
> mobile biological weapons labs, which are being studied by allied
> inspectors now in Iraq, are the same ones he described to the world
> last Feb. 5 at a U.N. presentation which was the result of four days
> and four nights of meetings with the CIA." "I stand behind that pres-
> entation," he said . . .
>
> In an article published on the same day as Powell's interview, Peter
> Beaumont and Antony Barnett reported in the Observer that there
> [are] mounting indications that these vans were for "balloons, not
> germs" . . .
>
> In fact, the American experts themselves concede that the van could,
> at best, serve only one stage of the process for biological weapons
> production. There would need to be three or four other stages in the
> process, or other complementary vans, to be able to produce Powell's
> less than heuristic claim . . .

I'll blog tomorrow about how Iraqis felt about WMD . . . and I'll
also update the recipe page. **posted by river @ 11:56 PM**

Saturday, December 06, 2003

LATEST DEVELOPMENTS . . .

Rain! It has been raining . . . I love the rain. I think most Iraqis love
the rain because it is a relative rarity in our dry part of the world. We

have only a couple of rainy months during the year and they're not that rainy . . . more like drizzly.

The air smells like rain. It's the most wonderful smell—wet dust. It's not the first time this year, but it's been somewhat continuous. Everyone has been praying for lightning because Iraqis love "chimeh" or truffles. Those are those little potato-like veggies that grow like underground mushrooms and taste like wet socks. It is believed that the more lightning during the rainy season, the better/larger/tastier the truffles later on . . . don't ask me why.

The topic of the moment is currently Samarra . . . or "Samir-reh" as we pronounce it. People are really confused about the whole thing. The US military are saying that 54 Iraqis are dead, with several wounded—almost all of them "insurgents," but the Iraqi police claim there are only 8 dead—two of them an elderly Iranian couple who had come on a pilgrimage to a religious site in Samirreh. There were only 8 corpses found after the battle and the police say that not a single one of the corpses was in fida'ieen clothes. So where did the other bodies go? Iraqi forces don't have them and American forces don't have them—as far as anyone knows . . . did they just disappear? People from the area claim that the American troops had losses too. Most people believe that the big number of dead was thrown out in order to legitimatize the "collateral damage," i.e. the civilians, like the Iranian tourists and the dozens who were injured and had nothing to do with it. If 54 are dead, then the extra 8 innocents who died won't really matter when one looks at the "bigger picture."

One thing everyone agrees on—there are dozens of wounded. The scenes in the hospital were terrible—so many injured, including some children. The troops are saying that the whole thing occurred outside of the city, but shelled houses, shattered glass and "collateral damage" all contradict that. Other reports confirm that a mosque, a hospital, and houses all came under heavy fire.

The other topic we've been discussing is the CPA's decision to start a militia, to fight the resistance against troops, composed of various militias belonging to the political parties involved with the GC people. Read more about it on Juan Cole.

Warlords annointed by Bremer

The WP reports that the US will create a new paramilitary force to fight terrorism in Iraq, and that it will draw for its personnel on the militias of five important political groupings in Iraq:

"The five parties that will contribute militiamen are Alawi's Iraqi National Accord, Ahmed Chalabi's Iraqi National Congress, the Shiite Muslim Supreme Council for the Islamic Revolution in Iraq and two large Kurdish parties, the Kurdistan Democratic Party and the Patriotic Union of Kurdistan. Kurdish members will be drawn from the ranks of pesh merga fighters who defended autonomous Kurdish areas from former president Saddam Hussein's army, officials said."

Ghazi al-Yawar, a Sunni member of the IGC, told the LA Times that this was a very bad idea, and that the militias should be disbanded rather than being legitimized.

Al-Yawar is right, of course. This step is ominous, moreover, because this genderamerie will report to the Interior Ministry, which is dominated by the appointees of ex-Baathist Iyad al-Alawi.

We're all worried about that. It basically means that Badir's Brigade (belonging to the SCIRI) and the Bayshmarga (with Talbani), amongst others, are going to be made legitimate. They are going to be given uniforms and weapons and allowed to basically do what they've been doing these last few months—terrorize the citizens—but with a CPA stamp of approval, this time around.

Muqtada Al-Sadr in the south is making some not-so-covert threats about how other militias might be tempted to join the resistance if they aren't given power, or at least some semblance of it.

This latest militia thing is a definite change from last month when these same militias were being ordered to disarm. My cousin is a wise man. The moment he heard the decision to disarm Badir's Brigade and the Bayshmarga a few weeks ago, he snorted with laughter and shook his head at my naïve, "FINALLY!"

"They'll take away their toys for about a week," he said, shaking his head, "and then put them in some fancy suits, with a badge on their arm, a monthly wage and bigger guns." Apparently, if you can't beat 'em, pretend you approve of what they're doing (and that you *really* can control them...no, *really*).

Salam Pax (dear_raed.blogspot.com) is blogging once more! He's blogging in orange because Raed, his co-blogger, blogs in white. For those who don't know him (is there anyone who doesn't?!) Salam is the Baghdad Blogger (thebaghdadblog.com/home) and he was blogging way before the war and he encouraged me, and others, to start a blog—he is daily reading.

Both Salam and Juan Cole mention the fact that the US rejected an Iraqi plan to hold a census by the summer (in order to allow voting) and that the Governing Council were supposedly shocked. I imagine they may have known, but, as we say in Iraqi Arabic "ghelisow" or they turned a blind eye to the whole issue because someone like Chalabi, or even Talbani, is very aware of the minimal support he would get from voters. Who needs a risky vote when you can be appointed?!

"U.S. Rejects Iraqi Plan To Hold Census by Summer," The New York Times, December 4, 2003, http://www.nytimes.com/2003/12/04/ international/middleeast/04CENS.html?hp

Iraqi census officials devised a detailed plan to count the country's entire population next summer and prepare a voter roll that would open the way to national elections in September. But American officials say they rejected the idea, and the Iraqi Governing Council members say they never saw the plan . . .

Informed Comment, http://www.juancole.com, December 5, 2003

Census Plan bypasses IGC

The Iraqi Census Bureau made up a plan that would have allowed a census to be completed by September 1, but the plan was immediately rejected by the US and did not reach the Interim Governing Council before their Nov. 15 vote on creating a transitional government through caucus elections. According to AFP, angry council members said they might have voted differently. The plan did not arrive from the Census Bureau because of a bureaucratic SNAFU.

> *Still, the US officials had seen the plan and rejected it and did not bother to bring it up with the IGC. The outcome looks manipulated even if it was not. Of course, the real reason for trying to get a new transitional government by July 1 is to get Iraq out of the news before the fall presidential campaign.*

COMPLETELY UNRELATED . . .

Is Something Burning (iraqrecipes.blogspot.com) has been updated.
posted by river @ 2:23 AM

Friday, December 12, 2003

KEROSENE AND GASOLINE . . .

The electricity has been terrible lately—it comes in fits and starts. The moment it goes off, we start running around the house unplugging things and flicking off the power switches—you don't want anything to be turned on when the power comes back either too high or too low. That's why I've been blogging less often. Every time there's electricity, we remember a long list of things that can only be done in an electrical world . . . like vacuum. Some say it's not only Baghdad—the north also seem to be having continuous electricity problems.

The most popular guy in the neighborhood these days [is] Abu Hassen. He lives on our street and he's going to purchase one of those large generators that will, supposedly, provide electricity to around 20 houses. The problem is that it can't accommodate any more than 20 houses (probably fewer) and anyone who wants to has to "sign up" for the electricity. When E. went to get us registered for a few amperes, Abu Hassen told him that he already had 30 families who wanted to sign on but he would put us on a waiting list (!).

Since the generators are expensive, Abu Hassen has been hesitant to buy one. E. says he has a nephew who works at one of the electric power stations in Baghdad who convinced him it would be a *great* investment because the power situation promises to be very erratic for a while yet.

The big problem now is that gasoline is hard to come by. This is a very frustrating issue for Iraqis. Gasoline was like water here. In fact, bottled water used to be far more expensive than gasoline and admittedly still is. The lines at the gas stations are long and tedious. E. and my cousin sometimes go to fill up the car and disappear for hours at a time. The gasoline is necessary for running the generators and now they're going to start rationing it. This will mean that within days, the price of gas is going to go up because people will start selling black market gasoline.

Kerosene is also hard to come by these days. Every time the kerosene man comes banging down our street, representatives from each household instantly run outside and stand impatiently at their gates, some greeting him with an energetic "Hello, habibi!" We need the kerosene for the "sopas" or the kerosene heaters, and the kerosene lamps. The weather is nice during the day, but it gets somewhat chilly during the evening. We light the kerosene heaters in the rooms and watch them carefully so that they don't start giving out poisonous fumes from burning kerosene. There have been entire families that died in their sleep from CO [carbon monoxide] poisoning from kerosene heaters.

The nicest thing about the heaters is the fact that there's always a kettle of water on top of them. This accomplishes two things it once: it keeps the air in the room from getting very dry, and it provides a ready kettle of hot water for the tea ritual during the evening. The sopa is also fantastic for heating bread. At night, when there is no hope of electricity, we sit around on the rug, a little distance away from the sopa, and drink sweet tea, with warm bread and some famous Iraqi salted white cheese, while listening to the radio or just talking about family matters, or political matters.

The sun sets quite early these days and, if there's no electricity, it gets a little bit depressing. E. and I often go out to the roof to enjoy the last few minutes of sun every evening. Sometimes, the electricity will return at night and the lights will flicker on suddenly, leaving us too dazzled for the first few moments to do anything but sit there, allowing our eyes to adjust to the abrupt change. **posted by river @ 2:21 AM**

MEANWHILE . . .

We heard the latest statement from Washington about Germany, France, Russia and Canada not being allowed to have anything to do with the reconstruction. Iraq no longer feels like a country—it feels like war spoils: the winning team gets the pickings. So how is the world supposed to be involved in the reconstruction of Iraq when they are being deliberately excluded?

It's a decision like this one that brings to light the complete uselessness of the Governing Council. Why is Washington calling the shots on the reconstruction issues? This means that even after a military occupation, we'll be under an economic occupation for years to come. Why aren't any of the new ministers or GC members saying anything about this? Somehow, I have a feeling that if they have anything to say, it'll be in accordance with this latest decision.

There was a demonstration in Baghdad yesterday of about 4,000 people. The parties who are a part of the GC took part in an "anti-terror" protest. The roads were closed for security reasons and helicopters were hovering over head. There were a couple of women's groups . . . I recognized some women from Al-Da'awa Al-Islamiya—Al-Jaffari's party. The Iraqi communist party and SCIRI were also involved. The irony is seeing SCIRI members hold up the "NO TERROR" banners (they could start by not terrorizing the Al-Iraqiya station because the anchorwomen don't wear hijabs . . .).

There were other demonstrations in some provinces, and they've all been lobbed together with the one in Baghdad. The truth is that some of them were actually anti-occupation demonstrations, like the one in Khaldiya. There were large crowds demonstrating in Khaldiya, demanding the release of boys and men who have been detained for over 3 months in American prison camps.

Today (well, technically, yesterday) there was another large demonstration in Baghdad which was a peaceful anti-occupation demonstration. The demonstrators were mainly university students and teachers who were opposing the raids occurring in some colleges and universities. They were demanding the release of three women who were detained when the Technology University in Baghdad was raided. Their spokesperson, a professor, I think, said that this was going to be the first demonstration in a long series of anti-occupation activism being organized by teachers and students.

There were some loud explosions a while ago . . . I just read it might have been inside of the "Green Zone." **posted by river @ 2:22 AM**

Tuesday, December 16, 2003

THE LATEST . . .

The electricity only returned a couple of hours ago. We've been without electricity for almost 72 hours   other areas have it worse. Today we heard the electricity won't be back to pre-war levels until the middle of next year.

We heard about Saddam's capture the day before yesterday, around noon. There was no electricity, so we couldn't watch tv. The first sign we got that something abnormal was occurring was the sound of a Klashnikov in the distance. I remember pausing in my negotiations with E. over who should fill the kerosene heaters and listening hard to the sounds of shooting. I grabbed the battery-powered radio and started searching the stations, skipping from one to the other. I finally located a station that was broadcasting in Arabic and heard that Saddam may have been caught.

We thought nothing of it at first . . . another false alarm. It happened on an almost weekly basis. When the sounds of shooting became more frequent, curiosity got the better of E. and he ran to our neighbor's house where they had a small generator running. Fifteen minutes later, he came back breathless with the words, "They've caught Saddam . . ." Everyone was shocked. We all clamored for the radio once again and tried to find out what was happening. The questions were endless—who? What? When? How?

It was only later in the evening that we saw the pictures on tv and saw the press-conference, etc. By then, Baghdad was a mess of bullets, and men waving flags. Our area and other areas were somewhat quiet, but central Baghdad was a storm of gunfire. The communist party [was] scary—it's like they knew beforehand. Immediately, their red flags and banners were up in the air and they were marching up and down the streets and around Firdaws Square. My cousin was caught in the middle of a traffic jam and he says the scenes were frightening.

The bullets are supposed to be an expression of joy . . . and they probably are—in a desert, far from buildings, streets crawling with vulnerable people and cars. In Baghdad, they mean chaos. People were literally ducking and running, trying to get out of the rain of firepower because what goes up must, eventually, come down.

Yesterday was almost as messy. Most parents kept their kids home. There have been pro-America demonstrations in some areas, and anti-America demonstrations in other areas. At around 6 pm yesterday evening, the chaos began in Amiriyah, a residential area in Baghdad. The streets were suddenly filled with anti-American demonstrators, some holding up pictures of Saddam. It lasted until around 11 pm and then the tanks pulled up and things settled down somewhat. Similar occurrences in A'adhamiya in Baghdad, and one or two other areas.

Today there were pro-America demonstrations in Baghdad organized by SCIRI and there were anti-America demonstrations in Tikrit, Falloojeh, Samirreh [Sammara] (where 11 Iraqis were killed—CPA claim they were "insurgents"), Baghdad, Imsayab and the biggest one was in Mosul. Thousands of students from the University of Mosul took to the streets with an anti-occupation demonstration and some of the residents joined them . . . the university president had to shut down the university—it was huge. I was surprised the CNN wasn't covering it. The troops broke it up by firing above the crowd and bringing in the helicopters. The demonstration in Samnara had a similar ending, except the firing was *in* the crowd and several people were wounded severely.

The question that everyone seems to be asking is the effect it will have on the resistance/insurgence/attacks. Most people seem to think that Saddam's capture isn't going to have a big effect. Saddam's role was over since April, many of the guerilla groups and resistance parties haven't been fighting to bring him back to power and I think very few people actually feared that.

Political analysts and professors in Iraq think that Saddam's capture is going to unite resistance efforts, as one of them put it, "People are now free to fight for their country's sovereignty and not Saddam."

The rumors have been endless ever since yesterday—and they all seem to be filtering in from Tikrit. Some of the rumors include people claiming that Saddam was actually caught a week ago, but the whole thing was kept quiet. Another rumor is that some sort of nerve gas was used in a limited sort of way on the area he was hiding in. Another rumor goes on about how he was "drugged"—something was added to his food . . . Others say he's being interrogated in Qatar . . . and on and on.

The GC seem equally confused with the commotion. Talabani claims it was a combined effort between the Bayshmarga (the Kurdish militia) and the troops, Chalabi, on the other hand, insisted the whole thing was completely an American effort. It's hard to tell who has the story right and who's getting it wrong . . .

People have differing opinions on where he should be tried and by whom—in Iraq or an international court? Others are wondering about the legitimacy of a court under occupation. The one thing everyone seems to agree upon is that it should be an open court and *everything* should be discussed. The question is, will the US allow that? Won't it bring forward certain political dealings with America in the '80s? Only time will tell . . .

Things are very frightening these days in Baghdad. Going from one area to another is like going from one city to another—the feelings and emotions vary so drastically it feels like only a matter of time before we may see clashes . . . **posted by river @ 9:58 PM**

Monday, December 22, 2003

QUESTIONS AND FEARS . . .

Baghdad has been a very tense place these last few days. Yesterday alone we heard around 8 explosions though none of the news channels seem to be covering them. There have also been several demonstrations—some anti-Saddam and some pro-Saddam and several anti-America. The most prominent anti-America demonstrations took place in A'adhamiya and Amiriya, two residential areas in Baghdad.

One demonstration in A'adhamiya included people from all over the city. The demonstrators were demanding the release of hundreds of people who have been detained over the last few weeks (there are thousands of detained Iraqis, overall). Most people imagine detained Iraqis as being bearded, angry men in their 30s or 40s shouting anti-imperialist slogans and whipping their heads about in a livid frenzy. They do not see the women—school teachers, professors and house-wives—being herded off to the infamous Abu Ghraib prison. They don't see the kids—some no more than 13 or 14 years old—who are packed away with bags over their heads, hands secured behind their backs. They don't see the anxious mothers and children, weeping with fear and consternation, begging in a language foreign to the soldiers to know where their loved ones are being taken.

The Amiriya demonstrations were pro-Saddam demonstrations led by a boys' high school in the area. Jo Wilding in Baghdad (http:// www. wildfirejo.org.uk/) describes the demonstrations in an internet article, and she has another article on some of the detentions:

"December 18th —Arresting Children," http://www.wildfirejo.org.uk/
feature/display/56/index.php

Schoolchildren arrested by armed US soldiers and masked translators for demonstrating against the occupation and in support of Saddam.

"Two days ago there was a demonstration after school finished, against the coalition and for Saddam. Yesterday the American army came and surrounded the whole block. They just crashed into the school, 6, 7, 8 into every classroom with their guns. They took the name of every student and matched the names to the photos they got from the day before and then arrested the students. They actually dragged them by their shirts onto the floor and out of the class."

They wouldn't give their names. The children at Adnan Kheiralla Boys' School in the Amiriyah district of Baghdad were still scared, still seething with rage. Another boy, Hakim Hamid Naji, was taken today. "They were kicking him," one of the pupils said. A car pulled up and a tall, thin boy ran into the school, talked briefly with staff and left again. The kids said the soldiers had come looking for this boy too.

**December 13th—Prisoners, http://www.wildfirejo.org.uk/feature/
display/53/index.php**

> . . . Sahib explained, "He was a taxi driver and he went out from home
> and just didn't come back, about 6 months ago. I didn't know what
> happened. First I went to a lot of hospitals and to the morgue and I
> did not find him, so I went to the American base and after that I went
> to the computer office and they gave me a paper and told me your
> son is in Abu Ghraib and gave me a paper with his name and a num-
> ber on and I came here but no one gave me any answers and the guy
> inside, the translator, just told them to go and get a lawyer . . .
>
> On the second of two days of protests for the rights of people detained
> without charge by the occupying powers, people stood waiting qui-
> etly, holding pieces of paper, queueing to talk to activists, NGO
> workers, journalists, anyone who would hear their story, anyone who
> might perhaps be able to help . . .
>
> Even if people are accused of genuine terrorist offences, or caught
> in the act of theft, for example, still there has to be due process, oth-
> erwise, as the families say, there is no difference between the Amer-
> icans and the old regime. Previously you could be detained on a
> trumped up charge and could disappear. Now, they say, you can be
> detained on no charge at all and disappear . . .

Gasoline is a big problem. A friend of ours quit her job a couple
of days ago because her husband can't afford to wait in long lines for
4 or 5 hours to fill up their battered Volvo so that he can drive her
across Baghdad every morning to the clinic she works in. Everyone has
been buying black-market gasoline of late, but we've been getting
leaflets and warnings threatening 7 – 10 years of prison if we buy or
sell black-market gasoline. Black-market gas simply means a surly,
dirty guy surrounded with yellowish plastic containers selling gas for
over 30 times its original price. He, inevitably, has a cigarette dan-
gling out of the side of his mouth and a furtive, hurried look about him.

We've been using candles most of the time instead of kerosene
lamps because the kerosene man hasn't been coming around these
last few days and we need the kerosene for the heaters. The kids really hate the candles. The other day, the electricity suddenly flashed on

at 8 pm after a 6-hour blackout. We were exalted. Everyone jumped for the television at once and a chorus of voices called out, "News! The movie! A song! Cartoons!" After flipping the channels, we settled for a movie.

We sat watching until one of the scenes faded into a darkened room. The camera focused on the couple sitting at a round table, gazing into each others eyes and smiling fondly across two elegant candles. It was a cozy, romantic candle-light dinner. I think the whole family was lost in the scene when suddenly, my cousin's youngest daughter spoke up, impatiently, "They have no electricity! They're using the candles . . ."

It took me about 15 minutes to try to explain to her that they had electricity but actually *chose* to sit in the dark because it was more "romantic." The difficulty of explaining romance to a 7-year-old is nothing compared to the difficulty of explaining the "romance" of a darkened room and candles—especially if the 7-year-old has associated candles to explosions and blackouts her whole life.

These last few days have been truly frightening. The air in Baghdad feels charged in a way that scares me. Everyone can feel the tension and it has been a strain on the nerves. It's not so much what's been going on in the streets—riots, shootings, bombings and raids—but it's the possibility of what may lie ahead. We've been keeping the kids home from school, and my cousin's wife learned that many parents were doing the same—especially the parents who need to drive their kids to school.

We've been avoiding discussing the possibilities of this last week's developments . . . the rioting and violence. We don't often talk about the possibility of civil war because conferring about it somehow makes it more of a reality. When we do talk about it, it's usually done in hushed tones with an overhanging air of consternation. Is it possible? Will it happen?

Sunnis and Shi'a have always lived in harmony in Iraq and we still do, so far. I'm from a family that is about half Shi'a and half Sunni. We have never had problems as the majority of civilized people don't discriminate between the two. The thing that seems to be triggering a lot of antagonism on all sides is the counterinsurgency militia being cultivated by the CPA and GC which will include Chalabi's thugs, SCIRI extremists and some Kurdish Bayshmarga.

The popular and incorrect belief seems to be that if you are a Kurd or Shi'a, this step is a positive one. Actually, the majority of moderate Kurds and Shi'a are just as exasperated as Sunnis about this new group of soldiers/spies that is going to be let loose on the population. It's just going to mean more hostility and suspicion in all directions, and if the new Iraqi force intends to be as indiscriminate with the detentions and raids as the troops, there's going to be a lot of bloodshed too.

I once said that I hoped, and believed, Iraqis were above the horrors of civil war and the slaughter of innocents, and I'm clinging to that belief with the sheer strength of desperation these days. I remember hearing the stories about Lebanon from people who were actually living there during the fighting and a constant question arose when they talked about the grief and horrors—What led up to it? What were the signs? How did it happen? And most importantly . . . did anyone see it coming? **posted by river @ 6:19 AM**

Wednesday, December 24, 2003

FILLING THE WATER TANK . . .

We filled the water tank today. Most Iraqi homes have a water tank or "tanki" on top of the roof. The water pressure was usually high enough to send the "municipal water" to the tank on the roof, and then the water goes from there to either the "gizer" or water heater (another tank heated by electricity, kerosene or coals) or directly to the cold water faucet. Because the water pressure is low these days in our area, the water barely makes it to a couple of faucets on the ground floor.

I realized the water tank was empty at around 10 am when I turned on the faucet in the kitchen and, instead of the sound of gushing, flowing water, the faucet sort of wheezed, spluttered and whined. The faucet and I groaned simultaneously. I called out E's name and he stumbled downstairs in two sweaters, pajama bottoms and mismatched socks (it's just so *cold* lately).

"E., the water is GONE! Not a single drop in any of the faucets . . . we have to fill up the tank." E. groaned and beat his head gently against the staircase railing, mumbling something under his breath. I didn't blame him. Filling up the water tank is no fun. It involves at least 3 people, several buckets, a lot of sloshing around in the water and mud and some interesting slips and spills.

E., of course, always gets roof duty. That means he gets to stand on the roof, next to the water tank, receive the pails of water, and dump them into the tank. I get hose duty, which has me standing outside IN THE COLD, filling up pails of cold, cold water from the garden hose while shifting from one foot to the other and trying to keep my thoughts away from the kerosene heater inside of the house. There should also be at least two people (we'll call them the couriers) to run the buckets from me, wielding the hose, to E. who empties them and sends them back down. This process is repeated around 12 to 15 times, or until either E., the couriers or I have dropped from sheer exhaustion.

The hard part about doing this during the winter is the fact that everyone involved is bound to get wet and cold, but it is necessary to do this chore because otherwise, it may take days and days for the tank to fill up. We have an electric water pump but there isn't enough electricity to run it long enough to fill the tank.

I took the final bucket upstairs to the roof myself because our courier (a twelve-year-old three houses away) claimed he had a soccer game to attend to. As I neared the water tank, I saw E. leaning against it conversing with a pigeon that seemed oblivious to his presence. We have seemingly millions of pigeons in Baghdad and some people are obsessed with them—E. is not one of those people . . . I thought he had finally lost it. "What are you talking about?!" I asked, awed.

"I was envying its wings . . ." he murmured, staring out into the distance.

"Ah . . . you'd like to fly away . . ." I nodded sagely.

"No . . . I just think it's fantastic he doesn't have to wait in line 8 hours for gas to get from one place to the next . . ." **posted by river @ 3:49 AM**

BEST ASIAN BLOG . . .

Check out *Flying Chair* (http://www.flyingchair.net/) for nominations on the best Asian blogs. I've been a little obsessed with blogs from Pakistan and Iran, personally. I love comparing the similarities and differences in our cultures. *Baghdad Burning is nominated for the Best Iraqi Blog on this page.* (http://www.flyingchair.net/vote.php?categoryID=26) Vote for your favorite. **posted by river @ 3:57 AM**

Friday, December 26, 2003

CHRISTMAS IN BAGHDAD . . .

Explosions and bombing almost all day yesterday and deep into the night. At some points it gets hard to tell who is bombing who? Resistance or Americans? Tanks or mortars? Cluster bombs or IEDs [improvised explosive devices]? Nothing on the news . . . to see the reports on CNN, Abu Dhabi, and Al-Arabia you'd think there was nothing going on in Baghdad beyond the usual thumps and thuds. Yesterday was *very* unusual. Embassies, mines, residential areas and the Green Zone . . . and the sirens. I hate the sirens. I can stand the explosions, the rattling windows, the slamming doors, the planes, the helicopters . . . but I feel like my heart is wailing when I hear the sirens.

The explosions haven't really put anyone in a very festive spirit. The highlight of the last few days, for me, was when we went to our Christian friends' home to keep them company on Christmas Eve. We live in a neighborhood with a number of Christian families and, under normal circumstances, the area would be quite festive this time of year—little plastic Santas on green lawns, an occasional plastic wreath on a door and some colored, blinking lights on trees.

Our particular friends (Abu Josef's family) specialized in the lights. Every year, a week before Christmas, they would not only decorate their own plastic tree (evergreens are hard to come by in Iraq), but they would decorate 4 different olive trees in the little garden in front of their home with long strings of red lights. Passing by their house, the scene of the green olive trees with branches tangled in little red lights always brought a smile . . . you couldn't help but feel the "Christmas spirit"—Christians and Muslims alike.

This year the trees weren't decorated because, as their father put it, "We don't want to attract too much attention . . . and it wouldn't be right with the electricity shortage." The tree inside of their house *was* decorated, however, and it was almost sagging with ornaments. The traditional tree ornaments were hanging, but the side of the tree was covered with not-so-traditional Pokemon toys. Their 8-year-old is an avid collector of those little Pokemon finger puppets and the bottom section of the tree was drooping with the weight of the little plastic figures which took Iraq by storm a couple of years ago.

Kids in Iraq also believe in Santa Claus, but people here call him "Baba Noel" which means "Father Noel." I asked the children what he looked like and they generally agreed that he was fat, cheerful, decked in red and had white hair. (Their impertinent 11-year-old explains that he's fat because of the dates, cheerful because of the alcohol and wears red because he's a communist!) He doesn't drop into Iraqi homes through the chimney, though, because very few Iraqi homes actually have chimneys. He also doesn't drop in unexpectedly in the middle of the night because that's just rude. He acts as more of an inspiration to parents when they are out buying Christmas gifts for the kids; a holiday muse, if you will. The reindeer are a foreign concept here.

The annual ritual around Christmas for many Christians in Baghdad used to be generally hanging out with family and friends on Christmas Eve, exchanging gifts and food (always food—if you're Iraqi, it's going to be food) and receiving guests and well-wishers. At 12 am, many would attend a Christmas service at their local church and light candles to greet the Christmas spirit. Christmas day would be like our first day of Eid—eating and drinking, receiving family, friends and neighbors and preparing for the inevitable Christmas party in the evening at either a friend's house or in one of the various recreational clubs in Baghdad. The most famous for their Christmas parties were the Hindiya club and the Armenian club.

This year, the Christmas service was early and many people didn't go because they either didn't have gasoline, or just didn't feel safe driving around Baghdad in the evening. Many of them also couldn't join their families because of the security situation. Abu Josef's family have aunts and uncles in a little village north of Mosul. Every year, the extended relatives come down and stay in their house for a week to celebrate Christmas and New Year. This year they've decided to stay in their village because it just isn't safe to leave their home and head for Baghdad.

At one point during the evening, the house was dark and there was no electricity. We sat, gathered around on the ground, eating date-balls and watching Abu Josef's dog chew on the lowest branch of the tree. The living room was lit by the warm light radiating from the kerosene heater and a few Christmas candles set on the coffee table. Abu Josef's phone suddenly rang shrilly and Abu Josef ran to pick it up. It was his brother in Toronto and it was the perfect Christmas gift because it was the first time Abu Josef got an overseas call since the war—we were all amazed. An Iraqi phone conversation goes like this these days:

III= Iraqi Inside Iraq

IOI= Iraqi Outside Iraq

Ring, ring

II: Alloo?

OI: ALLOO?!

II: ALLOOOO? MINNOOO? (Hello? Who is it?)

IOI: ABU (fill in the blank)??! Shlonkum? (How are you?)

III: Aaaagh! Is it really you?!

(Chorus of family in the background, "Who is it?! Who is it?!")

IOI: How are . . . (the voice cracks here with emotion) you?

III: We're . . . (the line crackles) . . . and is doing well.

IOI: I CAN'T HEAR YOU! Doing well? Thank God . . .

III: Alloo? Alloo . . . ? (speaker turns to speak to someone in the background, "Sshhh . . . I can't hear anything!" The family go silent and hold their breaths.)

III: Alloo? Alloo?!

IOI: Alloo? Yes, yes, your voice is back—are you ok?

III: Fine, fine.

IOI: Is my mother ok? My brothers and sisters?

III: All fine . . . we're fine, thank God.

IOI: Thank God (the voice cracks again)

III: How are you? (a vague echo with "you . . . you . . . you . . . ")

IOI: We're fine but terribly worried about all of YOU . . .

III: Don't worry—we're doing alright . . . no electricity or fuel, but we'll be alright . . .

IOI: (crackling line . . . fading voices) . . . tried and tried to call but . . . (more crackling line) . . . and we heard horrible . . . (static)

III: Alloo? Alloooooooo? Are you there? (silence on the other end)

III: Alloo? If you can hear me, I can't hear you . . . (the hovering relatives all hold their breath)

III: . . . I still can't hear you . . . if you can hear me just know that we're fine. We're ok. We're alive and wondering about your health. Don't worry . . . yallah, ma'a al salama . . . don't worry. Alloo . . . Alloo . . . ?

And everyone exhales feeling a bit more relieved and a little bit empty as the phone is returned to the cradle and the momentous event passes.

Although it's late—Merry Christmas.   **posted by river @ 5:25 PM**

By the turn of the year the Grand Ayatollah Ali al-Sistani, the most influential Sh'ia cleric in the country and a man who usually eschewed day to day political life, suddenly steps into the picture declaring that members of the interim government must be selected by direct vote. He opposes the US plan to hold regional caucuses, which appeared to many as just another device for perpetuating American rule, albeit under the table, because the US could manipulate the caucuses much more easily than if there was a direct vote. The US acknowledges the caucus system is less than democratic but insists this method will hasten matters and speed up the process of turning over the government to Iraqis by June 30. Al-Sistani is adamant and refuses to meet US officials. In frustration Washington asks the UN, whose advice it had shunned in going to war, to intercede. Meanwhile 100,000 Shiites take to the streets in Baghdad and in other cities around the country.

Events in the US are not helping Bush. David Kay, whom the Bush administration confidently predicted would bring home proof of Saddam's weapons of mass destruction, instead tells a Senate committee he can't find any evidence of their existence, and that pre-war intelligence was "almost all wrong." This sets off debate: Did the US get bad intelligence or did Bush manipulate the intelligence for his own ends? Or both? Meanwhile the insurgency mounts. Some 100-odd Iraqis die in suicide bombings in Erbil.

. . .

At the beginning of February Bush tries to quiet growing debate on his war policies by appointing an independent commission to study intelligence failures. On February 10, 54 people, mostly Iraqis, are killed in a bombing as they apply for work at a police station. The next day 47 die in an attack outside an army recruiting center. A UN official meets with al-Sistani and the UN says an election can't possibly be held until late 2004 or early 2005, and sets forth plans for restructuring the interim government to run the country until then.

In March the insurgency spreads and becomes more intense. Attacks in Karbala on a Muslim feast day kill over 100 and wound over 300. The Iraqi Governing Council puts out an interim constitution which includes a bill of rights, system of checks and balances. The attacks continue, with a reported 27 people killed and 41 wounded in a car bombing of a Baghdad hotel. The attack comes two days before the anniversary of the US invasion. At the end of the month, US forces close the Al-Hawza newspaper of Moqtada al-Sadr, the firey anti-American young radical Sh'ia cleric. Rumsfeld previously had applauded the renewal of a free press in Iraq as a sign of dawning freedom. Al-Hawza was closed for allegedly inciting anti-American violence. On March 31, Iraqi mobs kill and mutilate four American private security operatives in Falloojeh, then drag them through the streets and hang them from a suspension bridge. Falloojeh is west of Baghdad.

In retaliation the US lays siege to Falloojeh.

—James Ridgeway

> Monday, January 05, 2004

HAPPY NEW YEAR . . .

Technically, I haven't blogged for a year—not since 2003. We've been phone-less for the last few days. The line suddenly went dead on us around 4 days ago and came back only this afternoon.

So this is 2004. Not surprisingly, it feels much like 2003. We spent the transition from last year into this one at my aunt's house. She dropped by on the 30th and said that since no one was going anywhere this year, we should spend it together at her house. If there's one advantage to war, then it's the fact that families somehow find themselves closer together. Every year, we'd all be in a different place: parents at a gathering somewhere and E. and I with our friends . . . other people would spend it at one of the dozens of restaurants or clubs holding New Year parties.

This year, New Year's Eve was a virtual family reunion. We decided we'd gather at my aunt's house but it couldn't be too big a gathering otherwise we'd be mistaken for a "terrorist cell"—women, children, dishes of food and all.

We got there at around 6 pm and found out that the power had been coming and going all day and that the generator had just enough gasoline for around 3 hours of electricity. We decided we'd save it up for the last two hours of the year which turned out to be a wise decision because the electricity went out at around 8 pm and didn't come back until noon the next day! We're lucky we left our house early because E. found out that roadblocks were later set up in several areas that had the people trapped well into the next day.

Almost an hour after we got [to] Aunt K.'s house, a blast shook the whole area. I was preparing to light a bunch of candles set up in the middle of the table, when suddenly a huge "BOOM" shook the room, the windows and the family. E. and I ran outside to see what was happening and we found my aunt's neighbors standing around at their gates, looking as perplexed as we felt. We later found out that a bomb had exploded near a small fast-food place a few kilometers away. "Tea Time" is a little two-storey restaurant in Harthiya that sells hamburgers and other sandwiches full of fries and mayonnaise.

We sat around from 8 until 11 in the dark, munching on popcorn, trying to remember the latest jokes (most about the Governing Council) and trying to pretend that the candles were festive candles, not necessary candles.

While many people consider 2003 a "year," for us it has felt more like a decade. We started the year preparing for war. While the rest of the world was making a list of resolutions, we were making lists of necessary items for the coming battle. We spent the first two and a half months of 2003 taping windows, securing homes, stocking up on food, water and medication, digging wells and wondering if we would make it through the year.

March brought the war and the horror. The scenes we witnessed made every single day feel more like a week . . . some days felt like a year. There were days where we lost track of time and began counting not hours and minutes, but explosions. We stopped referring to the date and began saying things like, "The last time we saw my uncle was . . . the day the Americans bombed that market in Al Shu'la and dozens were killed."

They say the war ended in April, but it didn't end in April. April was just the beginning of another set of horrors . . . watching Baghdad burned and looted by criminals . . . seeing the carcasses of burnt cars and the corpses of charred humans on the roadside . . . watching the tanks and Apaches shoot right and left . . . realizing that it had turned from a war into a full-fledged occupation.

So we sat, the last few hours, thinking about the last few months and making conjectures about the future. In the background you could hear a few explosions, some gunfire, helicopters and planes. I kept thinking something terrible was going to happen and we'd never see the beginning of a new year.

At around 10 pm, they turned on the generator and we gathered around the television to watch the rest of the world celebrate their way into the New Year. The kids fell asleep on the living-room floor, in front of the kerosene heater, before the clock struck 12 and the thuds around us began getting heavier. Immediately after twelve, the sounds of warplanes and explosions got so heavy, we could hardly hear the television. There was nothing on the news, as usual. Al-Iraqiya was showing some lame fading in and out of its motto on a blue background while all hell was breaking loose outside. We found out the next day that a restaurant in A'arassat, a wealthy area in Karrada, had explosives planted in front of it.

What have the first few days of 2004 felt like? Exactly like the last few months of 2003. The last few days have been a series of bombs and explosions. A couple of nights ago they were using cluster bombs to bomb some area. Before the bomb drops, you can hear this horrible screaming sound. We call it "the elephant" because it sounds like an elephant shrieking in anger. I'm not sure what it is or what its purpose is. Someone said it's supposed to be some sort of warning signal to the troops on the ground to take cover in their tanks before the bomb hits. It's usually followed by a series of horrific explosions and then the earth shudders.

It's strange what you can get used to hearing or seeing. The first time is always the worst: the first time you experience cluster bombs, the first time you feel the earth shudder beneath you with the impact of an explosion, the first tanks firing at houses in your neighborhood, the first check-point . . . the first broken windows, crumbling walls, unhinged doors . . . the first embassy being bombed, the first restaurant . . . It's not that you no longer feel rage or sadness, it just becomes a part of life and you grow to expect it like you expect rain in March and sun in July.

May 2004 be better than 2003. **posted by river @ 1:12 AM**

Thursday, January 08, 2004

SPLITTING IRAQ . . .

Salam blogged about a subject close to every Iraqi's heart these last few days—the issue of federalism in Iraq and the Kurdish plan to embrace Kirkuk and parts of Mosul into the autonomous region in the north.

Where is Raed?, http://dear_raed.blogspot.com, January 6, 2004

Have you been noticing all the talk about Iraq as a federal country lately? Something made me itch every time I heard an Iraqi or CPA official talk about it, first I couldn't figure out [what] was bothering me, but during the long long drive to Amman I was finally able to put my finger on it. No one asked us what we thought of the idea.

I remember almost a month ago when Zibari (our minister for foreign affairs) talked about federalism and I thought "that's nice we are starting the discussion finally." I was wrong it was not a discussion; it was a done and made deal. It got so silly that Kurds and Arabs are having real trouble about the issue, the Kirkuk incident was. I can't remember anyone asking me what I thought about the whole issue, neither was it put to debate openly. Someone high and mighty suddenly decided that is what's good for you, and we are going thru the process of trying to fit into that prêt-á-porter [ready-made] federalism. "The Officials" are not discussing whether that system is good for us or not they are way beyond that point, they are discussing into how many pieces Iraq is going to be cut up. Along "ethnic" lines or by governorates.

Have I mentioned already that we were not asked?

Our new temporary head of state, Mr. Pachachi, promises the Kurds that they will get what they want. Which means that they will cut up Iraq into three parts and making sure that instead [of] making sure we all here live together peacefully our ethnic and religious differences get even more accentuated. Yes I know identity is important but you see my father is Sunni, my mother Sh'ia and our neighbors for years Kurds. There are no lines and none should exist, the situation in Kirkuk does create lines and make people choose sides. Although I find the idea of an independent state of Baghdad or Samaweh or Basra a bit funny; it is all one Iraq for me, but I think if we were force fed this federalism without being asked I hope they

182

> won't go for a federal state consisting of Kurdistan in the north, Sunni-stan in the middle and Sh'ia-stan in the south.

I can sum it up in two words: bad idea. First off, Kirkuk doesn't have a Kurdish majority as Talabani implies in every statement he makes. The Arabs and Turkomen in Kirkuk make up the majority. After the war and occupation, the KDP (led by Berazani) and PUK (led by Talabani) began paying party members to set up camp in Kirkuk and its outskirts to give the impression that there was a Kurdish majority in the oil-rich area. The weeks of May saw fighting between Kurdish Bayshmarga and Turkomen civilians because in some selected areas, the Turkomen were being attacked and forced to leave their homes and farms.

While Kurds and Turkomen generally get along in Iraq, there is some bitterness between them. Making Kirkuk a part of "Kurdistan," as some are fond of calling it, would result in bloodshed and revolt. The Arabs in Kirkuk would refuse and the Turkomen wouldn't tolerate it. To understand some of the bitterness between Turkomen and Kurds, one only has to look back at what happened in 1959 in the northern part of Iraq. During that time, the Iraqi communist party had control and was backing Abdul Kareem Qassim, who was president back then.

Many die-hard communists decided that the best way to promote communism in the region would be to attack religious figures, nationalists and socialists—especially in Mosul, a conservative, dominantly Sunni Arab city and Kirkuk. For several weeks in 1959, there were massacres in both areas. During this time, communist Kurds from Suleimaniyah and Arbil were given orders to control the rebellious region. For days, there were assassinations of innocents . . . people were shot, dragged in the streets, maimed and hung on lampposts as an "example" to those unwilling to support the communist revolution. Naturally, the people in Mosul and Kirkuk never forgot that—anyone over the age of 50 from that region will have at least six woeful stories to tell.

Mosul, on the other hand, is about 90% Sunni Arab, with around 5% Christian Arab and the rest a mix of Kurds, Yezidis, and some other Christian factions. Masslawis (people from Mosul) would *not* take kindly to a Kurdish rule.

183

Already, we've been hearing news of riots, demonstrations and assassinations in Kirkuk ever since Talabani suggested expanding the autonomous region. Turkomen and Arabs in Kirkuk are promising revolt and civil war if the Kurdish plan goes through.

How do I stand? I'm against splitting Iraq into areas that identify themselves ethnically or religiously. It won't work. It's almost every Iraqi's fear that Iraq will be torn into several pieces and the plan for an enlarged Kurdish region is just the first step to an independent Kurdish state or—Kurdistan—as they like to call it.

I believe that Kurds have the right to live equally as well as Arabs and people of other ethnicities—there is no argument to that. I have many Kurdish friends and we get along beautifully. I even have Kurdish relatives (through a cousin's marriage) and there's nothing nicer than an ethnically diverse family. In other words, I'm a champion of Kurdish rights.

Do I believe Kurds should have an independent Kurdish state? No. If every ethnic group in Iraq were to call for an independent state, we would have to split the country into more than 5 groups—the autonomous Kurdish region, the Sunni Arab region (including Mosul), the independent state of Kirkuk, the Republic of Baghdad, and the south would have to be split into 3 different states: one for Al-Hakim's supporters, one for Al-Sadr's supporters and another for Al-Sistani's supporters.

What is it that the Kurds can get in an independent "Kurdistan" that they can't get in a democratic, united Iraq? Some would say that they had complete rights even before the war. There were tens of thousands of Kurds living in Baghdad. In fact, some of Baghdad's most affluent families prior to the occupation were Kurdish families with several sprawling palaces in Baghdad and other palaces in Suleimaniyah and Arbil. The irony is that some of these wealthy Kurds, much to the scorn of their less fortunate brothers, made their fortunes off of smuggling weapons during the Iran-Iraq war. Now, after the war, the arms smugglers are speaking the loudest against war atrocities (you learn this in occupation: the incredibly rich and powerful suddenly grow consciences like our garden grows weeds). Their kids drove the fastest cars, went to the best schools (there was no law banning Kurds from any school or college) and spent their summers in Switzerland, Germany and England.

Kurds also had a couple of exclusive clubs based in Baghdad, like Nadi Salah Al-Din, where they held weddings, parties and social events and while Arabs were welcome to attend as guests, they weren't allowed as members. On the other hand, Kurds were allowed as members into any club in Iraq—which is their right, as a minority. A definite advantage Kurds had over Arabs was the fact that they weren't drafted into the army.

To say that all Kurds want an independent Kurdistan would be a lie. Many Kurds are afraid of expanding the autonomous region because they know it will lead to a lot of bloodshed and strife. The Kurds who've always lived in Baghdad, as opposed to those living in the north, are afraid that this step by the ambitious Kurdish leaders will lead to a "reaction" against Kurds outside of the autonomous zone. It's happening already—many people are bitter against Kurds because they feel that the splitting of Iraq will be at the hands of the Kurdish leaders.

Another thing Kurds seem to be worrying about of late is the fact that "there is blood," as they say, between Berazani and Talabani. For the time being, they are presenting a united front for the CPA and Washington, pretending that they couldn't get along better if they were brothers. The reality is that before the war, they were constantly wrangling for power in the north with supporters of one attacking the supporters of the other, with innocent people, all the while, falling victim to the power struggle . . . and that was before oil was involved. Imagine what happens if they get Kirkuk.

We all lived together before—we can live together in the future. Iraqis are proud of their different ethnicities, but in the end, we all identify ourselves as "Iraqi." Every Iraqi's nightmare is to wake up one morning and find Iraq split into several parts based on ethnicity and religion. Salam said it best when he said, "There are no lines and none should exist . . ." (http://dear_raed.blogspot.com/10733395931040 7798)

(By the way, Salam, did you hear Muwafaq Al-Rubai'i suggest that he wasn't satisfied with splitting Iraq into 3 parts? He's suggesting five . . . 3ud dai ka7ilheh, 3maha—sorry but that's just not translatable)
posted by river @ 4:38 AM

DARKNESS AND DUST . . .

The last few days we've sort of been on an electricity schedule—for every four hours of no electricity, we get two hours of electricity. It's not much, but it's an improvement on one or two hours for every fourteen of darkness.

The last few minutes of electricity, we run around the house switching off lights and appliances so that nothing is ruined. Sometimes the electricity doesn't go out immediately—it sort of dims, flashes back on and then stutters to a close. We're getting less generator time because there's still a gasoline problem and everyone is being really careful about the type of fuel they're using because the gas being sold on black market is sometimes mixed with kerosene.

A couple of days ago there was a lot of dust. Iraq is famous for its dust storms. Within a matter of hours, the horizon turns orange and everything looks slightly faded. The stucco houses take on a pale, peach hue and even the people look a little bit dull. It becomes difficult to breathe and it's almost catastrophic for people with allergies.

We've been dusting the last 24 hours because we found everything covered with a light film of dust. The kids spent the day drawing stick figures in the dust on the furniture which drove my mother just a little bit crazy—she rushed about the house wielding a rag and attacking everything with a smooth surface.

Everyone is feeling somewhat depressed these days. The weather isn't particularly good and the air feels charged with a combination of disappointment and impatience.

People are asking what the reaction is to the claims of the former American treasurer about Bush planning regime-change before September 11. Why is that such a shock to Americans? I haven't met a single Iraqi who thinks Iraq had ANYTHING to do with September 11. The claims were ridiculous and so blatantly contrived that it was embarrassing to see people actually believed them.

I sometimes wonder how the American people feel. After these last two wars with Afghanistan and Iraq, do the American people feel any safer? We watch the "terror alerts" announced on television— politicians with somber faces and dramatic pauses alerting the population that at any minute, there might be an explosion or an attack. It's amusing because Iraq has been at the red level for the last 9 months. Why is it a drama when collective America experiences some strain for a couple of weeks during the holiday, but it's ok for Iraqis to experience five times the strain and apprehension for the next five years? Apparently, we are more tolerant—our blood pressures don't go up, our hearts don't palpitate and our kids can't be traumatized.

We heard about the American embassies being closed and secured all over the world . . . diplomats being withdrawn from countries or asked to remain locked indoors. Is that part of the "war on terror?" Are Americans worldwide any safer? Do they sleep better at night now knowing that they are definitely safe from the fabled Iraqi WMD? We've forgotten what it feels like to feel completely safe.

posted by river @ 5:45 AM

SHARI'A AND FAMILY LAW . . .

On Wednesday our darling Iraqi Puppet Council decided that secular Iraqi family law would no longer be secular—it is now going to be according to Islamic Shari'a. Shari'a is Islamic law, whether from the Quran or quotes of the Prophet or interpretations of modern Islamic law by clerics and people who have dedicated their lives to studying Islam.

The news has barely been covered by Western or even Arab media and Iraqi media certainly aren't covering it. It is too much to ask of Al Iraqiya to debate or cover a topic like this one—it would obviously conflict with the Egyptian soap operas and songs. This latest decision is going to be catastrophic for females—we're going backwards.

Don't get me wrong—pure Islamic law according to the Quran and the Prophet gives women certain unalterable, nonnegotiable rights. The problem arises when certain clerics decide to do their own interpretations of these laws (and just about *anyone* can make themselves a cleric these days). The bigger problem is that Shari'a may be drastically different from one cleric to another. There are actually fundamental differences in Shari'a between the different Islamic factions or "methahib." Even in the same methahib, there are dozens of different clerics who may have opposing opinions. This is going to mean more chaos than we already have to deal with. We've come to expect chaos in the streets . . . but chaos in the courts and judicial system too?!

This is completely unfair to women specifically. Under the Iraqi constitution, men and women are equal. Under our past secular family law (which has been in practice since the '50s) women had unalterable divorce, marriage, inheritance, custody, and alimony rights. All of this is going to change.

I'll give an example of what this will mean. One infamous practice brought to Iraq by Iranian clerics was the "zawaj muta'a," which when translated by the clerics means "temporary marriage." The actual translation is "pleasure marriage"—which is exactly what it is. It works like this: a consenting man and woman go to a cleric who approves of temporary marriage and they agree upon a period of time during which the marriage will last. The man pays the woman a "mahar" or dowry and during the duration of the marriage (which can be anything from an hour, to a week, a month, etc.) the man has full marital rights. Basically, it's a form of prostitution that often results in illegitimate children and a spread of STDs.

Sunni clerics consider it a sin and many Shi'a clerics also frown upon it . . . but there are the ones who will tell you it's "halal" and Shari'a, etc. The same people who approve it or practice it would, of course, rather see their daughters or sisters dead before they allow *them* to practice it—but that's beyond the point.

Anyway, secular Iraqi family law considers it a form of prostitution and doesn't consider a "pleasure marriage" a legitimate marriage. In other words, the woman wouldn't have any legal rights and if she finds herself pregnant—the child, legally, wouldn't have a father.

So what happens if a married man decides to arrange a pleasure marriage on the side? In the past, his legitimate wife could haul him off to court and ask for a divorce because the man would be committing adultery under Iraqi family law. That won't be the case now. Under certain clerics, a pleasure marriage will be considered legal and the woman won't have a case for divorce. Under other clerics, he'll be committing adultery—so who gets to judge? The cleric she chooses, or the cleric he chooses?

Another example is in marriage itself. By tribal law and Shari'a, a woman, no matter how old, would have to have her family's consent to marry a man. By Iraqi law, as long as the woman is over 18, she doesn't need her family's consent. She can marry in a court, legally, without her parents. It rarely happened in Iraq, but it *was* possible.

According to Iraqi secular law, a woman has grounds to divorce her husband if he beats her. According to Shari'a, it would be much more difficult to prove abuse.

Other questions pose themselves—Shari'a doesn't outlaw the marriage of minors (on condition they've hit puberty). Iraqi secular law won't allow minors to marry until the age of at least 16 (I think) for women and the age of 18 for men.

By Iraqi civil law, parents are required to send their children to complete at least primary school. According to Shari'a, a father can make his son or daughter quit school and either work or remain at home. So what happens when and if he decides to do that? Does Shari'a apply or does civil law apply?

There are hundreds of other examples that I can think of and that make me feel outrage. I practice Islam, but do I want an Islamic government? No. I feel that because we have so many different methahib and religions, any religious government is bound to oppress some faction of society. It's already happening in the south where fundamentalist Shi'a are attacking Christian families and shops.

Juan Cole had something to say about the subject and he referred to an article written in Financial Times appropriately titled, "Iraqi plan for Sharia law "a sop to clerics," say women." Unfortunately, the writers of the article apparently have no background on secular Iraqi law beyond what the GC members have told them. The fundamentalist GC members claim that civil Iraqi law forced people to go against their doctrine, which isn't true because a large part of civil law was based on Shari'a or the parts of Shari'a that were agreed upon by all the differing Islamic factions (like the right to divorce) and taking into consideration the different religious groups in Iraq.

Informed Comment, http://www.juancole.com, January 15, 2004

The Financial Times, to its credit, picked up the story for Thursday (most of the Western press had ignored it initially). It looks to me as though IGC members tried to deceive Nicolas Pelham and Charles

> Clover with claims such as that the IGC decree implementing religious law was "voluntary" and anyway would not be implemented because it needed Paul Bremer's signature. You don't need a government law to have voluntary compliance with shariah or Islamic law. If someone wants to write a will in accordance with literalist approaches to Islamic law, they already can. What is objectionable is the government imposing religious law on people who may or may not want it, and that is what the IGC is trying to do. As for the claim that Bremer won't implement the law, just issuing the decree gives vigilante militias a pretext to pry into the private affairs of Iraqis and to impose religious practices on them.
>
> So, the response of the Bush administration to the September 11 attack on the United States by a group of radical Islamist extremists has been to abolish secular law for Iraqi women and impose a fundamentalist reading of Islamic law on them. Yes, it all makes perfect sense.

Women are outraged . . . this is going to open new doors for repression in the most advanced country on women's rights in the Arab world! Men are also against this (although they certainly have the upper-hand in the situation) because it's going to mean more confusion and conflict all around.

What happens when all the clerics agree that a hijab isn't "preferred" but necessary? According to this new change in the "ahwal shakhsiya" laws or "personal circumstances" laws, all women will have to cover their heads and according to Shari'a, if a woman's husband decides that she can't continue her education or work, she'll have to remain a house-wife.

Please don't misunderstand—any oppression to women isn't a reflection on Islam. It's a reflection on certain narrow minds, ignorance and the politicization of religion. Islam is a progressive religion and no religion is clearer on the rights of women—it came during a time when women had no rights at all.

During the sanctions and all the instability, we used to hear fantastic stories about certain Arab countries like Saudi Arabia, Kuwait, Oman, and Qatar, to name a few. We heard about their luxurious lifestyles—the high monthly wages, the elegant cars, sprawling homes and malls . . . and while I always wanted to visit, I never once remember yearning to live there or even feeling envy. When I analyzed my feelings, it always led back to the fact that I cherished the rights I had as an Iraqi Muslim woman. During the hard times, it was always a comfort that I could drive, learn, work for equal pay, dress the way I wanted and practice Islam according to my values and beliefs, without worrying whether I was too devout or not devout enough.

I usually ignore the emails I receive telling me to "embrace" my new-found freedom and be happy that the circumstances of all Iraqi women are going to "improve drastically" from what we had before. They quote Bush (which in itself speaks volumes) saying things about how repressed the Iraqi women were and how, now, they are going to be able to live free lives.

The people who write those emails often lob Iraq together with Saudi Arabia, Iran and Afghanistan and I shake my head at their ignorance but think to myself, "Well, they really need to believe their country has the best of intentions—I won't burst their bubble." But I'm telling everyone now—if I get any more emails about how free and liberated the Iraqi women are *now* thanks to America, they can expect a very nasty answer.   **posted by river @ 7:55 PM**

Tuesday, January 20, 2004

STILL BROODING . . .

My head has been spinning these last few days with decision No. 173 on changing Family Law to Shari'a. I've been darkly mulling over the endless possibilities. I'm not the only one—everyone I talk to is shaking their head in dismay. How is this happening? How are we caving in to fundamentalism?

Talabani was saying that the decision wasn't taken or passed because it didn't get enough votes by the GC, but all the signs say that the decision was made and might be implemented as soon as they get Bremer's signature. Nisreen Barwari, the only female minister on the cabinet, was out demonstrating with several of the women's rights parties a few days ago against the decision. Christopher Allbritton over at Back to Iraq 3.0 has written something on the subject and so has the Washington Post.

Back to Iraq 3.0, January 14, 2004
http://www.back-to-iraq.com/archives/000647.php

About 100 Iraqi women, led by a minister of the Iraqi Governing Council, marched in Baghdad Tuesday to protest proposed changes that would scrap the secular family affairs code and place it under Islamic religious law.

From the article: "Iraq's 1959 civil code governing family affairs was considered the most progressive in the Middle East, making polygamy difficult and guaranteeing women's custody rights in the case of divorce."

Nasreen Mustafa Sideek Barwari, Iraqi minister of public works, led the march. I interviewed Barwari in Arbil in July 2002 and came away impressed. She's Harvard educated, smart, poised and truly wants what's best for the people of Iraq—men and women alike. She's Kurdish, by the way . . .

"Women in Iraq Decry Decision To Curb Rights," The Washington Post,
January 16, 2004, http://www.washingtonpost.com/ac2/
wp-dyn/A21321-2004Jan15?language=printer

For the past four decades, Iraqi women have enjoyed some of the most modern legal protections in the Muslim world, under a civil code that prohibits marriage below the age of 18, arbitrary divorce and male favoritism in child custody and property inheritance disputes.

Saddam Hussein's dictatorship did not touch those rights. But the U.S.-backed Iraqi Governing Council has voted to wipe them out, ordering in late December that family laws shall be "canceled" and such issues placed under the jurisdiction of strict Islamic legal doctrine known as sharia.

This week, outraged Iraqi women—from judges to cabinet ministers— denounced the decision in street protests and at conferences, saying it would set back their legal status by centuries and could unleash emotional clashes among various Islamic strains that have differing rules for marriage, divorce and other family issues . . .

> *"This new law will send Iraqi families back to the Middle Ages,"* Hakki said. *"It will allow men to have four or five or six wives. It will take away children from their mothers. It will allow anyone who calls himself a cleric to open an Islamic court in his house and decide about who can marry and divorce and have rights. We have to stop it . . .*

The question is, even if the personal status laws aren't going to be subjected to change now—immediately—what about the future? What does that say about 6 months from now when Bremer's signature isn't necessary?

Two days ago, there was a conference on women's rights in the elegant Nadi Al-Sayd (or Hunting Club) in Baghdad led by the major women's rights groups and they were condemning decision No. 173 saying that it'll be a blow to women's rights in Iraq. The frightening thing was that one of the more secular members of the GC was championing the decision and claiming that it was going to be a "great advance" in the rights of Iraqi women. He didn't explain how or why, but he condescendingly sat in front of the angry mob of women and gave them a mysterious Mona Lisa smile that, I assume, was supposed to be reassuring.

Seeing some of the GC members give press conferences these days reminds me of the time I went to watch my cousin's daughter "graduate" from kindergarten. They had about 20 kids up on this little stage with their teacher, Miss Basma, standing benevolently in their midst. As long as she was on the stage, they all stood correctly; simultaneously reciting a poem they had learned just for the occasion. The moment Miss Basma stepped down, there was a stampede—20 students rushed for the only microphone on the stage all at once, grappling to see who could reach it first and drown out the other voices with their own.

Now we face a similar situation. Miss Basma—er, I mean Bremer—has been off the stage (in Washington and New York) and there has been a rush to grab the metaphorical microphone. For example, while the decision on family law seems almost definite, Talabani adamantly denies it . . . other members only reluctantly discuss it.

A couple of weeks ago, when federalism was all the rage with the GC, Talabani made statements on how the decision was almost final: federalism based on ethnicity was just around the corner. The same week, Ibraheim Al-Ja'affari, head of Al-Da'awa Al-Islamiya Party, also made an appearance on either LBC or Al-Arabia, claiming that there was no chance Iraq was going to be split up. Adnan Al-Pachichi then gave a press conference stating that while federalism was an option, it wasn't going to be immediate or "loose."

There is now talk of it being some sort of a tradeoff or compromise—federalism for the Kurds on the GC, and Shari'a for the Shi'a Islamic groups . . . It doesn't matter in the end—the Iraqi people will be the losers.

Meanwhile, there have been huge demonstrations in the south these last few days and in Baghdad, demanding elections. The roads were blocked in Baghdad in the areas around the demonstration and there were helicopters overhead all day. Most of the demonstrators were supporters of Sistani who has made himself a national figure in this mess. He was eerily silent about the occupation in the beginning and now he is probably the most influential challenger of the GC. He fluctuates—one day, he claims that if elections aren't held there'll be a fatwa ordering civil disobedience. On another day, he claims that the decision to hold elections should be made by Kofi Annan. The most significant thing he has said so far is that even if elections are held, people from abroad shouldn't be able to run (i.e. 95% of the GC).

I watched the meeting today between some GC members, Bremer and Kofi Annan on CNN. They didn't seem to come to any conclusion except that *maybe* Kofi would send a delegation to assess the situation in Iraq. Meanwhile, 100,000 Shi'a and Sunnis demonstrated in Baghdad today (although the Shi'a outnumbered the Sunnis by far on this occasion), holding up pictures of Sistani, Al-Sadr and some others. It wasn't violent, but it was angry, forceful and frightening. This has been the largest demonstration since the war.

I'm torn on the topic of elections. While I want elections because it's the "democratic" thing to do, I'm afraid of the outcome. All the signs lead one to believe that elections will lead to a theocracy (which I dread). The current GC is *not* representative of the Iraqi people—neither Sunnis nor Shi'a approve of them . . . but will elections bring about a more representative group of would-be leaders? Furthermore, what if the Iraqi "majority" *do* want a theocracy like the one in Iran? If the choice boils down to a democracy styled like the one in America or a theocracy styled like the one in Iran, how do you think a Muslim country is going to choose?

For more info on Al-Sistani, check out his site—it's in Arabic, Farsi, English, French and Urdu (sistani.org) . . . quite impressive. His biography is here: Sistani's Biography and for those who were *very* interested in temporary marriage, check this out.

http://www.sistani.org/html/eng/main/index.php?page=
1&lang=eng&part=1

> *For more than half a century, the school of the late Grand Ayatullah Imam Abul-Qassim al-Khu'i has been an undepletable spring that enriched Islamic thought and knowledge.*
>
> *From his school graduated dozens of jurists, clergymen, and dignitaries who took it upon themselves to continue his ideological path which was full of achievements and sacrifices in the service of the faith, knowledge, and society.*
>
> *Among those are outstanding professors of parochial schools, specially Holy Najaf and Qum. Some of them have attained the level of "ijtiihad"—competence to deduce independent legal judgment enabling them to assume the office of supreme religious authority.*
>
> *Others reached lofty levels qualifying them for shouldering the responsibilities of teaching and education. Most distinguished among those towering figures is His Eminence Grand Ayatullah al-Sayyid Ali al-Hussani al-Sistani.*
>
> *He ranks among the brightest, the most qualified and knowledgeable of Imam al-khu'i's former students*
>
> *http://www.sistani.org/html/eng/main/index.php?page=3&lang=eng&part=1*
>
> *In a permanent marriage, the period of matrimony is not fixed, and it is forever. The woman with whom such a marriage is concluded is called da'ima (i.e. a permanent wife).*
>
> *In a fixed time marriage (Mut'ah), the period of matrimony is fixed, for example, matrimonial relation is contracted with a woman for an hour, or a day, or a month, or a year, or more. However, the period fixed for the marriage should not exceed the span of normal lives of the spouses, because in that case, the marriage will be treated as a permanent one. This sort of fixed time marriage is called Mut'ah or Sigha.*

posted by river @ 5:48 AM

THE INSOMNIAC . . .

It's 4 a.m. as I write this and will probably be 5 a.m. before I post it. Salam (dear_raed.blogspot.com) was commenting the other day on my weird blogging hour (it was around 5:30 a.m.). I've been an insomniac since before the war. My sleeping hours are strange and disconnected—rather like a cat. During the war it was almost impossible to sleep. The nights were full of bombing. We'd stay up, huddled together in a room, listening to the planes and explosions, sometimes venturing outside to search the horizon for signs of burning.

After the war, the looting and pillaging kept everyone up. We'd take turns staying up and listening for prowlers or break-ins. My job was always to make the tea. Guns make me very nervous and I'd stand brewing the tea and eying the gun over the cupboard warily. We'd sit, listening to the radio, the sky . . . waiting for the creak of the gate that would send everyone into a flurry of action—grab the guns, gather the family.

Now, sleep doesn't come very easily. I toss and turn in bed as one thought crowds out the other. And thoughts are like chickens—once one of them starts squawking, the whole bunch of them join in. I've tried every single technique—counting sheep, reciting the periodic table, counting down from 100 . . . none of it works. I end up more alert than ever.

It's often the anxiety that keeps one awake, although we've learned to live with it. There are moments when I'm busy doing something that needs concentration when I can sort of forget about the past and the future and concentrate on the very immediate present. There are other moments when I'll be watching something on tv—a movie or song—and I'll lose myself in the story . . . but as soon as the commercials begin, so the nagging feeling returns. After a while, the prickly feeling of anxiousness dulls and turns blunt. Have you ever left the house and worried that you didn't turn off the oven or the iron? That's what the feeling turns into—except it lasts all day . . . and night . . . and week . . . and month, after month, after month until you don't notice it except at night.

Sometimes, sleep just seems like a waste of time and electricity.

For example, the day before yesterday, our area had no electricity almost the whole day. Friday is our "laundry day" so it was doubly frustrating. We stood around looking at the pile of clothes that needed washing. My mother deliberated washing them by hand but I convinced her it would be a bad idea—the water was cold, the weather was miserable and the clothes wouldn't even feel clean. We waited all day for the electricity and once or twice, it flashed on for all of 20 minutes. Finally, at 12 p.m., my mother stated, "Tomorrow, if there's no electricity, we'll wash them by hand. That's that."

I crawled into bed at 1 a.m., tired with waiting and actually looking forward to maybe sleeping . . . and it began—first the procession of sheep, then the elements . . . and just as I found my eyelids getting heavy, I felt it—the electricity was on. I could hear the distant whir of the refrigerator as it adjusted itself to the current. I groped on my bedside table and found my clock, brought it close to my face and peered into the very heart of it—2 a.m.

Two voices began chattering in my head—the one that was counting sheep was slurred and drowsy . . . it said, "Go to sleep. You need some sleep—who cares about the electricity?" The other voice, alert and anxious, cried out, "Are you serious?! Think of the possibilities—the computer, the television, the washer . . . !!" The sleepy voice groaned and cursed as I hauled myself out of bed and into the corridor, fumbling for the light switch. I finally found the light and, after several hours of dark, it assaulted me.

I squinted around for a couple of minutes and listened to the silence . . . except it was no longer silent. E. had beat me to the television and was switching from channel to channel, trying to find something interesting and my mother had already made her way downstairs to load up the washer. The house was alive.

E. was watching a Lebanese "reality tv" show where around 20 young people were gathered to train to become singers and dancers. It focused on their daily routine of . . . singing and dancing. E. scoffed, "That's not reality . . . are we even living in the same universe?!" No. It's not reality . . . reality is the washer, clanging away at 2:30 a.m. because you don't know when there'll be electricity again . . . and imaginary sheep that mock you in the dark, night after night.
posted by river @ 4:59 AM

Saturday, January 31, 2004

THE BIG EID . . .

We've been cleaning again these last few days. The "Big Eid" or "Eid Al Kabeer" or "Al Eid Al Adh'ha" is on Sunday and everyone has been hectically taking down curtains for washing, polishing furniture and rearranging sock drawers.

The "Big Eid" is known as the big one because it lasts a day longer than the other Eid, "Eid Al Futtur." During the Big Eid, Muslims from all over the world go to Mecca in Saudi Arabia and visit "Bayt Allah" or "God's House" which was built by the Prophet Abraham. Visiting Mecca is one of the five pillars of Islam which include fasting, "shahada" or bearing witness to God and the Prophet, prayer, visiting Mecca (at least once during the lifetime), and "Zekat" or charity.

After visiting Mecca and taking part in certain Islamic rituals, a man becomes a "Hajji" or "one who has done the Haj" and a woman becomes a "Hijjiya." That is why it is quite common to see people in Muslim countries calling an elder "Hajji" or "Hijjiya." It is assumed that by the time a man or woman reaches a certain age, they have gone to visit Mecca and gained the prestigious and respectful title of Hajji or Hijjiya.

The whole Islamic world celebrates this occasion. In Iraq, the festivities include visiting family and friends, lots of good food and money handed out to the younger kids in the family to spend on candy and other things that will ruin the teeth and complexion.

Like the "Eid Al Fittur," the house has to be very, very clean. For those of you who don't know her, I blogged about the Martha Stewart of Baghdad a few months ago. She has been emotionally terrorizing the area for the last few days by making daily appearances in her garden and in front of her house, washing down windows, wringing out clothes and keeping a hawkish eye on the front doors of all the neighbors.

Yesterday, our street which normally rings with the cries of children playing street football was eerily silent. I stood at our gate, pondering the sudden disappearance of half a dozen rowdy boys. I caught one of our 9-year-old neighbors dodging from his house to the one across the street. He scampered in what I imagine he must have thought a stealthy fashion . . . he actually looked like a lizard escaping the scorching sun.

"Haydar!" I called out to him before he had a chance to close the gate behind him. He halted in mid-scurry and turned around. His little shoulders sagged with relief as soon as he saw it was me. I waved him over and he rushed towards me with an expression of consternation, looking over his shoulder.

"What are you hiding from?" I asked sternly. It seemed a more diplomatic question than the one that really flashed in my mind: what have you done?

He pushed up the big glasses he wore and pointed to the dreaded house across the street. "I'm hiding from Umm Maha!" Ahhh, I nodded my head sagely and he rushed on, "Yesterday, she made Mahmud pick up alllllllllllllll the litter up and down the street . . . and today she wanted me to sweep the sidewalks of all the houses . . . "

"Well, just tell her that you won't." I said, not believing I was actually promoting anarchy. He shook his head emphatically as he slipped off the glasses and rubbed the bridge of his nose, "I can't do that . . . I can't. She scares me and . . . " His voice slipped to a whisper, " . . . she told Mahmud to take a bath yesterday because she says he smelled like sheep . . . she scares me." I secretly agreed with him because, well, she terrifies me a little bit too.

"So is that why you're all hiding?" I was referring to the little mob we had running our street. On their good days, they would play gently, as little boys tend to do—pushing, shoving, scraping knees and elbows and stubbing toes. On their bad days, they'd end up blocking the road from both ends with broken bricks and tin cans of sand (to represent goal posts) and fighting at the top of shrill voices as to who would get to be Ronaldo or Beckham.

I sympathized with him and he looked up at me for some sort of solution. "Well, next time she catches you, just tell her you're running some errands for me." I offered helpfully. He was dubious, but he silently accepted and I allowed him to scurry back across the street.

This morning, I went out to the roof to hang some clothes that had been washed. I saw Umm Maha on her own roof, across the street. She wasn't hanging clothes, she was hanging out some relatively large rugs that she had washed—by hand of course—just that morning. I balked—no one cleans their rugs until the summer or immediately before putting them away in late spring. You just didn't do that. First, there was every chance it would rain on them and second, you'd just have to clean them AGAIN before putting them away.

I waved at Umm Maha just as she looked up from her task and she smiled and waved back. "I hope it rains . . . " I muttered and shook out the shirt I had in my hands, knowing that somehow it wouldn't. It didn't dare rain on Umm Maha's rugs.

Other than the cleaning, nothing feels festive. It's just normal—electrical outages, explosions and helicopters. Students now have their mid-year holiday and sometimes you can see them in the street although everyone is at home by 7 or 8 pm, which is a contrast to the past when the fun didn't start until 7 or 8 pm. Anyone who can is spending the holiday in either Syria or Jordan. It's hard to believe that those two countries have become havens to Iraqis . . . Baghdad was always the place everyone wanted to be.   **posted by river @ 2:16 AM**

A WHOLE BUNCH OF LINKS . . .

I have a lot of links to share.

There are several new Iraqi bloggers. The first blog to introduce is the Iraqi Agora (iraqibloggers.blogspot.com)—a group blog by Iraqis inside and outside of Iraq. It's basically a blog for Iraqis too lazy to begin their own blog. The truth is that 3 of the contributing bloggers (Salam (dear_raed.blogspot.com), Liminal (www.shlonkombakazay. blogspot.com) and I have our own blogs. The guy calling himself "Liminal" is a twenty-something Iraqi living in the US and you'll have to read his personal blog to learn more about him. Hurria is an Iraqi woman who has lived abroad for a long time and has some fantastic opinions about . . . everything. Torshe is another Iraqi abroad and is new to blogging but you won't want to miss him either. You'll have to be patient with the group blog because we're still getting it on its feet (and Liminal is doing most of the work). I have two other contributors inside of Iraq interested in blogging on it.

Another Iraqi blog is Iraqi's Iraqi Spirit (iraqispirit.blogspot.com) by an Iraqi network engineer in his 30s and he warns you that his blog is not meant to be politically correct.

For those of you who want Iraqi music, check it out at this site: www.iraqimusic.com. It has some fantastic classics as well as some of the more modern songs, available as downloadable MP3 files.

This link came from B. from North Ireland and it's a link to a site he *insisted* I check out. Physicians for Human Rights (phrusa.org). They have a special page devoted to Iraq and have apparently done some extensive work in the region. Check out what they have to say about cluster bombs.

Bulletin #6 —May 6, 2003, http://www.phrusa.org/research/iraq/
bulletin_050603.html

Detailed Minefield and Cluster Bomb Target Site Information Must Be Made Available to Protect Civilian Populations and Reconstruction Personnel

Physicians for Human Rights (PHR) calls on the Coalition Forces to immediately release to civilians and those involved with peacekeeping and reconstruction detailed maps of known mine fields and cluster bomb drop sites. To date, the large-scale maps released through the Humanitarian Operations Center (HOC) do not provide adequate information to assess Iraqi populations at risk or provide security information for humanitarian aid workers . . .

---

posted by river @ 2:39 AM

Friday, February 13, 2004

FAMILY CRISIS . . .

I haven't been blogging for several reasons. The main reason is that since the fourth day of Eid we've been coping with a family crisis.

Eid started out normal enough, under the circumstances. The first day consisted of explosions, and a few family members and neighbors, interspersed with bouts [of] electricity. We spent the first two days at home, so thoroughly exhausted with Eid preparations, we didn't enjoy Eid itself very much.

On the fourth day of Eid, one of my uncles absolutely insisted on a family reunion of sorts at his house. His wife had been slaving over the stove all day and anyone who couldn't come had better have a good excuse.

And so we went. We packed ourselves off to his house, across Baghdad, at 4 p.m. and he promised dinner would be served promptly at 7 (which is an obscene hour to eat dinner for Iraqis, but everyone wanted to be home early). The house was crowded with uncles and aunts, grandparents, nieces, nephews, and shrieking children (two of whom I didn't recognize).

Dinner was served at seven. It consisted of "timen ala quzi" or rice and lamb garnished with sultanas, almonds and all sorts of spices, a Lebanese salad, chicken soup and two different kinds of bread. For a brief 30 minutes, we forgot politics and occupation and sat concentrating on the steaming array of food piled before us. Even the children calmed down enough to enjoy the feast. The local generator was humming in the background and we sat enjoying the food and light and feeling that it really was Eid. After all, we were family and gathered together . . . what could be more Eid-like than that?

After sweet tea and fresh fruit, the family began to disperse. At nine, we sat around with my uncle, his wife, my cousin and her husband and her husband's parents. The children had fallen into a sort of lethargic stupor in front of the television, watching a children's song in Arabic with a bunch of crazy rabbits bouncing about on the screen.

The elders soon began the usual discussion—politics. Politics in Iraq isn't discussed like in any other place. You see, we don't sit around with lit cigars and cups of tea debating this politician or that one—that's much too tame and boring. That is left for Brits in wood-paneled studies, surrounded by leather-bound books. No. We have to do it the Iraqi way—mobile expressions, erratic hand signals, and an occasional table—pounding to emphasize a particularly salient point.

The younger generation (E., a couple of cousins, and I) instantly backed out of the conversation. Old/new names were suddenly being dragged into the limelight of the dispute and I, personally, was lost at the Iraqi monarchy. They left me behind during the '50s and I got up to help clear the tea cups which were beginning to rattle ominously as the conversation got more heated.

My uncle and his daughter's father-in-law were soon deep into an argument over some conspiracy dealing with the monarchy. I saw a smile hovering on the lips of my cousin as her father-in-law began to light the wrong end of the cigarette. She winked covertly at her husband and he gracefully rose with the words, "Well, dad—should we drop you and mom off at home? It's getting late and I don't want to have to drive back alone . . . L., the children and I are spending the night here tonight "

And they were off in a matter of minutes. The argument was soon forgotten, adults bundled in coats and cigarettes properly lit. My cousin's husband, A., hustled his parents outside and into his battered old Brazilian-made Volkswagen. We stayed behind to help clear up the mess—which was considerable. Rice was strewn everywhere, little fingers had made little marks up and down the walls, the tables and across the television screen. Ashtrays had to be emptied, cups washed and children undressed and put to bed.

By the time the initial mess was cleared, it was almost 10 pm. Where was A., my cousin's husband? He had left over an hour earlier and his parents' house was only 15 minutes away. My mother suggested that his parents had maybe insisted he step down for a cup of tea or something else to eat . . . my cousin, L., shook her head emphatically—he wouldn't do that because he knew she'd worry. His parents didn't have a working telephone and any delay simply meant additional worry. Her brow puckered and I suddenly felt queasy.

We went over the possibilities—perhaps the road to his parents' house was blocked and he had to take an alternate route? Maybe they needed to purchase something on the way home? There *must* be a logical, rational reason. A. was a logical, rational, and—above all— careful man. We were supposed to be on our way home by 10:30. In modern-day Iraq, you just don't stay out longer than that. We couldn't leave my uncle and his family in the mess they were in. We sat around longer.

My father and uncle couldn't take it anymore—they got into our car and went to A.'s parents' house to see what had happened—and drag A. home by his ear if necessary. L. was angry by then, convinced that A. was OK and that he was simply dallying around at his mother's house. I was dubious, but supported the theory because it seemed like the easiest one to accept.

We sat around quietly for 30 minutes while my father and uncle went to look for A. L. was furiously polishing the coffee table and I sat channel-surfing, trying to find something to take my mind off of the possibilities.

Half an hour later, the men came home—trying not to look grim and worried. A.'s parents were safe at home—had, in fact, been home for over an hour. A. dropped them off at the door, watched them walk inside, honked his horn twice and left. L. went paler than she normally is and sat down dully on the couch. She was suddenly sure he was dead. What could have happened? Where had he gone? Someone mentioned a flat tire but L.'s father said that they hadn't seen his car along the way . . .

And so we reviewed the possibilities. He had been detained by Americans. His car had been hijacked. He had been abducted. He had been killed. He had a car accident and his beat-up old vehicle was overturned in some ditch . . . the possibilities were endless and each one was worse than the one before.

Going home was no longer an option. We sat around in the living room with my uncle's family, watching the seconds creep by on the clock and willing A. to walk through the door. E. spent the night pacing the driveway and peering out into the dark, silent street. I joined him outdoors a couple of times and he confessed that he was very worried—any disappearance at this time of night couldn't be good.

We spent the night making conjectures and trying to find logical reasons for A.'s disappearance. In the end, we agreed that if he wasn't back by 10 a.m., we'd go to the police and the family would start a separate search.

At 8 a.m., I was putting the kettle on in preparation for morning tea. The house was silent but no one was asleep. No one had slept all night. E. was still pacing; my father and uncle were closed up in the living room, trying to decide on a course of action and L. was trying not to cry. Suddenly, just as I lit the stove, the phone rang. It never sounded so shrill. I ran to the living room and found that my uncle had already jumped to answer it and was barking, "Elloo?" L. ran into the room and stood wringing her hands nervously.

It was A.'s best friend and business partner, S. He had heard from A. just a few minutes before . . . he had been abducted and was being held for a ransom of $15,000. A. and S. are partners and share a small shop in a mercantile neighborhood in Baghdad. They sell everything from Korean electrical ovens to fluorescent light bulbs and make just enough money to support their respective families. We'd be given 3 days to get the money—a place would be agreed upon where we'd give them the money and they'd release A. later on.

We panicked. The whole house broke down. L. fell to the floor crying and shouting that they'll kill him—she just knew they'd kill him like they were killing others. We tried to calm her down and finally decided to give her a couple of valiums to ease the stress. We sat debating on what to do—go to the police? No way. In some areas, the police were actually working with abductors for a certain amount of money and there was nothing they were willing to do anyway.

We spent the rest of the day rushing to sell gold, collect money and my uncle took a broken L. to the bank to empty the account—they've been saving up to build or buy a house. A.'s parents were soon at my uncle's house and we had a difficult time breaking the news to them. His mother cried and wanted to rush home for her few pieces of gold and his father sat, stunned, chain-smoking and trying to make sense of the situation. S., A.'s friend, came over with money—looking harrowed and tired.

To make a long, terrible story short—we had the money by the middle of the next day. L. had almost lost her wits and the only way the rest of us stayed sane was with the hope that A. would soon be back at home, with us.

The money was handed over on the third day after his abduction. But no A. came back. They told my uncle and S., who had gone with him, that A. would be set free in the next couple of days. My uncle and S. came home almost in tears—like we had sent them on a mission and they had failed us.

I can't even begin to describe the next couple of days. If it was bad before—it suddenly became worse. We hear about abductions ALL THE TIME . . . but to actually experience it is something else. It's like having a part of you torn away. To think that A. might not come back was more horrible than anything we'd experienced so far. Watching his parents deteriorate from one minute to the next and knowing his wife was dying a little bit inside every hour that passed by was so nerve-

wracking that I'd run outside every hour to breathe in some fresh air—
not the stale stuff inside of the house contaminated with depression,
frustration and fear.

On the fifth day after A.'s abduction, we were all sitting in the living room. There was no electricity and L. had fallen into a valium-
induced sort of calm. We suddenly heard a feeble clang of the
gate—like someone was knocking, but not very hard. E. jumped up,
ran to the door and called out, "Who is it?!" A moment later he ran
back—it was A . . . he had come home.

I won't describe the crying, screaming, shouting, jumping, hobbling (A. was limping) and general chaos that followed A.s entrance.
Apparently, his abductors had been watching the house for the last
couple of weeks. As soon as A. dropped off his parents, they had followed with two cars and forced him to the side of the road on a seclud-
ed street. Four armed men forced him out of the car, put a bag over
his head after kicking him around and threw him into a minivan with
some more men.

After several hours of abuse and interrogation about his assets
(which they seemed to have thought much more than he actually had),
they let him make a call to his business partner who was supposed
to call his family for the money.

(And if you could have seen him the moment he described this—
you'd know ALL about the tenacity of the Iraqi sense of humor—here
was A., with a gash on his head, a bluish bruise on the side of his face,
a back bruised with kicks and punches, feet bleeding after walking over
one kilometer barefoot and he was cracking jokes: "They actually only
wanted $5,000," he said at one point, "but I was outraged—told
them I was worth AT LEAST $20,000 – five is just an insult to my per-
sonal worth . . . we agreed on $15,000 in the end . . .")

They had kept him in a slum on the outskirts of Baghdad where
police and troops don't dare set up camp. He was transferred from one
hovel to the next and at each one he says there were abducted
people. Some of the abductions were political—some religious and
many were for the money. He says the worst part was not being able
to see anything around him, but being able to hear the others being
beaten . . . and anticipating another kick or punch from any random
direction.

I saw him again yesterday and he still looks haggard and tired. L. says he can't sleep all night—he keeps waking in the middle of the night with a nightmare or some sort of hallucination—thinking he's still caught.

And so that's how we've been spending our last few days. It has been a nightmare and I've had to examine a lot. Everything has felt so trivial and ridiculous . . . the blog, the electrical situation, the insomnia, the "reconstruction," the elections, the fictional WMD . . . politics and politicians . . . I've been wondering about all those families who can't pay the ransom or the ones whose sons and daughters come home on a stretcher instead of on foot or in a garbage bag, as we heard about one family . . . and I've also realized how grateful we should be just being able to make the transition from one day to the next in a situation like ours . . . **posted by river @ 4:16 PM**

Sunday, February 15, 2004

DEDICATED TO THE MEMORY OF L.A.S.

So Happy Valentine's Day . . . although it's the 15th. It still feels like the 14th here because I'm not asleep . . . it's the extension of yesterday.

Do you know what yesterday marked? It marked the 13th anniversary of the Amiriyah Shelter massacre—February 13, 1991. Can you really call it an "anniversary?" Anniversary brings to mind such happy things and yet is there any other word? Please send it along if you know it.

February 12, 1991, marked one of the days of the small Eid or "Eid Al-Fitr." Of course it also marked one of the heaviest days of bombing during the Gulf War. No one was in the mood for celebration. Most families remained at home because there wasn't even gasoline to travel from one area to the next. The more fortunate areas had bomb shelters and people from all over the neighborhood would get together inside of the shelter during the bombing. That year, they also got together inside of the shelters to celebrate Eid Al-Fitr with their neighbors and friends.

Iraqis don't go to shelters for safety reasons so much as for social reasons. It's a great place to be during a bombing. There's water, electricity and a feeling of serenity and safety that is provided as much by the solid structure as by the congregation of smiling friends and family. Being with a large group of people helps make things easier during war—it's like courage and stamina travel from one person to the next and increase exponentially with the number of people collected.

So the families in the Amiriyah area decided they'd join up in the shelter to have a nice Eid dinner and then the men and boys over the age of 15 would leave to give the women and children some privacy. Little did they know, leaving them behind, that it would be the last time they would see the wife/daughter/son/fiancé/sister/infant . . .

I can imagine the scene after the men left at around midnight— women sat around, pouring out steaming istikans of tea, passing out Eid kilaycha and chocolate. Kids would run around the shelter shrieking and laughing like they owned the huge playground under the earth. Teenage girls would sit around gossiping about guys or clothes or music or the latest rumor about Sara or Lina or Fatima. The smells would mingle—tea, baked goods, rice . . . comfortable smells that made one imagine, for a few seconds, that they were actually at home.

The sirens would begin shrieking—the women and children would pause in the midst of eating or scolding, say a brief prayer in their heart and worry about their loved ones above the ground—the men who refused to remain inside of the shelter in order to make room for their wives and kids.

The bombs fell hard and fast at around 4 a.m. The first smart bomb went through the ventilation, through the first floor of the shelter—leaving a gaping hole—and to the bottom "basement" of the shelter where there were water tanks and propane tanks for heating water and food. The second missile came immediately after and finished off what the first missile missed. The doors of the advanced shelter immediately shut automatically—locking over 400 women and children inside.

It turned from a shelter into an inferno; explosions and fire rose from the lower level up to the level that held the women and children and the water rose with it, boiling and simmering. Those who did not burn to death immediately or die of the impact of the explosions, boiled to death or were steamed in the 900+ ° F heat.

We woke in the morning to see the horrors on the news. We watched as the Iraqi rescue workers walked inside of the shelter and came out crying and screaming—dragging out bodies so charred, they didn't look human. We saw the people in the area—men, women and children—clinging to the fence surrounding the shelter and screaming with terror; calling out name after name . . . searching for a familiar face in the middle of the horror.

The bodies were laid out one beside the other—all the same size—shrunk with heat and charred beyond recognition. Some were in the fetal position, curled up, as if trying to escape within themselves. Others were stretched out and rigid, like the victims were trying to reach out a hand to save a loved one or reach for safety. Most remained unrecognizable to their families—only the size and fragments of clothing or jewelry indicating the gender and the general age.

Amiriyah itself is an area full of school teachers, college professors, doctors and ordinary employees—a middle-class neighborhood with low houses, friendly people and a growing mercantile population. It was a mélange of Sunnis and Shi'a and Christians—all living together peacefully and happily. After the 13th of February, it became the area everyone avoided. For weeks and weeks the whole area stank of charred flesh and the air was thick and gray with ash. The beige stucco houses were suddenly all covered with black pieces of cloth scrolled with the names of dead loved ones. "Ali Jabbar mourns the loss of his wife, daughter, and two sons . . . "; "Muna Rahim mourns the loss of her mother, sisters, brothers and son . . . "

Within days, the streets were shut with black cloth tents set up by the grief-stricken families to receive mourners from all over Iraq who came to weep and ease some of the shock and horror. And it was horrible. Everyone lost someone—or knew someone who lost several people.

My first visit to the shelter came several years after it was bombed. We were in the neighborhood visiting a friend of my mother. She was a retired schoolteacher who quit after the Amiriyah bombing. She had no thoughts of quitting but after schools resumed in April of 1991, she went on the first day to greet her class of 2nd graders. She walked into the classroom and found only 11 of her 23 students. "I thought they had decided not to come . . . " I remember her saying to my mother in hushed tones, later that year," . . . but when I took attendance, they told me the rest of the children had died in the shelter . . . " She quit soon after that because she claimed her heart had broken that day and she couldn't look at the children anymore without remembering the tragedy.

I decided to pay my respects to the shelter and the victims. It was October and I asked the retired teacher if the shelter was open (hoping in my heart of hearts she'd say "no"). She nodded her head and said that it was indeed open—it was always open. I walked the two short blocks to the shelter and found it in the midst of houses—the only separation being a wide street. There were children playing in the street and we stopped one of them who was kicking around a ball. Is there anyone in the shelter? He nodded his head solemnly—yes the shelter was "maskoon."

Now the word "maskoon" can mean two different things in Arabic. It can mean "lived in" and it can also mean "haunted." My imagination immediately carried me away—could the child mean haunted? I'm not one who believes in ghosts and monsters—the worst monsters are people and if you survive war and bombs, ghosts are a piece of cake . . . yet something inside of me knew that a place where 400 people had lost their lives so terribly—almost simultaneously—had to be "haunted" somehow by their souls...

We walked inside and the place was dark and cold, even for the warm October weather. The only light filtering in came from the gaping hole in the roof of the shelter where the American missiles had fallen. I wanted to hold my breath—expecting to smell something I didn't want to . . . but you can only do that for so long. The air didn't smell stale at all; it simply smelled sad—like the winds that passed through this place were sorrowful winds. The far corners of the shelter were so dark, it was almost easy to imagine real people crouching in them.

The walls were covered with pictures. Hundreds of pictures of smiling women and children—toothy grins, large, gazelle eyes and the gummy smiles of babies. Face after face after face stared back at us from the dull gray walls and it felt endless and hopeless. I wondered what had happened to their families, or rather their remaining families after the catastrophe. We knew one man who had lost his mind after losing his wife and children inside of the shelter. I wondered how many others had met the same fate . . . and I wondered how much life was worth after you lost the people most precious to you.

At the far end of the shelter we heard voices. I strained my ears to listen and we searched them out—there were 4 or 5 Japanese tourists and a small, slight woman who was speaking haltingly in English. She was trying to explain how the bomb had fallen and how the people had died. She used elaborate hand gestures and the Japanese tourists nodded their heads, clicked away with their cameras and clucked sympathetically.

"Who is she?" I whispered to my mother's friend.

"She takes care of the place . . . " she replied in a low voice.

"Why don't they bring in someone who can speak fluently—this is frustrating to see..." I whispered back, watching the Japanese men shake hands with the woman before turning to go.

My mother's friend shook her head sadly, "They tried, but she just refuses to leave. She has been taking care of the place since the rescue teams finished cleaning it out . . . she lost 8 of her children here." I was horrified with that fact as the woman approached us. Her face was stern, yet gentle—like that of a school principal or . . . like that of a mother of 8 children. She shook hands with us and took us around to see the shelter. This is where we were. This is where the missiles came in . . . this is where the water rose up to . . . this is where the people stuck to the walls.

Her voice was strong and solid in Arabic. We didn't know what to answer. She continued to tell us how she had been in the shelter with 8 of her 9 children and how she had left minutes before the missiles hit to get some food and a change of clothes for one of the toddlers. She was in the house when the missiles struck and her first thoughts were, "Thank God the kids are in the shelter . . . " When she ran back to the shelter from her house across the street, she found it had been struck and the horror had begun. She had watched the corpses dragged out for days and days and refused to believe they were all gone for months after. She hadn't left the shelter since—it had become her home.

She pointed to the vague ghosts of bodies stuck to the concrete on the walls and ground and the worst one to look at was that of a mother, holding a child to her breast, like she was trying to protect it or save it. "That should have been me . . . " the woman who lost her children said and we didn't know what to answer.

It was then that I knew that the place was indeed "maskoon" or haunted . . . since February 13, 1991 it has been haunted by the living who were cursed with their own survival.

Important Side Note: For those of you with the audacity to write to me claiming it was a legitimate target because "American officials assumed it was for military purposes" just remember Protocol 1 of the 1977 Geneva Conventions, Part IV, Section 1, Chapter III, Article 52: . . . 3. In case of doubt whether an object which is normally dedicated to civilian purposes, such as a place of worship, a house or other dwelling or a school, is being used to make an effective contribution to military action, it shall be presumed not to be so used. (Like that would matter to you anyway.) **posted by river @ 4:15 AM**

Friday, February 20, 2004

DUMB AND DUMBER . . .

Ok, I just read this article in the New York Times and I had to share. Actually, someone sent it to me and they seem highly satisfied with it. The title is: Arabs in US Raising Money to Back Bush, and it is written by a Leslie Wayne who, apparently, knows very little about geography. I just love when articles like this find their way into the New York Times.

"Arabs in U.S. Raising Money to Back Bush," The New York Times Februrary 17, 2004, http://www.nytimes.com/2004/02/17/politics/campaign/17MONE.html?pagewanted=1

> *Wealthy Arab-Americans and foreign-born Muslims who strongly back President Bush's decision to invade Iraq are adding their names to the ranks of Pioneers and Rangers, the elite Bush supporters who have raised $100,000 or more for his re-election.*

> ... the attacks of Sept. 11, 2001 and the war in Iraq have been a catalyst for some wealthy Arab-Americans to become more involved in politics. And there are still others who have a more practical reason for opening their checkbooks: access to a business-friendly White House. Already their efforts have brought them visits with the president at his ranch in Crawford, Tex., as well as White House dinners and meetings with top administration officials . . .

The article basically states that a substantial sum of the money supporting Bush's presidential campaign is coming from affluent Arab-Americans who support the war on Iraq. The fun part about the article is that it goes on and on about "Arab"-Americans—not Muslim-Americans or even Asian-Americans but specifies Arab-Americans giving you the impression that the article is going to be about people who were originally from Iraq, Saudi Arabia, Syria, Egypt, Libya, Yemen, the United Arab Emirates, Bahrain, Oman, Qatar, Tunisia, Morocco, Palestine, Lebanon . . . you know—an Arab country where the national language is Arabic and the people are generally known as Arabs.

The article is dumb, but apparently the author thinks that the readers are even dumber. Of the 5 prominent "Arabs" the author gives as examples in the article (supporters of Bush), two are Iranian and the third is a Pakistani! Now this is highly amusing to an Arab because Pakistanis aren't Arabs and while Iran is our neighbor, Iranians are, generally speaking, not Arabs and I'm sure you can confirm that with Iranian bloggers . . .

One of the Iranian contributors is a Mr. Mori Hosseini who claims to know all about the region because he was born in Iran and lived there before moving to the US at the tender, prepubescent age of 13. He must be Iran's Chalabi—keep an eye on him. I predict he'll either be given contracts to build homes in Iraq or suddenly have important information on Iranian WMD he has been hiding since the age of 13.

I just wish all those prominent Arabs who supported the war—you know, the ones living in Washington and London who attend State dinners and parties at the White House holding silk handkerchiefs in one hand (to wipe away the tears for the "homeland") and cocktails in the other hand—would pack their Louis Vuitton bags, and bring all that money they are contributing to that war-hungry imbecile in the White House to Iraq or Iran or wherever they wish the spread of democracy and help "reconstruct" and "develop" their own countries. One wonders with that $200,000 how many homes Mr.Hosseini could have rebuilt in Bam, for example . . . but then again, if they don't bomb Iran into the pre-industrial era, how will Mr. Hosseini get all those huge contracts in the future? **posted by river @ 1:08 AM**

Wednesday, February 25, 2004

ANGRY ARABS AND AMERICAN MEDIA . . .

We were all watching Al-Itijah Al-Mu'akis or "The Opposite Direction" on Al-Jazeera. It was pretty good today. We had just cleared the dinner table and were settling down to watch some film when E. turned the channel to Al-Jazeera expecting a news brief. I instantly recognized the man in the lemon yellow shirt with his longish curly hair pulled back in a ponytail—Asa'ad Abu Khalil. I remembered him from an interview he did on Al-Arabia or Al-Jazeera—I can't remember which— immediately after the war, slamming Radio Sawa. Tonight, "The Opposite Direction" was hosting Asa'ad Abu Khalil, better known as The Angry Arab (angryarab.blogspot.com), and Ibraheim Al-Ariss, a writer for Al-Hayat newspaper which is based in Lebanon but is funded by some rich Saudi.

The subject was American propaganda in Arab media. Asa'ad Abu Khalil was brilliant. He discussed the effects of American propaganda on current Arab media and the way the current American government was pressuring certain Arab publications and networks into a pro-America stance. Unfortunately, his argument was way above Al-Ariss's head. Al-Ariss apparently thinks that pro-American propaganda is nothing less than a front-page headline saying, "WE LOVE AMERICA!!!"

Asa'ad Abu Khalil was discussing the more subtle changes taking place in some newspapers—the change in terminology, the fact that some newspapers have stopped covering the news and taken to translating articles directly from New York Times or some other American news outlet. He almost gave Ibraheim Al-Iriss, a reddish, portly man, an apoplectic fit. Poor Ibraheim fell short of pounding the table with his fists and throwing crumpled papers at Abu Khalil, who kept admirably cool. In other words, Asa'ad Abu Khalil ibarid il gallub.

(Iraqi phrase alert: ibarid il gallub, translated to "cools the heart" is basically used to refer to something or someone who eases the mind—and heart—by saying or doing something satisfactory.)

I get really tired of the emails deriding Al-Jazeera and Al-Arabiya for their news coverage, telling me they're too biased towards Arabs, etc. Why is it ok for CNN to be completely biased towards Americans and BBC to be biased towards the British but Al-Jazeera and Al-Arabiya have to objective and unprejudiced and, preferably, pander to American public opinion? They are Arab news networks—they SHOULD be biased towards Arabs. I agree that there is quite a bit of anti-America propaganda in some Arabic media, but there is an equal, if not more potent, amount of anti-Arab, anti-Muslim propaganda in American media. The annoying thing is that your average Arab knows much more about American culture and history than the average American knows about Arabs and Islam.

I wish everyone could see Al-Hurra—the new "unbiased" news network started by the Pentagon and currently being broadcast all over the Arab world. It is the visual equivalent of Sawa—the American radio station which was previously the Voice of America. The news and reports are so completely biased, they only lack George Bush and Condi Rice as anchors. We watch the reports and news briefs and snicker . . . it is far from subtle. Interestingly enough, Asa'ad Abu Khalil said that Sawa and Al-Hurra are banned inside of America due to some sort of law that doesn't allow the broadcast of blatant political propaganda or something to that effect. I'd love to know more about that.

A channel like Al-Hurra may be able to convince Egyptians, for example, that everything is going great inside of Iraq, but how are you supposed to convince Iraqis of that? Just because they broadcast it hourly, it doesn't make it true. I sometimes wonder how Americans would feel if the Saudi government, for example, suddenly decided to start broadcasting an English channel with Islamic propaganda to Americans.

Important note to those of you who are going to email me: The last few days, I have received at least 3 emails saying, "I read your blog and don't agree with what you say but we have a famous saying in America—I don't agree with what you say but I'll die for your right to say it." Just a note—it's not your famous American saying, it is French and it is Voltaire's famous saying:"I do not agree with a word you say, but I will fight to the death for your right to say it." **posted by river @ 1:23 AM**

Sunday, February 29, 2004

ASHOURA . . .

The tension in the air is almost electric. Everyone feels it. It is the beginning of the Islamic year or Muharam, the first month of the Hijri year. This time of the Hijri year is important because of certain historical events that occurred hundreds of years ago. The Prophet Mohammed's remaining family were killed, and some captured, in Karbala, in south-east Iraq. It's a long, sad and involved story.

The Prophet Mohammed's grandchildren, their children, wives and entourage all came to Iraq because they were encouraged by the people in the region to receive the leadership of the Islamic nation, or Khilafah. Before they could get to Karbala—more near the area of Kouffa—they were surrounded by Yazeed's army. Yazeed was a distant relative of the Prophet and wanted to become the Khalifa—or leader of the Islamic world. Yazeed also believed he had a right to be the Khalifah because his father, Ma'awiya, had claimed his right as Khalifah in opposition to the Imam Ali—the Prophet's cousin and also his son-in-law.

The Khilafah (or caliph-hood) was not hereditary. The Prophet Mohammed, upon his deathbed, ordered that the Khilafah would always be through general agreement of the "Sahhaba" who were a group of select respected, devout and influential people in Mecca. Three Khalifas after the Prophet's death, when the third Khalifah Othman bin Affan was killed, the problems began.

Anyway, after the Prophet's family were trapped in Kouffa, they were systematically killed and some taken as prisoner during the first ten days of Muharam. On the tenth day, Imam Al-Hussein, the Prophet's grandson was killed in the most gruesome way during a battle in Kouffa. He was beheaded and his head was taken to Yazeed.

The people of Kouffa and Karbala have always felt guilty for not helping Al-Hussein and his family and followers—for sending for them and then abandoning them when Yazeed's army attacked. This guilt is "remembered" every year by doing certain things—like cooking huge pots of steaming porridge for the poor and making special foods for neighbors and family. Sunnis and Shi'a alike do this, usually. My mother makes "harrisa," the porridge, for the whole family every year—it's the best part of Muharam.

Sometimes people have a "qirraya" at their house. This is often a women's affair. Women from all over the neighborhood gather at one of the houses and they send for a specialized group of women who sort of sing out the story of the "Maqtal" or the killing of Imam Al-Hussein and his family. I attended one of these qirrayas a few years ago and it was emotional and charged. The qirrayas often end in tears because the story of the "Maqtal" is so terrible, that it is difficult to stay dry-eyed when hearing about it.

This year, another ritual has been added to the ones mentioned above—the "Latmiya." This is done strictly by Shi'a—and not all Shi'a. Many moderate Shi'a frown upon the process of beating oneself with chains because the sight of it is just so . . . terrible. E. and I watched from the rooftop a couple of days ago as a procession of about 50 black-clad men passed down the main road. It was frightening. They had beards, wore head-to-toe black, with the exception of a green bandanna or piece of cloth tied around the wrist and they held up green and black flags and banners and pictures of Imam Al-Hussein on a green background. They were beating their chests to a certain beat and chanting something incoherent. These processions were banned before and, quite frankly, I wish they could be confined to certain areas now. The sight of so much violence (even if it is towards oneself) is just a little bit unnerving.

On tv, we saw much bigger Latmiyas in the south—especially Karbala where Imam Al-Hussein is buried. The men hold chains and beat their backs with them, sometimes to the point where their clothes tear and their bodies are bloodied. I don't like the ritual. It doesn't feel sacred or religious and many Muslims consider it a wrong, since it is considered "haram," or a sin, to disfigure the body. This year, Karbala is going to be especially crowded because, in addition to Iraqis, there are going to be thousands and thousands of Iranians who have somehow gotten into Iraq.

Ashoura, or the tenth day of Muharam, is in a couple of days and everyone is really worried about what might happen on this day. Dozens of buildings all over Baghdad are shrouded in black cloth. It is a depressing and sobering sight. E. was in Baghdad University a few days ago and he says that someone draped black cloth all over the buildings there and even over the department balconies. There were even signs offering "Latmiya" lessons and some of the more religiously bent Shi'a have given orders to the department cafeterias that there will be no music allowed and the only stuff they can play are taped "qirrayas."

The electrical situation is almost stable at around 10 hours of electricity a day at this point. Everything is a little bit frightening right now and I can't help but wish we could remain without electricity during the day and have it as soon as it gets dark. There have been a string of assassinations these last couple of weeks and some of them are just inexplicable . . . doctors, teachers, professors, religious figures . . . Baghdad is quite depressing and all this black cloth isn't helping any.
posted by river @ 2:19 AM

Wednesday, March 03, 2004

ASHOURA TRAGEDY . . .

The explosions in Karbala and Kadhimiya were horrible. We heard the ones in Kadhimiya from a distance. There were a couple of dull thuds and we didn't know what it was. We found out later on the news and everyone has been horrified ever since. It's so hard to believe this has happened. The shots on Al-Arabia and the other channels were terrible—body parts everywhere—people burning alive . . . who could do this? We've all been asking each other that . . . who would have anything to gain from this?

Fingers are being pointed everywhere. Everyone has been afraid that this will be the metaphorical straw that breaks the camels back—except it's not a straw . . . it's more like an iron anchor that is just to heavy to carry. Fortunately, the reactions have been sane, yet sorrowful. Sunnis and Shi'a are sticking together . . . more now than ever before. It's like this catastrophe somehow made everyone realize that there are outside forces trying to drive us all apart and cause unrest or "fitna." People are refusing to believe that this was done by Iraqis. It's impossible. It's inexcusable and there is nothing that can justify it.

We were extremely worried because we have some relatives who make the annual trip to Karbala every year. They live in an area with no working telephones so E. and my cousin had to go over there and check things out for themselves. We found out that they had decided against going this year because the situation was so unstable. I'm worried now about Salam—he wrote on his blog that he was going to Karbala this year with his family. I hope he's ok.

I guess we've all been expecting some sort of attack or riots or something . . . this tragedy was still unexpected. You sometimes think that you've seen all the violence there is—every single type—and there is nothing that will shock you anymore. This was a shock, and a painful one too. Today was an official day of mourning over the victims who died in Karbala and Kadhimiya. The mosques have been offering prayers for the victims and the mosque sheikhs have been condemning the bombings.

Before Ashoura, there was a lot of talk about civil war. We talk about it like it concerns a different set of people, in another country. I guess that is because none of us can believe that anyone we know could be capable of senseless violence. After this massacre, and after seeing the reactions of Sunnis and Shi'a alike, my faith in the sense and strength of Iraqis has been reaffirmed. It has been like a large family—with many serious differences—reuniting after a terrible tragedy to comfort each other and support one another. **posted by river @ 10:10 PM**

. . .

SISTANI AND THE GREEN ZONE . . .

Today was a mess. It feels like half of Baghdad was off-limits. We were trying to get from one end to the other to visit a relative and my cousin kept having to take an alternate route. There's a huge section cut off to accomodate the "Green Zone" which seems to be expanding. We joke sometimes saying that they're just going to put a huge wall around Baghdad, kick out the inhabitants and call it the "Green City." It is incredibly annoying to know that parts of your city are inaccessible in order to accomodate an occupation army.

Another section was cut off because there was some sort of crisis unfolding in or around the Ministry of Health. We later learned that former employees—some fired before the war and others fired during the occupation—had invaded the ministry and were trying to break into the minister's office. They were demanding work and some channels even mentioned a hostage situation. All we know is that there was a huge, angry mob outside of the ministry and tanks, cars and angry soldiers facing them. They say almost 1,300 employees working with the Ministry of Health have been fired since the end of the war. This includes doctors, nurses, hospital guards, etc.

Today the Iraqi Puppet Council was attempting to sign the Basic Law document which is sort of a prelude to a permanent constitution. I want to read it and see what it's about. They had everything set up in an elegant conference room—chrome and gray chairs with name tags on them, expensive pens ready for the GC members, a podium, a bunch of little kids ready to sing and a little orchestra to play music. They didn't sign the long-awaited document. Some of the Shi'a members of the council refused to sign it because, apparently, there had been disagreements to the presidency, women's rights, federalism and, generally, the constitution—should they ever decide to draft one.

Al-Sistani appears to be running the show, along with Bremer. I don't know why they don't just set up an office for him in the Green Zone—it would make things much easier for the GC members. They wouldn't have to keep running down to Karbala to beg for his approval.

It's unbelievable. Sistani is a respectable cleric. He has millions of followers both inside and outside of Iraq . . . but when you get down to it, he is Iranian. How is it that an Iranian cleric is moulding the future of Iraq?

His opinion is important in many ways—but he seems to have some sort of invisible veto within the Council. All he has to do is murmur disapproval in the ears of one of his followers and it is immediate dissent with his followers. It is so frustrating. How is Iraq going to be secular and, well, *Iraqi* if we have a cleric of Iranian origin making conditions and rules?!

You can read more about the constitutional mess over at Juan Cole and Back to Iraq.

Informed Comment, http://juancole.com, March 6, 2004

On Friday, five Shiite members of the Interim Governing Council suddenly pulled out of signing the Basic Law they had agreed to, with the rest of the IGC, last Monday.

A huge formal signing ceremony had been arranged, attended by hundreds of people and the press, who just kept waiting for hours and hours as the five were holed up with Ahmad Chalabi. Finally the Coalition Provisional Authority announced that nothing would happen, and everyone went home.

The whole performance was a huge embarrassment for the Bush administration, which had counted on enacting the Basic Law as a prelude to finding a way to hand sovereignty over to an Iraqi government of some description on June 30. That deadline seems increasingly shaky . . .

The issues over which the five revolted were: the presidency, federalism, women's rights, and the permanent constitution. The Basic Law had stipulated that there would be a president and two vice presidents. It said that the constitution could be annulled if any three of Iraq's provinces objected to it (a provision inserted by the 5 Kurdish representatives). They also withdrew their support for a provision that 25% of seats in parliament should ideally go to women . . .

Back to Iraq, http://www.back-to-iraq.com/archives/000694.php
March 5, 2004

Well, seems I spoke too soon this morning when I said the interim Iraqi constitution would be signed "in a couple of hours." Five Shi'ite clerics refused to sign the charter today, saying the document didn't give the Shi'a enough power in a newly sovereign Iraq.

Iraqi leaders said the Shiites wanted to strike a provision that would allow a minority of the country's voters to block the implementation of a permanent constitution, which is to be written next year. And the Shiites are holding out for an expansion of the Iraqi presidency, which, by most accounts, will likely turn out to be held by a Shiite.

The Kurds and Sunni members of the Iraqi Governing Council blasted the Shi'ite decision not to sign as a grab for power, which it is. Instead of a single president and two deputies, as currently outlined in the Transitional Administrative Law as the constitution is called, the Shi'a are asking for a collective presidency of three Shi'a, one Kurd and one Sunni. The Shi'a also, on the word of Grand Ayatollah Sayyid Ali Husaini Sistani, want to remove safeguards that would give Kurds a veto over the final, permanent charter, which is to be hashed out next year. Today's draft allowed for two-thirds of voters in any three provinces to veto the permanent charter via a referendum. The Kurds, coincidentally enough, control three provinces in the north of the country.

---

posted by river @ 11:53 PM

Friday. March 12. 2004

SPRING . . .

Discussions around the dinner table mainly focus on the Transitional Law these days. I asked a friend to print out the whole thing for me and have been looking it over these last two days. I watched only a part of the ceremony because the electricity went out in the middle of it and I didn't bother watching a recap of it later on.

The words look good on paper—as words often do. Some parts of it sound hauntingly like our last constitution. The discussions about the Transitional Law all focus on the legitimacy of this document. Basically, an occupying power brought in a group of exiles, declared Iraq "liberated," declared the constitution we've been using since the monarchy annulled and set up a group of puppets as a Governing Council. Can these laws be considered legitimate?

Furthermore, just how sincere are these puppets about this new Transitional Law? For example, there's a lovely clause that reads, "No one may be unlawfully arrested or detained, and no one may be detained by reason of political or religious beliefs." Will the American troops discontinue the raids and arbitrary detentions (which are still quite common) come June 30? Or is the Transitional Law binding only to Iraqis?

One example of an arbitrary detention we heard about the other day was of a man who was arrested in Tikrit. They raided his home and gathered the 25-year-old man, two brothers and an elderly uncle. They got the usual treatment: a bag on the head, and hands behind their backs. They were taken to a place outside of Tikrit and thrown into a barn-like area with bags on their heads—still tied up. For 3 days, they were kicked and cursed by the troops. In between the kicking and cursing, a hefty soldier would scream questions at them and an interpreter would translate, "Are you part of Al-Qaeda?! Do you know Osama bin Laden?!" On the third day, one of the young men struck up a deal with who he gathered was their "head"—the man who gave all the orders. They agreed that one of the soldiers would accompany the man back to the city and wait while he came up with $300/detainee. The rest of the men would be freed a couple of days later.

And it worked. Two days later, his three relatives came walking home after being dropped off on the side of the road. Basically, they paid a ransom for their freedom. Just one of the many stories about life in the "New Iraq"—no wonder Chalabi was so jubilant while signing the Transitional Law document. The country is currently like an unguarded bank—especially for those who bear arms.

The general attitude towards the document is a certain weariness. Iraqis are weary of everything "transitional" and "temporary." I guess, after almost a year of instability and strife, we just crave something more definite and substantial.

Spring is in the air—and that means dust storms and a mellow sun for Iraqis. We're enjoying the weather because by the end of April, summer will be in full swing and the heat will come in almost palpable waves. The mornings are slightly cool and by noon we've shed the jackets. We no longer need the "sopas" or kerosene heaters at home— which is a relief to E. who has been designated the job of filling them up and making sure the kerosene tank in the yard is always full (the kerosene man has become a dear friend).

These last few days have brought back memories of the same dates, last year. What were we doing in early March? We were preparing for the war . . . digging wells, taping up windows, stocking up on candles, matches, kerosene, rice, flour, bandages, and medicine . . . and what are we doing now? Using them.   **posted by river @ 11:02 PM**

Friday, March 19, 2004

EXPLOSIONS . . .

The explosion two days ago was a colossal one. Our area isn't very close to the area that got bombed, but we heard it loud and clear. It was one of several explosions during this last week . . . but it was the biggest. The moment it happened, E. and I started trying to guess where the noise was coming from. It has become a sort of morbid game.

Al-Jazeera almost instantly began covering the explosion and we found out that E. was right—it was in Karrada (I get the direction wrong 90% of the time and E. chauvinistically assures me that a warped sense of direction is quite common to most females). A hotel in the middle of a residential area was bombed and the stories vary in a strange sort of way. People in the area claim they heard the hissing of a rocket and then an explosion. Others say that it was an instant explosion. One news network is claiming that 32 bodies have been taken out of the rubble . . . another mentioned 17 and the Iraqi police are saying that only 6 were found. Reports on the nationalities of the deceased also vary—the Iraqi police are claiming all the residents of the hotel were Iraqi and the Americans are saying that there were some Americans and Brits among the dead. Who to believe?

Last Saturday and Sunday there were demonstrations in Baghdad. Students weren't allowed into Baghdad University because the university guards (ironically appointed by the Americans) wouldn't let anyone in. They are part of Sistani's gang and since Sistani's followers have diligently been objecting [to] the TAL document signed by the Puppet Council, the guards decided that college would be closed for a couple of days. The students had to watch the dean of the engineering college beg to be let in, and refused.

I found out about the demonstrations because I was supposed to have a job interview on Saturday and my potential employers called me postponing it until further notice because their guards—avid Sistani fans—had decided to take the day off to join the demonstration objecting the TAL. Sistani's followers would not be out protesting the transitional law document if they didn't have explicit directions from him—so

Mustansiryia University (another major university in Baghdad) is full of student protests because the dean of the college of science requested that after the arba'een (40th day after the death of Imam Al-Hussein), the students take down the black flags and pictures of Al-Sadr and Sistani. The more conservative Shi'a students immediately took offence and decided that they wouldn't attend classes until the dean was fired. In retaliation, Sunni students decided they would organize a *protest* to the strike organized by the Shi'a students . . .

We also heard that one of the assistant deans of the college of engineering in Baghdad University was assassinated recently. It's terrible news and the subject has been on my mind a lot lately. I don't know why no one focuses on this topic in the news. It's like Iraq is suffering from intellectual hemorrhaging. Professors and scientists are being assassinated right and left—decent intelligent people who are necessary for the future of Iraq. Other scientists are being detained by the Americans and questioned about—of all things—Al-Qaeda.

The stories they tell after being let go are incredible. Most of the scientists are college professors and have dedicated their lives to teaching and research. Many are detained only because they specialize in a certain field, like heredity, for example. One man who was recently let go told about the ridiculous interrogation that lasted 3 days and involved CIA and military police. They showed him picture after picture of his family, confiscated from the family home during a raid, and kept pointing at his two teenage sons and their friends and asking, "Aren't they a part of Al-Qaeda?!"

And it doesn't stop with the scientists. Doctors are also being assassinated by some mysterious group. It started during the summer and has been continuing since then. Iraq has some of the finest doctors in the region. Since June, we've heard of at least 15 who were killed in cold blood. The stories are similar—a car pulls up to the clinic or office, a group of men in black step down and the doctor is gunned down—sometimes in front of the patients and sometimes all alone, after hours. One doctor was shot brutally in his house, in front of his family. There was a rumor that Badir's Brigade (the SCIRI militia led by Al-Hakeem) had a list out of 72 doctors that had to be killed for one reason or another. They include Sunni, Shi'a and Christian doctors.

Scientists, professors and doctors who aren't detained or assassinated all seem to be looking for a way out. It seems like everyone you talk to is keeping their eyes open for a job opportunity outside of the country. It depresses me. When I hear someone talking about how they intend to leave to Dubai or Lebanon or London, I want to beg them to stay . . . a part of me wants to scream, "But we need you here! You belong here!" Another more rational part of me knows that some of them have no options. Many have lost their jobs and don't know how to feed their families. Others just can't stand the constant worrying about their children or spouse. Many of the female doctors and scientists want to leave because it's no longer safe for women to work like before. For some, the option is becoming a housewife or leaving abroad to look for the security to work.

Whatever the reason, the brains are slowly seeping out of Iraq. It's no longer a place for learning or studying or working . . . it's a place for wealthy contractors looking to get wealthier, extremists, thieves (of all ranks and origins) and troops . . . **posted by river @ 10:22 AM**

Saturday, March 20, 2004

THE WAR ON TERROR . . .

I'm feeling irritable and angry today. It's exactly a year since the war on Iraq began and it seems to be weighing heavily on everyone.

Last year, on this day, the war started during the early hours of the morning. I wasn't asleep . . . I hadn't slept since Bush's ultimatum a couple of days before. It wasn't because I was scared but because I didn't want to be asleep when the bombs started falling. The tears started falling with the first few thuds. I'm not very prone to tears, but that moment, a year ago today, I felt such sorrow at the sound of those bombs. It was a familiar feeling because it wasn't, after all, the first time America was bombing us. It didn't seem fair that it was such a familiar feeling.

I felt horrible that Baghdad was being reduced to rubble. With every explosion, I knew that some vital part of it was going up in flames. It was terrible and I don't think I'd wish it on my worst enemy. That was the beginning of the "liberation" . . . a liberation from sovereignty, a certain sort of peace, a certain measure of dignity. We've been liberated from our jobs, and our streets and the sanctity of our homes . . . some of us have even been liberated from the members of our family and friends.

A year later and our electricity is intermittent, at best, there constantly seems to be a fuel shortage and the streets aren't safe. When we walk down those streets, on rare occasions, the faces are haggard and creased with concern . . . concern over family members under detention, homes raided by Americans, hungry mouths to feed, and family members to keep safe from abduction, rape and death.

And where are we now, a year from the war? Sure—we own satellite dishes and the more prosperous own mobile phones . . . but where are we *really*? Where are the majority?

We're trying to fight against the extremism that seems to be upon us like a black wave; we're wondering, on an hourly basis, how long it will take for some semblance of normality to creep back into our lives; we're hoping and praying against civil war . . .

We're watching with disbelief as American troops roam the streets of our towns and cities and break violently into our homes . . . we're watching with anger as the completely useless Puppet Council sits giving out fat contracts to foreigners and getting richer by the day—the same people who cared so little for their country that they begged Bush and his cronies to wage a war that cost thousands of lives and is certain to cost thousands more.

We're watching sardonically as an Iranian cleric in the south turns a once secular country into America's worst nightmare—a carbon copy of Iran. We're watching as the lies unravel slowly in front of the world—the WMD farce and the Al-Qaeda mockery.

And where are we now? Well, our governmental facilities have been burned to the ground by a combination of "liberators" and "Free Iraqi Fighters"; 50% of the working population is jobless and hungry; summer is looming close and our electrical situation is a joke; the streets are dirty and overflowing with sewage; our jails are fuller than ever with thousands of innocent people; we've seen more explosions, tanks, fighter planes and troops in the last year than almost a decade of war with Iran brought; our homes are being raided and our cars are stopped in the streets for inspections . . . journalists are being killed "accidentally" and the seeds of a civil war are being sown by those who find it most useful; the hospitals overflow with patients but are short on just about everything else—medical supplies, medicine and doctors; and all the while, the oil is flowing.

But we've learned a lot. We've learned that terrorism isn't actually the act of creating terror. It isn't the act of killing innocent people and frightening others . . . no, you see, that's called a "liberation." It doesn't matter what you burn or who you kill—if you wear khaki, ride a tank or Apache or fighter plane and drop missiles and bombs, then you're not a terrorist—you're a liberator.

The war on terror is a joke . . . Madrid was proof of that last week . . . Iraq is proof of that everyday.

I hope someone feels safer, because we certainly don't. **posted by river @ 11:02 PM**

Saturday, March 27, 2004

SISTANISTAN . . .

The telephone wasn't working these last few days. It will do that every once in a while—disappear coyly. We pick up the receiver and instead of a dial tone hear nothing but a strange sort of silence laced with static. It almost drove me crazy because I couldn't connect to the internet. I spent the days hovering anxiously around the telephone, picking it up every few minutes and calling out "Allooo? Alloooooooo?" E. asked around and learned that the lines in the whole area were down.

I was in Karrada yesterday—a popular area in central Baghdad. It's a mercantile district where you can find everything from butchers to ice cream shops. The stores are close together and it's the ideal area to go looking for something you're not sure you'll find. You'll find it in Karrada—whether it's a gold bracelet or fuzzy slippers or the complete, unabridged collection of the late Al-Hakeem's religious lectures on CD.

My uncle is planning a trip to Jordan so we had to buy him some luggage. I had been looking forward to the shopping trip for at least 4 days which is how long it takes to get the routine familial permission these days. First, I have to make a declaration of intent; I have to tell the parents that I intend to go out and purchase something. Then, I have to specify the area where I intend to make the purchase, after which comes locating a free male relative with some extra time on his hands to join me in the adventure. The final step is setting the date and time and getting the final household authorization.

For those of you wondering, YES, it annoys me beyond anything that, at my age, I have to get parental permission to leave the house. It's a trend that started after the war and doesn't look like it's going to abate any time soon. I comfort myself with the thought that it's not specific to my household or even my gender—all parents seem to be doing it lately . . . where are you going? To do what? Who is going with you? What time will you be back? Is it absolutely necessary?

If E. and I are half an hour late, we can come home expecting to see one of the parents standing outside, in the driveway, pacing anxiously and peering out into the street every once in a while. I can't really blame them—with all the abductions, explosions and detentions. On the other hand, if one of the parents are late, E. and I also end up in the driveway, squinting into the night and mumbling about people who never phone to say they're going to be late.

Karrada was quite crowded with people coming and going. Women, of course, were a startling minority. Karrada used to be full of women—mothers, daughters and wives sometimes alone and sometimes dragging along a weary male. As we got out of the car, my confidence and enthusiasm began to wane. I was one of the few women on the street not wearing a hijab, or head-cover. One, two, three women passed by with the hijab covering their hair . . . the fourth one had gone a step further and was wearing an abbaya or black cloak . . . I tugged gently at the sleeves of my shirt which were cuffed almost to my elbows. They slid down once more to my wrists and I was suddenly grateful that I had decided to wear a long denim skirt.

We walked the few meters to the display of suitcases on the side-walk. The suitcases were mostly new but some were used and a little faded around the edges. I wondered if they had been hijacked from some unfortunate Iraqi who had come from abroad. E. and my cousin stood haggling with the suitcase man. He was showing them a Korean knockoff of Samsonite and swearing it was the original. For those who have never shopped in Iraq—nothing costs as much as the first price they give you. If the man says 10,000 Iraqi Dinars, you can instantly challenge him with, "I'll buy it for 7,000" and be quite confident that he'll give in the end with some minor grumbling.

I studied the streets and surrounding shops while I waited. The street was crowded with cars—mostly old ones. Few people dare to drive around in decent vehicles. The traffic flow kept stopping every few minutes and a choir of honking and swearing would instantly start up. Heads would pop out of car windows and eyes would strain to see what could possibly be keeping the long line of cars in front.

There were some strange-looking people in the street—heads covered in turbans, black and white . . . women shrouded from top to bottom in black cloth . . . men with long beards and abbayas. I was getting quite a few critical stares—why wasn't this girl wearing a hijab? The rational person in me was asking the same question—why aren't you wearing one? Is it too much to ask for you to throw something on top of your head when you leave the house? Everyone else is doing it . . . most of the women you know are just flinging on a head-cover to avoid those disapproving glares and harsh words. Ever since the war, even some Christian women have been pressured into hiding their hair—especially in the south. And on and on went the rational voice . . . The stubborn voice—the one that blogs—tried to drown out common sense with, "Blah, blah, blah, blah, blah . . . we won't be pressured . . . "

I focused my attention on the shops around me, staring hard at the displays in the windows. Many of the windows showed posters of the Imam Hussein, Al-Sadr, one or more of the Hakeems and there were so many pictures of Sistani both outside and inside of shops that I decided the area should change its name from Karrada to "Sistanistan."

After almost 10 minutes of selecting and bartering, E. and my cousin had decided on one large black suitcase and a smaller one. E. counted out the money patiently as the suitcase man swore he was being robbed by selling the suitcases for such a meager sum. My cousin went to open the trunk of the car and I helped the suitcase man wrap the luggage in a large plastic bag.

Before we got into the car to go home, E. asked me if there was anything else I wanted to get—did I want to see the shops? A part of me *did* want to take a more thorough look around, but another part of me was both physically and mentally exhausted with the rare outing. I just wanted to get back to the safety of our home where I didn't have to feel like some sort of strange outcast.

This time of year is the closest we get to spring. April promises to be hot and sticky . . . I used to constantly yearn to be outside— not just on the roof or in the garden—but on a street or sidewalk with people coming and going around me. That need hits me less and less of late . . . **posted by river @ 2:54 PM**

RAED IN THE MIDDLE . . .

Raed of Where is Raed? (dear_raed.blogspot.com) has started his own blog! You can check out Raed's independent views at Raed in the Middle (raedinthemiddle.blogspot.com) . . . **posted by river @ 3:08 PM**

Monday, March 29, 2004

TALES FROM ABU GHRAIB . . .

At precisely 5 p.m., yesterday afternoon, my mother suddenly announced that we were going to go visit a friend of hers who had recently had a minor operation. The friend lived two streets away and in Iraqi culture, it is obligatory to visit a sick or healing friend or relative. I tried to get out of the social call with a variety of tired excuses. It was useless—my mother was adamant.

We left the house at around 5:40, with me holding a box of chocolate and arrived at the friend's house less than five minutes later. After the initial greetings and words of sympathy and relief, we all filed into the living room. The living room was almost dark; the electricity was out and the drapes were open to let in the fading rays of sun. "The electricity should be back at six . . . " my mother's friend said apologetically, "That's why we haven't lighted the kerosene lamps."

Just as we were settling down, a figure sitting at the other end of the living room rose in a hurry. "Where are you going?!" cried out my mother's friend, Umm Hassen. She then turned to us and made a hasty introduction, "This is M.—she's a friend of the family . . . she's here to see Abu Hassen . . . " I peered hard across the darkening room to get a better look at the slight figure, but I couldn't make out her features. I could barely hear her voice as she said, "I really have to be going . . . it's getting dark . . ." Umm Hassen shook her head and firmly declared, "No—you're staying. Abu Hassen will drive you home later."

The figure sat down and an awkward silence ensued as Umm Hassen left the living room to bring tea from the kitchen. My mother broke the silence with a question, "Do you live nearby?" She asked the figure. "Not really . . . I live outside of Baghdad . . . on the southern edges, but I'm staying with some relatives a few streets away." I listened to the voice carefully and could tell that the girl was young— no more than 20 or 25 . . . probably less.

Just as Umm Hassen walked into the room with the tea tray, the lights in the house flickered back to life and we all murmured a prayer of thanks. As soon as my eyes adjusted to the glaring yellow lights, I turned to get a better look at Umm Hassen's guest. I had been right—she was young. She couldn't have been more than 20. She was wearing a black shawl, thrown carelessly over dark brown hair which was slipping out from under the head cover. She clutched at a black handbag and as the lights came back on, she shrank into herself at the far end of the room.

"Why are you sitting all the way over there?" scolded Umm Hassen fondly, "Come over here and sit." She nodded towards a large armchair next to our couch. The girl rose and I noticed for the first time just how slight her figure was—the long skirt and shirt hung off of her thin body like they belonged to someone else. She settled stiffly in the big chair and managed to look even smaller and younger.

"How old are you, M.?" my mother asked kindly. "Nineteen." came the reply. "And are you studying? Which college are you in?" The girl blushed furiously as she explained that she was studying Arabic literature but postponed the year because . . . "Because she was detained by the Americans." Umm Hassen finished angrily, shaking her head. "She's here to see Abu Hassen because her mother and three brothers are still in prison."

Abu Hassen is a lawyer who has taken on very few cases since the end of the war. He explained once that the current Iraqi legal system was like a jungle with no rules, a hundred lions, and thousands of hyenas. No one was sure which laws were applicable and which weren't; nothing could be done about corrupt judges and police and it was useless taking on criminal cases because if you won, the murderer/thief/looter's family would surely put you in your grave . . . or the criminal himself could do it personally after he was let out in a few weeks.

This case was an exception. M. was the daughter of a deceased friend and she had come to Abu Hassen because she didn't know anyone else who was willing to get involved.

On a cold night in November, M., her mother, and four brothers had been sleeping when their door suddenly came crashing down during the early hours of the morning. The scene that followed was one of chaos and confusion . . . screaming, shouting, cursing, pushing and pulling followed. The family were all gathered into the living room and the four sons—one of them only 15—were dragged away with bags over their heads. The mother and daughter were questioned—who was the man in the picture hanging on the wall? He was M.'s father who had died 6 years ago of a stroke. You're lying, they were told—wasn't he a part of some secret underground resistance cell? M.'s mother was hysterical by then—he was her dead husband and why were they taking away her sons? What had they done? They were supporting the resistance, came the answer through the interpreter.

How were they supporting the resistance, their mother wanted to know? "You are contributing large sums of money to terrorists." The interpreter explained. The troops had received an anonymous tip that M.'s family were giving funds to support attacks on the troops.

It was useless trying to explain that the family didn't have any "funds"—ever since two of her sons lost their jobs at a factory that had closed down after the war, the family had been living off of the little money they got from a "kushuk" or little shop that sold cigarettes, biscuits and candy to people in the neighborhood. They barely made enough to cover the cost of food! Nothing mattered. The mother and daughter were also taken away, with bags over their heads.

Umm Hassen had been telling the story up until that moment, M. was only nodding her head in agreement and listening raptly, like it was someone else's story. She continued it from there . . . M. and her mother were taken to the airport for interrogation. M. remembers being in a room, with a bag over her head and bright lights above. She claimed she could see the shapes of figures through the little holes in the bag. She was made to sit on her knees in the interrogation room while her mother was kicked and beaten to the ground.

M.'s hands trembled as she held the cup of tea Umm Hassen had given her. Her face was very pale as she said, "I heard my mother begging them to please let me go and not hurt me . . . she told them she'd do anything—say anything—if they just let me go." After a couple hours of general abuse, the mother and daughter were divided, each one thrown into a separate room for questioning. M. was questioned about everything concerning their family life—who came to visit them, who they were related to and when and under what circumstances her father had died. Hours later, the mother and daughter were taken to the infamous Abu Ghraib prison—home to thousands of criminals and innocents alike.

In Abu Ghraib, they were seperated and M. suspected that her mother was taken to another prison outside of Baghdad. A couple of terrible months later—after witnessing several beatings and the rape of a male prisoner by one of the jailors—in mid-January, M. was suddenly set free and taken to her uncle's home where she found her youngest brother waiting for her. Her uncle, through some lawyers and contacts, had managed to extract M. and her 15-year-old brother from two different prisons. M. also learned that her mother was still in Abu Ghraib but they weren't sure about her three brothers.

M. and her uncle later learned that a certain neighbor had made the false accusation against her family. The neighbor's 20-year-old son was still bitter over a fight he had several years ago with one of M.'s brothers. All he had to do was contact a certain translator who worked for the troops and give M.'s address. It was that easy.

Abu Hassen was contacted by M. and her uncle because he was an old family friend and was willing to do the work free of charge. They have been trying to get her brothers and mother out ever since. I was enraged—why don't they contact the press? Why don't they contact the Red Cross?! What were they waiting for?! She shook her head sadly and said that they *had* contacted the Red Cross but they were just one case in thousands upon thousands—it would take forever to get to them. As for the press—was I crazy? How could she contact the press and risk the wrath of the American authorities while her mother and brothers were still imprisoned?! There were prisoners who had already gotten up to 15 years of prison for "acting against the coalition" . . . she couldn't risk that. They would just have to be patient and do a lot of praying.

By the end of her tale, M. was crying silently and my mother and Umm Hassen were hastily wiping away tears. All I could do was repeat, "I'm so sorry . . . I'm really sorry . . . " and a lot of other useless words. She shook her head and waved away my words of sympathy, "It's ok—really—I'm one of the lucky ones . . . all they did was beat me. **posted by river @ 11:35 PM**

The US siege of Falloojeh leaves some 500 Iraqis and 36 Americans dead by early April. The opposition to the American occupation grows quickly as a result of Falloojeh. Local Shia militias take control of Najaf and Kut. On April 9, 200,000 Muslims, most of them Shia, fill the largest Sunni mosque in Baghdad in protest against the US. The US responds by announcing its intent to "kill or capture" Moqtada al-Sadr, who grows steadily in popularity as he fights the Americans. Two members of the Iraqi Governing Council resign in protest against the American invasion of Falloojeh, and on April 11, the US orders a cease-fire to allow for talks. With the November US presidential election in mind, the Bush administration predicts success. "Our military is . . . performing brilliantly. See, the transition from torture chambers and rape rooms and mass graves and fear of authority is a tough transition. And they're doing the good work of keeping this country stabilized as a political process unfolds," the President says in Iowa on April 15. Four days later Bush is sounding a somewhat different note in Pennsylvania. "We're facing supporters of the outlaw cleric, remnants of Saddam's regime that are still bitter that they don't have the position to run the torture chambers and rape rooms," he says. "They will fail because they do not speak for the vast majority of Iraqis who do not want to replace one tyrant with another. They will fail because the will of our coalition is strong. They will fail because America leads a coalition full of the finest military men and women in the world."

Bush says he will send more troops in mid-April and names John Negroponte as ambassador to Iraq to replace Bremer in the American embassy as of June 30. Hostage taking is a growing method of guerrilla warfare. Three Japanese are taken hostage, then released; then an Italian hostage is murdered. Meanwhile, there is a mortar attack on a Baghdad jail killing 22. A bomb goes off in Basra killing 68 people. Children on a school bus are among the dead. More fighting erupts in Falloojeh. The insurgents step up attacks on Iraq's oil industry, and there is an attack on the main oil facility in Iraq. Towards the end of the month, the US changes course yet again and decides the Baathist workers and members of Saddam's military whom it fired on taking over the country are not so bad after all, and starts hiring them back. Commanders in Baghdad insist there is a peace deal in Falloojeh, but as they talk, the US attacks the city with 500-pound bombs.

With the US facing a widening insurgency, losing control of much of the Central Iraq, the Abu Ghraib prison scandal breaks. The prison was a notorious torture jail under Saddam, and now photos are released showing American GIs torturing Iraqi prisoners.

At month's end, US forces are set to pull out of Falloojeh, leaving it in the hands of a new Iraqi security force, headed by a former Saddam general. Estimates now are that at least 600 people have been killed by coalition forces in Falloojeh and aid agencies say the way civilians are being treated potentially breaches the Geneva convention. In addition to untargeted fire and the high number of civilian deaths, the most widespread concern is caused by the prevention of civilians from leaving Falloojeh in order to seek refuge elsewhere.

In May the fighting continues as the Abu Ghraib scandal unfolds with more photos, stories by Seymour Hersh in the New Yorker and by other journalists. Senator John Warner, the Republican chairman of the Senate Armed Services Committee, conducts hearings in an effort to get to the bottom of the scandal. The inquiry almost immediately loses traction and begins to look like a public relations event for Warner and other members of the committee. Both members of Congress and high-ranking Pentagon officials fall all over one another attempting to push the scandal out of the news or, at the very least, confine it to a handful of soldiers. "I'm not a lawyer. My impression is that what has been charged thus far is abuse, which I believe technically is different from torture," says Secretary of Defense Donald Rumsfeld in a Pentagon Operational Update briefing on May 4.

The Pentagon stages an elaborate court martial for one soldier in Baghdad which is little more than a photo-op to demonstrate how serious the military is about cleaning up the prison scandal. A day later in an interview with Al Arabiya Television, Bush explains, "It's very important for people, your listeners, to understand in our country that when an issue is brought to our attention on this magnitude, we act—and we act in a way where leaders are willing to discuss it with the media. And we act in a way where, you know, our Congress asks pointed questions to the leadership. . . . Iraq was a unique situation because Saddam Hussein had constantly defied the world and had threatened his neighbors, had used weapons of mass destruction, had terrorist ties, had torture chambers."

As Abu Ghraib remains a topic of press interest, Nick Berg is beheaded and his grisly countenance fills the media. Hostage beheadings become a new form of warfare. There are later news reports that Central Command's senior commander, Lt. General Ricardo S. Sanchez personally signed off on the use of police dogs to intimidate prisoners at Abu Ghraib and ultimately he is removed from the command. Defense Secretary Rumsfeld visits the troops to rally morale. Hersh traces Abu Ghraib torture to expansion of a special program authorized personally by Rumsfeld. The month closes with Iraqi police raiding the office of Ahmed Chalabi, once the US choice to run Iraq but now banished from sight. The US military stands behind the Iraqi police.

By June the US is working overtime to get a sufficient grip on the country to permit the holding of elections as promised. By now Iraq has emerged as a central issue in the US presidential campaign. At this point, it is not a question of whether democracy in Iraq will succeed. It must succeed, or at least be seen to succeed.

Ayad Allawi, an old CIA retainer, is earmarked to become Iraq'a interim prime minister. He is immediately placed into the spotlight when two people tell an Australian journalist they witnessed him personally carrying out summary executions of prisoners lined up against a wall. As the deadline for the transfer of power to a new interim Iraqi government approaches, the insurgents strike repeatedly, killing Iraqi civilians, politicians and foreign civilians living and working in the country. On June 28, two days before the June 30 deadline, the occupation hands over "sovereignty" to Iraq.

The insurgency continues. Now foreign journalists and civilians are directly in the line of fire. Several are kidnapped, held as hostages, traded back and forth among different groups, and threatened with beheading. The Senate Intelligence Committee in early July blames George Tenet and the CIA as the main source of erroneous information on weapons of mass destruction used by the Bush administration. The Abu Ghraib scandal briefly surfaces once more with a Pentagon report admitting at least 94 confirmed instances of death in custody, sexual and physical assault and other abuses on the US's watch in Iraq and Afghanistan. At the end of July a suicide car bomb kills 68 in central Baquba. The bomb is aimed at a police recruiting center. Insurgents and police clash in Baghdad with more deaths. US forces hit Najaf at the beginning of August, killing 300 members of the militia. The US is fighting the Mahdi Army, soldiers supporting al-Sadr. On August 12, fighting intensifies, US war planes pound fighters in Kut and 68 are killed. Shia districts in Baghdad and Basra erupt in violence. In Najaf the US cordons off the most sacred mosque and ancient cemetery. It isn't until August 27 after almost 3 weeks of fighting that Ayatollah al-Sistani manages to broker a peace deal between al-Sadr and US and Iraqi forces. A reporter for the Observer (UK) on August 29 describes Najaf in the aftermath of the siege—"whole areas of the city are now in ruins; scores of civilians are dead and tens of thousands of people have left—or lost—their homes. The hotels and restaurants that serve the pilgrim trade to the ancient town are smashed hulks, the roads are littered with ordnance, much of the world-famous cemetery has been shot to pieces."

Meanwhile, Iraq's oil fields, on whose production the country's economy depends, are the targets of insurgency and many have to be shut down.

—James Ridgeway

RIOTS, STAR GAZING AND CRICKET CHOIRS . . .

There have been demonstrations by Al-Sadr's followers in Baghdad and Najaf. In Baghdad they are gathered near the Green Zone and the Sheraton hotel by the thousands—a huge angry mob, mostly in black. In Najaf, they were just outside of the Spanish troops' camp. The demonstration in Najaf was shot at by the soldiers and they say that at least 14 are dead and dozens are wounded . . . An Iraqi friend in Diwaniya was telling me that they had to evacuate the CPA building in Najaf because it was under attack. He says there's talk of Jihad amongst the Shi'a.

Let me make it very clear right now that I am *not* a supporter of Al-Sadr. I do not like clerics who want to turn Iraq into the next Iran or Saudi Arabia or Kuwait . . . but it makes me really, really angry to see these demonstrations greeted with bullets and tanks by the troops. Why allow demonstrations if you're going to shoot at the people? The demonstrators were unarmed but angry—Al-Sadr's newspaper was shut down recently by Bremer and Co. and his deputy is said to have been detained by the Spaniards down south (although the Spanish troops are denying it). His followers are outraged, and believe me—he has a healthy number of followers. His father was practically revered by some of the Shi'a and he apparently has inherited their respect.

Today Bremer also announced the fact that we now have an official "Ministry of Defense." The irony of the situation wasn't lost on Iraqis—the head of the occupation announcing a "Ministry of Defense." To defend against what? Occupation? Ha, ha . . . or maybe it's to secure the borders from unwelcome foreigners carrying guns and riding tanks? Or perhaps the Ministry of Defense should be more concerned with the extremists coming in from neighboring countries and taking over (but no—Bremer deals with them on the Puppet Council) . . . so many things to do for a Ministry of Defense.

There's also a new "Mukhaberat" or "National Iraqi Intelligence Organization" (or something to that effect). The irony is that while the name is new and the head is Ali Abd Ul Ameer Allawi (a relative of the Puppet Council President Ayad Allawi), the faces of the new Mukhaberat promise to be some of the same as the old. They've been contacting the old members of the Iraqi Mukhaberat for months and promising them lucrative jobs should they decide to join the new Iraqi intelligence (which, we hope, will be an improvement on American intelligence— I'd hate to have us invade a country on false pretenses).

The weather is quite nice lately (with the exception of dust every once in a while). We spend the electricity-less evenings out in the little garden. We pull out plastic chairs and a little plastic table and sit around gazing at the sky, which is marvelously clear on many nights. E. is thinking of starting a "count the stars" project. He's going to allot a section of the sky to each member of the family and have them count the number of stars in their designated astral plot. I'm thinking of starting a "cricket choir" with some very talented six-legged pests located under a dried-out rose bush . . .

In a few days, I'll have to go up and wash out the roof or "sattih." Last year, we'd sleep on top of the roof on the hot nights without electricity. We lay out thin mattresses on the clean ground and wet some sheets to cover ourselves with. It's not too bad until around 6 a.m. when the sun rises high in the sky and the flies descend upon the sleepers like . . . well, like flies.

These last couple of weeks have been somewhat depressing for most people. You know how sometimes you look back at the past year and think to yourself, "What was I doing last year, on this same day?" Well we've been playing that game constantly lately. What was I doing last year, this very moment? I was listening for the sirens, listening for the planes and listening to the bombs fall. Now we just listen for the explosions—it's not the same thing.

I haven't been sleeping very well either. I've been having disturbing dreams lately . . . Dreams of being stuck under rubble or feeling the earth shudder beneath me as the windows rattle ominously. I know it has to do with the fact that every day we relive a little bit of the war—on television, on the radio, on the internet. I'm seeing some of the images for the very first time because we didn't have electricity last year during the war and it really is painful. It's hard to believe that we lived through so much . . . **posted by river @ 9:35 PM**

Wednesday, April 07, 2004

TEAPOTS AND KETTLES . . .

Now it seems we are almost literally reliving the first few days of occupation . . . I woke up to the sound of explosions and gunfire last night and for one terrible moment I thought someone had warped me back a whole year and we would have to relive this last year of our life over and over again . . .

We haven't sent the kids to school for 3 days. The atmosphere is charged and the day before yesterday, Baghdad was quiet and empty, almost . . . the calm before the storm. The area of A'adhamiya in Baghdad is seeing street fighting: the resistance and Americans are fighting out in the streets and Al Sadr city was bombed by the troops. They say that dozens were killed and others wounded. They're bringing them in to hospitals in the center of the city.

Falloojeh has been cut off from the rest of Iraq for the last three days. It's terrible. They've been bombing it constantly and there are dozens dead. Yesterday they said that the only functioning hospital in the city was hit by the Americans and there's nowhere to take the wounded except a meager clinic that can hold up to 10 patients at a time. There are over a hundred wounded and dying and there's nowhere to bury the dead because the Americans control the area surrounding the only graveyard in Falloojeh; the bodies are beginning to decompose in the April heat. The troops won't let anyone out of Falloojeh and they won't let anyone into it either—the people are going to go hungry in a matter of days because most of the fresh produce is brought from outside of the city. We've been trying to call a friend who lives there for three days and we can't contact him.

This is supposed to be "retaliation" for what happened last week with the American contractors—if they were indeed contractors. Whoever they were, it was gruesome and wrong . . . I feel for their families. Was I surprised? Hardly. This is an occupation and for those of you naïve enough to actually believe Chalabi and the Bush administration when they said the troops were going to be "greeted with flowers and candy" then I can only wish that God will, in the future, grant you wisdom.

This is crazy. This is supposed to be punishment for violence but it's only going to result in more bloodshed on both sides . . . people are outraged everywhere—Sunnis and Shi'a alike. This constant bombing is only going to make things worse for everyone. Why do Americans think that people in Baghdad or the south or north aren't going care what happens in Falloojeh or Ramadi or Nassriyah or Najaf? Would Americans in New York disregard bombing and killing in California?

And now Moqtada Al-Sadr's people are also fighting it out in parts of Baghdad and the south. If the situation weren't so frightening, it would almost be amusing to see Al-Hakeem and Bahr Ul Iloom describe Al-Sadr as an "extremist" and a "threat." Moqtada Al-Sadr is no better and no worse than several extremists we have sitting on the Governing Council. He's just as willing to ingratiate himself to Bremer as Al-Hakeem and Bahr Ul Iloom. The only difference is that he wasn't given the opportunity, so now he's a revolutionary. Apparently, someone didn't give Bremer the memo about how when you pander to one extremist, you have to pander to them all. Hearing Abdul Aziz Al-Hakeem and Bahr Ul Iloom claim that Al-Sadr is a threat to security and stability brings about visions of the teapot and the kettle . . .

Then Bremer makes an appearance on tv and says that armed militias will *not* be a part of the New Iraq . . . where has that declaration been the last 12 months while Badir's Brigade has been wreaking havoc all over the country? Why not just solve the problem of Al-Sadr's armed militia by having them join the police force and army, like the Bayshmarga and Badir's Brigade?! Al-Sadr's militia is old news. No one was bothering them while they were terrorizing civilians in the south. They wore badges, carried Klashnikovs and roamed the streets freely . . . now that they've become a threat to the "Coalition," they suddenly become "terrorists" and "agitators."

Now there's an arrest warrant with his name on it, although the Minister of Justice was on tv claiming he knew nothing about the arrest warrant, etc. He basically said that he was washing his hands of any move against Moqtada Al-Sadr. Don't get me wrong—I'd love to see Moqtada behind bars, but it will only cause more chaos and rage. It's much too late for that . . . he has been cultivating support for too long. It's like a contest now between the prominent Shi'a clerics. The people are dissatisfied—especially in the south. The clerics who weren't given due consideration and a position on the Governing Council are now looking for influence and support through the people. You can either be a good little cleric and get along with Bremer (but have a lot of dissatisfied people *not* supporting you) or you can be a firebrand cleric and rally the masses . . .

It's like the first few days of occupation again . . . it's a nightmare and everyone is tense. My cousin and his family are staying with us for a few days because his wife hates to be alone at home with the kids. It's a relief to have them with us. We all sit glued to the television—flipping between Al-Jazeera, Al-Arabia, CNN, BBC and LBC, trying to figure out what is going on. The foreign news channels are hardly showing anything. They punctuate dazzling reportages on football games and family pets with a couple of minutes worth of footage from Iraq showing the same faces running around in a frenzy of bombing and gunfire and then talk about "Al-Sadr the firebrand cleric," not mentioning the attacks by the troops in Ramadi, Falloojeh, Nassriyah, Baghdad, Koufa, etc.

Over the last three days, over 150 Iraqis have been killed by troops all over Iraq and it's maddening. At times I feel like a caged animal—there's so much frustration and anger. The only people still raving about "liberation" are the Iraqis affiliated with the Governing Council and the Puppets, and even they are getting impatient with the mess.

Our foreign minister Hoshyar Zibari was being interviewed by some British journalist yesterday, making excuses for Tony Blair and commending him on the war. At one point someone asked him about the current situation in Iraq. He mumbled something about how there were "problems" but it wasn't a big deal because Iraq was "stable" . . . what Iraq is he living in?

And as I blog this, all the mosques, Sunni and Shi'a alike, are calling for Jihad . . . **posted by river @ 3:44 PM**

Friday, April 09, 2004

OCCUPATION DAY —APRIL 9, 2003

The last few days, I've been sorely trying to avoid a trip down memory lane. I flip the channel every time they show shots of Baghdad up in flames, I turn off the radio as they begin to talk about the first few days of occupation, and I quietly leave the room as family members begin, "Remember how . . ." No, I don't *want* to remember some of the worst days of my life. I wish there was some way one could selectively delete certain memories as one does files on a computer . . . however, that's impossible.

Today, I'm letting my mind wander back to last April quite freely. April 9, 2003 in particular. The day our darling Puppet Council has chosen to represent [as] our "National Day" . . . the day the occupation became not a possibility, but a definite reality.

The day began with heavy bombing. I remember waking up at 5 AM to a huge explosion. The hair almost stood on my head. We were all sleeping in the living room because the drapes were heavy and offered some small security against shattering glass. E. instantly jumped up and ran to make sure the Klashnikov was loaded properly and I tried to cover my cousin's children better with the heavy blankets. The weather was already warm, but the blankets would protect the kids against glass. Their older daughter was, luckily, still sound asleep—lost in a dream or nightmare. The younger one lay in the semi-dark, with eyes wide open. I sensed her trying to read my face for some small reassurance . . . I smiled tightly, "Go back to sleep . . . "

After a few more colossal explosions, we all knew sleep would be useless. It was still too early for breakfast and no one was in the mood anyway. My mother and I got up to check the bags we had packed by the door. We had packed the bags during the first few days of war . . . they contained some sturdy clothes, bottles of water, important documents (like birth certificates and ID papers), and some spare money. They were to remain by the door in case the ceiling came crashing down or the American tanks came plowing through the neighborhood. In either case, we were given specific instructions to run for the door and take out the bags, "Don't wait for anyone—just run and take the bags with you . . ." came the orders.

Our area was one of the more volatile areas. We had helicopters hovering above, fighter planes and explosions. An area just across the main street had been invaded by tanks and we could hear the gun shots and tanks all night. My mother stood, unsure, at the window, trying to see the street. Were we supposed to evacuate? Were we supposed to stay in the house and wait? What was going to happen? E. and my cousin volunteered to ask the neighbors their plans.

They came back 5 minutes later. E. was pale and my cousin looked grim. Everyone on our street was in the same quandary—what was to be done? E. said that while there were a few men in the streets in our immediate area, the rest of Baghdad seemed almost empty. We negotiated leaving the house and heading for my uncle's home on the other side of Baghdad, but my cousin said that that would be impossible—the roads were all blocked, the bridges were cut off by American tanks and even if we were lucky enough to get anywhere near my uncle's area, we risked being shot by a tank or helicopter. No, we would wait it out at home.

My cousin's wife was wide awake by then. She sat in the middle of her two children and held them close on either side. She hadn't spoken to her parents in almost a week now . . . there were no telephones to contact them and there was no way to get to their area. She was beyond terrified at this crucial point . . . she was certain that they were all dead or dying and the only thing that seemed to be keeping her functioning was the presence of her two young daughters.

At that point, my mind was numb. All I could do was react to the explosions—flinch when one was particularly powerful, and automatically say a brief prayer of thanks when another was further away. Every once in a while, my brain would clear enough to do some mindless chore, like fill the water pots or fold the blankets, but otherwise, I felt numb.

It was almost noon when the explosions calmed somewhat and I risked going outside for a few moments. The planes were freely coming and going and, along with the sound of distant gunshots, only they pierced the eerie silence. My mother joined me outside a few minutes later and stood next to me under a small olive tree.

"In case we have to leave, there are some things I want to be sure you know . . . " she said, and I nodded vaguely, studying a particularly annoying plane we were calling "buggeh" or "bug," as it made the sound of a mosquito while it flew. We later learned it was a "surveyor" plane that scanned certain areas for resistance or Iraqi troops.

"The documents in the bag contain the papers for the house, the car . . . " I was alert. I turned to her and asked, "But why are you telling me this—you know I know. We packed the stuff together . . . and *you* know everything anyway . . . " She nodded assent but added, "Well, I just want to be sure . . . in case something happens . . . if we . . . "

"You mean if we get separated for some reason?" I finished quickly. "Yes, if we get separated . . . fine. You have to know where everything is and what it is . . ." By then, I was fighting hard against tears. I swallowed with difficulty and concentrated harder on the planes above. I wondered how many parents and kids were having this very same conversation today. She continued talking for a few moments and seemed to introduce a new and terrible possibility that I hadn't dared to think about all this time—life after death. Not eternal life after death—that was nothing new—but the possibility of *our* life, mine and E.'s, after *their* death.

During the war, the possibility of death was a constant. There were moments when I was sure we'd all be dead in a matter of seconds—especially during the horrific "shock and awe" period. But I always took it for granted that we'd all die together—as a family. We'd either survive together or die together . . . it was always that simple. This new possibility was one I refused to think about.

As we sat there, she talking, and I retreating further and further into the nightmare of words, there was a colossal explosion that made the windows rattle, and even seemed to shake the sturdy trees in the little garden. I jumped, relieved to hear that sound for the very first time in my life . . . it was the end of that morbid conversation and all I could think was, "saved by the bomb."

We spent the rest of the day listening to the battery-powered radio and trying to figure out what was happening around us. We heard stories from the neighbors about a massacre in A'adhamiya—the Americans were shooting right and left, deaths and looting in the south . . . The streets were unsafe and the only people risking them were either the people seeking refuge in other areas, or the looters who began to descend on homes, schools, universities, museums and governmental buildings and institutions like a group of vultures on the carcass of a freshly dead lion.

Day faded into night . . . the longest day of my life. The day we sensed that the struggle in Baghdad was over and the fear of war was nothing compared to the new fear we were currently facing. It was the day I saw my first American tank roll grotesquely down the streets of Baghdad—through a residential neighborhood.

And that was April 9 for me and millions of others. There are thousands who weren't so lucky—they lost loved ones on April 9 . . . to guns and tanks and Apaches . . . and the current Governing Council want us to remember April 9 fondly and hail it our "National Day" . . . a day of victory . . . but whose victory? And whose nation? **posted by river @ 4:28 PM**

ONE YEAR LATER —APRIL 9, 2004

April 9, 2004

Today, the day the Iraqi Puppets hail "National Day," will mark the day of the "Falloojeh Massacre" . . . Bremer has called for a truce and ceasefire in Falloojeh very recently and claimed that the bombing will stop, but the bombing continues as I write this. Over 300 are dead in Falloojeh and they have taken to burying the dead in the town football field because they aren't allowed near the cemetery. The bodies are decomposing in the heat and the people are struggling to bury them as quickly as they arrive. The football field that once supported running, youthful feet and cheering fans has turned into a mass grave holding men, women and children.

The people in Falloojeh have been trying to get the women and children out of the town for the last 48 hours but all the roads out of the city are closed by the Americans and refugees are being shot at and bombed on a regular basis . . . we're watching the television and crying. The hospital is overflowing with victims . . . those who have lost arms and legs . . . those who have lost loved ones. There isn't enough medicine or bandages . . . what are the Americans doing?! This is collective punishment . . . is this the solution to the chaos we're living in? Is this the "hearts and minds" part of the campaign?

A convoy carrying food, medication, blood and doctors left for Falloojeh yesterday, hoping to get in and help the people in there. Some people from our neighborhood were gathering bags of flour and rice to take into the town. E. and I rummaged the house from top to bottom and came up with a big sack of flour, a couple of smaller bags of rice, a few kilos of assorted dry lentil, chickpeas, etc. We were really hoping the trucks could get through to help out in the city. Unfortunately, I just spoke with an Iraqi doctor who told me that the whole convoy was denied entry . . . it seems that now they are trying to get the women and children out or at least the very sick and wounded.

The south isn't much better . . . the casualties are rising and there's looting and chaos. There's an almost palpable anger in Baghdad. The faces are grim and sad all at once and there's a feeling of helplessness that can't be described in words. It's like being held under water and struggling for the unattainable surface—seeing all this destruction and devastation.

Firdaws Square, the place where the statue was brought down, is off-limits because the Americans fear angry mobs and demonstrations . . . but it doesn't matter because people are sticking to their homes. The kids haven't been to school for several days now and even the universities are empty. The situation in Baghdad feels very unstable and the men in the neighborhood are talking of a neighborhood watch again—just like the early days of occupation.

Where are the useless Governing Council? Why isn't anyone condemning the killings in the south and in Falloojeh?! Why aren't they sitting down that fool Bremer and telling him that this is wrong, wrong, wrong, wrong??? If one of them were half a man or even half a human, they would threaten to resign their posts if there isn't an immediate ceasefire . . . the people are enraged. This latest situation proves that they aren't Iraqi—they aren't here for the welfare of the Iraqi people.

The American and European news stations don't show the dying Iraqis . . . they don't show the women and children bandaged and bleeding—the mother looking for some sign of her son in the middle of a puddle of blood and dismembered arms and legs . . . they don't show you the hospitals overflowing with the dead and dying because they don't want to hurt American feelings . . . but people *should* see it. You should see the price of your war and occupation—it's unfair that the Americans are fighting a war thousands of kilometers from home. They get their dead in neat, tidy caskets draped with a flag and we have to gather and scrape our dead off of the floors and hope the American shrapnel and bullets left enough to make a definite identification . . .

One year later, and Bush has achieved what he wanted—this day will go down in history and in the memory of all Iraqis as one of the bloodiest days ever . . .   **posted by river @ 4:32 PM**

Sunday, April 11, 2004

ONE OF THOSE COUNTRIES . . .

We've taken to sleeping in the living room again. We put up the heavy drapes the day before yesterday and E. and I re-taped the windows looking out into the garden. This time, I made them use the clear tape so that the view wouldn't be marred with long, brown strips of tape. We sleep in the living room because it is the safest room in the house and the only room that will hold the whole family comfortably.

The preparations for sleep begin at around 10 p.m. on days when we have electricity and somewhat earlier on dark nights. E. and I have to drag out the mats, blankets and pillows and arrange them creatively on the floor so that everyone is as far away from the windows as possible, without actually being crowded.

. . .

Baghdad is calm and relatively quiet if you don't count the frequent explosions. Actually, when we don't hear explosions, it gets a
bit worrying. I know that sounds strange but it's like this—you know
how you see someone holding a rifle or gun and aiming at something,
ready to fire? You cringe and tense up while waiting for the gunshot
and keep thinking, "It's coming, it's coming . . . ." That's how it feels
on a morning without explosions. Somehow, you just *know* there are
going to be explosions . . . it's only a matter of time. Hearing them is
a relief and you can loosen up after they occur and hope that they'll
be the last of the day.

The hostage situations are a mess. I watch television and it feels
like I'm watching another country. All I can think is, "We've become
one of *those* countries . . . " You know—the ones where hostages
are taken on a daily basis and governments warn their civilians of visiting or entering the country. It's especially sad because even during
those long years during the blockade and in between wars and bombings, there were never any attacks on foreigners. Iraqis are hospitable,
friendly people who always used to treat foreigners with care . . . now,
everyone is treated like a potential enemy.

The case of the Japanese hostages is especially sad—I'm so
sorry for their families and friends specifically, and the Japanese
people in general. We keep hearing conflicting reports about their situation. This morning I heard that the kidnappers agreed to free them
but someone else told me that it was just a rumor . . . it's so hard to
tell. It's heart-breaking to see them on television and I wish there was
something that could be done. Will the Japanese government pull out
the troops? Not likely . . . three people won't matter to them. I hope
they come out of this alive and well and I hope they don't hold a
grudge against Iraqis. There's hostility towards Japan because of the
fact that they sent soldiers . . . Japan became one of "them" when
they decided to send over troops and these are the consequences. I'm
so sorry . . . in spite of the fact that dozens of Iraqis are abducted and
killed each day, I'm really sorry.

They say around 600 Iraqis were killed in Falloojeh—120 children and 200 women . . . it's an atrocity and horribly sad. They have
let one or two convoys in and the rest were sent back. The refugees
from the area are flowing into Baghdad and it's horrible to see them.

Women and children with tear-stained faces, mostly in black, carry-ing bundles of clothes and bottles of water. The mosques are gather-ing food and clothes for them . . . one of the storage areas for the refugee stuff was hit by an American tank today in A'adhamiya and the scene is chaotic . . . scattered food, medication, bandages, blan-kets, etc.

The south is a bit calmer because of the "Arba'een" of the Imam Hussein which will last for a couple of days . . . no one knows what will happen after. **posted by river @ 5:56 PM**

Wednesday, April 14, 2004

MEDIA AND FALLOOJEH . . .

There has been a lot of criticism about the way Al-Arabia and Al-Jazeera were covering the riots and fighting in Falloojeh and the south this last week. Some American spokesman for the military was ranting about the "spread of anti-Americanism" through networks like the abovementioned.

Actually, both networks did a phenomenal job of covering the attacks on Falloojeh and the southern provinces. Al-Jazeera had their reporter literally embedded in the middle of the chaos—and I don't mean the lame embedded western journalists type of thing they had going at the beginning of the war (you know—embedded in the Green Zone and embedded in Kuwait, etc.). Ahmed Mansur, I believe his name was, was actually standing there, in the middle of the bomb-ing, shouting to be heard over the F-16s and helicopters blasting away at houses and buildings. It brought back the days of "shock and awe" . . .

I know it bothers the CPA terribly to have the corpses of dead Iraqis shown on television. They would love for Al-Jazeera and Al-Ara-bia to follow Al-Hurra's example and show endless interviews with pro-occupation Iraqis living abroad and speaking in stilted Arabic. These interviews, of course, are interspersed with translated documentaries on the many marvels of . . . Hollywood. And while I, personally, am very interested in the custom leather interiors of the latest Audi, I couldn't seem to draw myself away from Al-Jazeera and Al-Arabia while 700+ Iraqis were being killed.

To lessen the feelings of anti-Americanism, might I make a few suggestions? Stop the collective punishment. When Mark Kimmett stutters through a press conference babbling about "precision weapons" and "military targets" in Falloojeh, who is he kidding? Falloojeh is a small city made up of low, simple houses, little shops and mosques. Is he implying that the 600 civilians who died during the bombing and the thousands injured and maimed were all "insurgents?" Are houses, shops and mosques now military targets?

What I'm trying to say is that we don't need news networks to make us angry or frustrated. All you need to do is talk to one of the Falloojeh refugees making their way tentatively into Baghdad; look at the tear-stained faces, the eyes glazed over with something like shock. In our neighborhood alone there are at least 4 families from Falloojeh who have come to stay with family and friends in Baghdad. The stories they tell are terrible and grim and it's hard to believe that they've gone through so much.

I think western news networks are far too tame. They show the Hollywood version of war—strong troops in uniform, hostile Iraqis being captured and made to face "justice" and the White House turkey posing with the Thanksgiving turkey . . . which is just fine. But what about the destruction that comes with war and occupation? What about the death? I don't mean just the images of dead Iraqis scattered all over, but dead Americans too. People should *have* to see those images. Why is it not ok to show dead Iraqis and American troops in Iraq, but it's fine to show the catastrophe of September 11 over and over again? I wish every person who emails me supporting the war, safe behind their computer, secure in their narrow mind and fixed views, could actually come and experience the war live. I wish they could spend just 24 hours in Baghdad today and hear Mark Kimmett talk about the death of 700 "insurgents" like it was a proud day for Americans everywhere . . .

Still, when I hear talk about "anti-Americanism" it angers me. Why does America identify itself with its military and government? Why does being anti-Bush and anti-occupation have to mean that a person is anti-American? We watch American movies, listen to everything from Britney Spears to Nirvana and refer to every single brown, fizzy drink as "Pepsi."

I hate American foreign policy and its constant meddling in the region . . . I hate American tanks in Baghdad and American soldiers on our streets and in our homes on occasion . . . why does that mean that I hate America and Americans? Are tanks, troops and violence the only face of America? If the Pentagon, Department of Defense and Condi are "America," then yes—I hate America. **posted by river @ 8:10 PM**

Friday, April 23, 2004

I JUST CAN'T EXPLAIN . . .

I haven't written for the last week or so because I simply haven't felt like it. It sometimes feels like homework and I actually end up feeling guilty when I don't write. I avoid looking at the computer because it sometimes seems to look back at me rebukingly, wondering why I haven't been blogging or at least checking my emails. The truth is that there's so much going on around us that I can't even begin to try to summarize it into a meagrer blog. The current situation in the south and the supposed truce in Falloojeh has me worried and angry all at once. There's nothing that can describe the current feeling in the air . . . it's like that Morrissey song:

Now my heart is full
Now my heart is full
And I just can't explain
So I won't even try to

There's a sort of truce going on in Falloojeh but the problem is that we still hear of people being killed on both sides and areas being bombed in the city. The refugees are still in Baghdad and neighboring cities. We heard that, for a couple of days, the troops were letting in around 80 families a day—now that number seems to have dwindled to 15 families a day. The refugees seem anxious to get back to their homes and many of them left behind family members in the city.

The situation in the south, especially Karbala, is also worrisome. There are stories of clashes between troops and Al-Sadr's militia. There have also been explosions in Basra and Baghdad but they hardly register on the news anymore. Iraqis take it in stride along with dust storms, blackouts and mosquitos. It has become a part of life and one simply has to find a way to live around it, just as one finds a way around American road blocks and concrete walls that are rising ever higher.

There is a sort of muggy, heavy heat lately. It's not the usual dry Iraqi heat that we're accustomed to. It's more of a moist, clammy heat that feels almost solid. The electrical situation is still quite bad in many areas. We're on a schedule of 3 hours of electricity and then three hours of darkness. While it was tolerable during the cool winter months, the hellish summer months promise to be torture.

I think I'll blog some more tomorrow . . . just wanted to tell all those concerned that I'm ok—I'm alive and I definitely have more to say.   **posted by river @ 10:10 PM**

Monday, April 26, 2004

OF CHALABI, FLAGS AND ANTHEMS . . .

There are two different kinds of strain. There's the physical strain of carrying 40 pails of water up and down the stairs to fill the empty water tank on the roof—after the 4th or 5th pail of water, you can literally see your muscles quivering under your skin and without the bucket of water, your arms somehow feel weightless—almost nonexistent. Then there's mental strain . . . that is when those forty buckets of water are being emptied in your head and there's a huge flow of thoughts and emotions that threaten to overwhelm you.

I think everyone I know is suffering from that mental strain. You can see it in the eyes and hear it in the taut voices that threaten to break with the burden of emotion. We're all watching things carefully and trying to focus on leading semi-normal lives all at once. The situation in the south seems to be deteriorating and we hear of fresh new deaths every day. Fighting has broken out in Falloojeh again and I'm not quite sure what has happened to the ceasefire. It's hard to know just what is going on. There's a sense of collective exhaustion in the air.

I've been reading articles about Chalabi being (very hopefully) on his way out. I can't believe it took this long for Washington to come to the conclusion that he is completely useless. Did anyone there actually believe he was going to be greeted as the leader of a new era? We were watching him carefully during the last few weeks, trying to see what he would do or say during the attacks on Falloojeh and all the fighting in the south. That was a crucial time . . . we were waiting for some reaction from the Puppets—any reaction. Some condemning words . . . some solidarity with the Iraqis being killed and left homeless and there was a strange sort of silence. One of them threatened to step down, but that was only after outraged Iraqis showed an inclination to eat them alive if something wasn't done about the situation . . .

Chalabi has only lately ventured out from under his rock (in the usual flashy tie) to cry out that Lakhdhar Il Braheimi, the special UN representative sent by Kofi to check out the possibility of elections, is completely and totally biased against Shi'a. So now Chalabi seems to consider himself a champion of Shi'a everywhere in Iraq. The amusing thing about this is the fact that, apparently, no one has told Chalabi that he has become the joke of the Shi'a community. We (Sunnis and Shi'a) tease each other with things like, "So . . . the Shi'a man of the moment is Chalabi, ah?!" and the phrase is usually received with an indignant outcry and a comparison of the man of the moment to . . . Britney Spears, for example.

I stare at him when he gives his speeches on television and cringe with the thought that someone out there could actually have thought he was representative of any faction of Iraqi society. I can hardly believe that he was supposed to be the one to target the Iraqi intellectuals and secularists. He's the tasteless joke Bush and Co. sent along with the soldiers and tanks to promote democracy—rather like one of those plastic blowup dolls teenage boys practice dancing with before the prom.

I also heard today that the Puppets are changing the flag. It looks nothing like the old one and at first I was angry and upset, but then I realized that it wouldn't make a difference. The Puppets are illegitimate, hence their constitution is null and void and their flag is theirs alone. It is as representative of Iraq as they are—it might as well have "Made in America" stitched along the inside seam. It can be their flag and every time we see it, we'll see Chalabi et al. against its pale white background.

My email buddy and fellow Iraqi S.A. in America said it best in her email, "I am sure we are all terribly excited about the extreme significance of the adoption by the completely illegitimate Iraq Puppet Council of a new national piece of garishly colored cloth. Of course the design of the new national rag was approved by the always tastefully dressed self-declared counter terrorism expert viceroy of Iraq, Paul Bremer, who is well known for wearing expensive hand-stitched combat boots with thousand dollar custom tailored suits and silk designer ties.

"The next big piece of news will be the new pledge of allegiance to said national rag, and the empire for which it stands. The American author of said pledge has yet to be announced."

For the coming national anthem, may I suggest Chalabi, Allawi, Hakeem and Talabani in a gaudy, Iraqi version of "Lady Marmalade?"
posted by river @ 11:37 PM

Friday, April 30, 2004

THOSE PICTURES . . .

The pictures are horrific. I felt a multitude of things as I saw them . . . the most prominent feeling was rage, of course. I had this incredible desire to break something—like that would make things somehow better or ease the anger and humiliation. We've been hearing terrible stories about Abu Ghraib Prison in Baghdad for a while now, but those pictures somehow spoke like no words could.

"Shock, outrage over prison photos," cnn.com, May 1, 2004
http://www.cnn.com/2004/WORLD/meast/04/30/iraq.photos/

Photographs showing the apparent abuse of Iraqi prisoners by both American and British troops have been greeted with shock and outrage worldwide . . .

> The photographs of alleged abuse by U.S. soldiers, which were first broadcast Wednesday on CBS' "60 Minutes II" in the United States, were shown Friday by Arab television networks . . .
>
> The U.S. military said six U.S. soldiers have been charged with abusing inmates at Abu Ghurayb prison, which was infamous under Saddam Hussein's reign . . .
>
> CBS said it has dozens of pictures purportedly showing a range of abuses.
>
> Some of the images published on one London, England-based newspaper's Web site show naked, hooded prisoners. In one, a male and a female soldier smile as they pose with prisoners.
>
> One picture shows what is apparently an Iraqi prisoner standing on a box with his head covered and wires attached to his hands . . .

Seeing those naked, helpless, hooded men was like being slapped in the face with an ice cold hand. I felt ashamed looking at them— like I was seeing something I shouldn't be seeing and all I could think was, "I might know one of those faceless men . . . " I might have passed him in the street or worked with him. I might have bought groceries from one of them or sat through a lecture they gave in college . . . any of them might be a teacher, gas station attendant or engineer . . . any one of them might be a father or grandfather . . . each and every one of them is a son and possibly a brother. And people wonder at what happened in Falloojeh a few weeks ago when those Americans were killed and dragged through the streets . . .

All anyone can talk about today are those pictures . . . those terrible pictures. There is so much rage and frustration. I know the dozens of emails I'm going to get claiming that this is an "isolated incident" and that they are "ashamed of the people who did this" but does it matter? What about those people in Abu Ghraib? What about their families and the lives that have been forever damaged by the experience in Abu Ghraib? I know the messages that I'm going to get—the ones that say, "But this happened under Saddam . . . " Like somehow, that makes what happens now OK . . . like whatever was suffered in the past should make any mass graves, detentions and torture only minor inconveniences now. I keep thinking of M. and how she was "lucky" indeed. And you know what? You won't hear half of the atrocities and stories because Iraqis are proud, indignant people and sexual abuse is not a subject anyone is willing to come forward with. The atrocities in Abu Ghraib and other places will be hidden away and buried under all the other dirt the occupation brought with it . . .

It's beyond depressing and humiliating . . . my blood boils at the thought of what must be happening to the female prisoners. To see those smiling soldiers with the Iraqi prisoners is horrible. I hope they are made to suffer . . . somehow I know they won't be punished. They'll be discharged from the army, at best, and made to go back home and join families and cronies who will drink to the pictures and the way "America's finest" treated those "Dumb I-raki terrorists." That horrible excuse of a human, [Brigadier General] Janis Karpinski, will then write a book about how her father molested her as a child and her mother drank herself into an early death—that's why she did what she did in Abu Ghraib. It makes me sick.

Where is the Governing Council? Where are they hiding now?

I want something done about it and I want it done publicly. I want those horrible soldiers who were responsible for this to be publicly punished and humiliated. I want them to be condemned and identified as the horrible people they are. I want their children and their children's children to carry on the story of what was done for a long time—as long as those prisoners will carry along with them the humiliation and pain of what was done and as long as the memory of those pictures remains in Iraqi hearts and minds . . . **posted by river @ 11:03 PM**

Friday, May 07, 2004

JUST GO . . .

People are seething with anger—the pictures of Abu Ghraib and the Brits in Basrah are everywhere. Every newspaper you pick up in Baghdad has pictures of some American or British atrocity or another. It's like a nightmare that has come to life.

Everyone knew this was happening in Abu Ghraib and other places . . . seeing the pictures simply made it all more real and tangible somehow. American and British politicians have the audacity to come on television with words like, "True the people in Abu Ghraib are criminals, but . . . " Everyone here in Iraq knows that there are thousands of innocent people detained. Some were simply in the wrong place at the wrong time, while others were detained "under suspicion." In the New Iraq, it's "guilty until proven innocent by some miracle of God."

People are so angry. There's no way to explain the reactions—even pro-occupation Iraqis find themselves silenced by this latest horror. I can't explain how people feel—or even how I personally feel. Somehow, pictures of dead Iraqis are easier to bear than this grotesque show of American military technique. People would rather be dead than sexually abused and degraded by the animals running Abu Ghraib prison.

There was a time when people here felt sorry for the troops. No matter what one's attitude was towards the occupation, there were moments of pity towards the troops, regardless of their nationality. We would see them suffering the Iraqi sun, obviously wishing they were somewhere else and somehow, that vulnerability made them seem less monstrous and more human. That time has passed. People look at troops now and see the pictures of Abu Ghraib . . . and we burn with shame and anger and frustration at not being able to do something. Now that the world knows that the torture has been going on since the very beginning, do people finally understand what happened in Falloojeh?

I'm avoiding the internet because it feels like the pictures are somehow available on every site I visit. I'm torn between wishing they weren't there and feeling, somehow, that it's important that the whole world sees them. The thing, I guess, that bothers me most is that the children can see it all. How do you explain the face of the American soldier, leering over the faceless, naked bodies to a child? How do you explain the sick, twisted minds? How do you explain what is happening to a seven-year-old?

There have been demonstrations in Baghdad and other places. There was a large demonstration outside of the Abu Ghraib prison itself. The families of some of the inmates of the prison were out there protesting the detentions and the atrocities . . . faces streaked with tears of rage and brows furrowed with anxiety. Each and every one of those people was wondering what their loved ones had suffered inside the walls of the hell that makes Guantanamo look like a health spa.

And through all this, Bush gives his repulsive speeches. He makes an appearance on Arabic tv channels looking sheepish and attempting to look sincere, babbling on about how this "incident" wasn't representative of the American people or even the army, regardless of the fact that it's been going on for so long. He asks Iraqis to not let these pictures reflect on their attitude towards the American people . . . and yet when the bodies were dragged through the streets of Falloojeh, the American troops took it upon themselves to punish the whole city.

He's claiming it's a "stain on our country's honor" ("Bush Apologizes, Calls Abuse "Stain" on Nation" Washington Post, May 7, 2004, http://www.washingtonpost.com/ac2/wp-dyn?pagename=article&contentId=A6866-2004May6&notFound=true) . . . I think not. The stain on your country's honor, Bush dear, was the one on the infamous blue dress that made headlines while Clinton was in the White House . . . this isn't a "stain" this is a catastrophe. Your credibility was gone the moment you stepped into Iraq and couldn't find the WMD . . . your reputation never existed.

So are the atrocities being committed in Abu Ghraib really not characteristic of the American army? What about the atrocities committed by Americans in Guantanamo? And Afghanistan? I won't bother bringing up the sordid past, let's just focus on the present. It seems that torture and humiliation are common techniques used in countries blessed with the American presence. The most pathetic excuse I heard so far was that the American troops weren't taught the fundamentals of human rights mentioned in the Geneva Convention . . . Right—morals, values and compassion have to be taught.

All I can think about is the universal outrage when the former government showed pictures of American POWs on television, looking frightened and unsure about their fate. I remember the outcries from American citizens, claiming that Iraqis were animals for showing "America's finest" fully clothed and unharmed. So what does this make Americans now?

We heard about it all . . . we heard stories since the very beginning of the occupation about prisoners being made to sit for several hours on their knees . . . being deprived of sleep for days at a time by being splashed with cold water or kicked or slapped . . . about the infamous "red rooms" where prisoners are kept for prolonged periods of time . . . about the rape, the degradations, the emotional and physical torture . . . and there were moments when I actually wanted to believe that what we heard was exaggerated. I realize now that it was only a small fragment of the truth. There is nothing that is going to make this "better." Nothing.

Through all of this, where is the Governing Council? Under what rock are the Puppets hiding? Why is no one condemning this? What does Bremer have to say for himself and for the Americans? Why this unbearable silence?

I don't understand the "shock" Americans claim to feel at the lurid pictures. You've seen the troops break down doors and terrify women and children . . . curse, scream, push, pull and throw people to the ground with a boot over their head. You've seen troops shoot civilians in cold blood. You've seen them bomb cities and towns. You've seen them burn cars and humans using tanks and helicopters. Is this latest debacle so very shocking or appalling?

The number of killings in the south has also risen. The Americans and British are saying that they are "insurgents" and people who are a part of Al-Sadir's militia, but people from Najaf are claiming that innocent civilians are being killed on a daily basis. Today the troops entered Najaf and there was fighting in the streets. This is going to cause a commotion because Najaf is considered a holy city and is especially valuable to Shi'a all over the world. The current situation in the south makes one wonder who, now, is going to implement a no-fly zone over areas like Falloojeh and Najaf to "protect" the people this time around?

I sometimes get emails asking me to propose solutions or make suggestions. Fine. Today's lesson: don't rape, don't torture, don't kill and get out while you can—while it still looks like you have a choice . . . Chaos? Civil war? Bloodshed? We'll take our chances—just take your Puppets, your tanks, your smart weapons, your dumb politicians, your lies, your empty promises, your rapists, your sadistic torturers and go. **posted by river @ 1:49 PM**

Saturday, May 15, 2004

LAST FEW DAYS . . .

That video of Nick Berg is beyond horrible. I haven't been able to watch it whole. It makes me sick to my stomach and I can hardly believe it happened. His family must be devastated and I can't even imagine what they must have felt. With all of this going on—first Abu Ghraib and now this, I haven't felt like writing anything.

Ansar Al Islam [is] a fundamentalist militant group—mostly Kurdish—based in the north of Iraq. They made a name for themselves recently and chose the Kurdish autonomous region as "home" with the full knowledge of the CIA, who had more control over the region than the former regime. Since the beginning of the war, they have been responsible for various explosions and attacks—or so they say. The beheading has nothing to do with Islam. I'm still hoping—albeit irrationally—that the whole thing was some sort of grotesque setup.

I was sick to my stomach when I first saw the video on some news channel and stood petrified, watching the screen and praying that they wouldn't show it whole because for some reason, I couldn't take my eyes off of it. I feel horrible. Was I shocked? Was I surprised? Hardly. We've been expecting this since the first pictures of the torture of Iraqi prisoners broke out. There's a certain rage in many people that is frightening. There's a certain hunger and need for revenge that lame apologies from Bush and surprise visits from Rumsfeld won't appease.

I think beheading was the chosen method of "execution" because the group wanted to shock Americans and Westerners in the worst possible way. The torturers at Abu Ghraib and other prisons chose sexual degradation because they knew that nothing would hurt and appall Iraqis and Muslims more than those horrible, sadistic acts. To Iraqis, death is infinitely better than being raped or sexually abused. There are things worse than death itself and those pictures portrayed them.

Foreigners in Iraq are being very, very careful and with good reason. Many of the companies have pulled out their staff and are asking the remaining workers and contractors to be extra careful and as inconspicuous as possible.

The assumption that Al Zarqawi himself was doing the beheading seems a little far-fetched. So now the heads of terrorism in the world seem to be Osama bin Laden, Aimen Al Dhawahiri and Abu Mussa'ab Al Zarqawi. Here's some food for thought—Ossama is from Saudi Arabia, Al Dhawahiri is Egyptian and Al Zarqawi is Jordanian. Which countries in the region are America's best allies? Let's see now . . . did you guess Saudi Arabia, Jordan and Egypt?! Fantastic! You win a trip to . . . Falloojeh!! (And no—it doesn't count if you give Saudi Arabia a little slap on the wrists and poke Egypt in the ribs—you're still buddies).

They let out around 300+ prisoners today while that sadistic fiend Rumsfeld was in town. Apparently, setting 300 prisoners free of the thousands currently detained is supposed to mollify Iraqis—quite like Bush's lame half-apology to King Abdallah of Jordan. What is King Abdallah to us? What does it matter if Bush gets down and begs him for forgiveness? What in God's name does he represent to the Iraqi people?

Karbala and Najaf in the south are war zones. There are Shi'a fighters in the streets and American tanks and helicopters are bombing certain areas. Today they bombed the oldest cemetery in Najaf (and one of the holiest in Iraq). It has caused quite an uproar and Al Sadr is currently calling for people to join him in the south. We are seeing another inflow of refugees into Baghdad . . . this time from the southern region. They are using the same tactics they used in Falloojeh on the "insurgency." So why was it an intifadhah, or popular uprising, in 1991 and now suddenly it's an insurgency? The people fighting in the streets of Najaf and Karbala aren't trained warriors or former regime members . . . they are simply people who are tired of empty promises and hollow assurances.

There are rumors that Badir's Brigade have been fighting alongside the Americans against Sadr's group and that doesn't bode well for SCIRI. The Puppets and spokespeople for the group have issued disclaimers but people sense that the Hakeems and Al-Da'awa leaders are eager to see Moqtada et al. crushed as soon as possible.

The end-of-the-year examinations have started in most of the schools. The school administrations are trying to get them over with as soon as humanly possible. It's already unbearably hot and dusty and the heat gets worse as summer progresses. Last year examinations were held in June and July and children were fainting in the summer heat in schools with no electricity. We're hoping to avoid that this year.

We're all donating money to the school in the area so they can remain hooked up to the local power generator during the day while the kids are being tested. You can see them in the streets and trapped behind car windows looking flushed and wilted. We're all praying that they'll be able to finish the year without anything drastic happening (well, relatively drastic).

The air feels stale and stagnant in Baghdad lately. There's disappointment and exhaustion and a certain resignation to the anger and fear that seem to have taken over during recent weeks. **posted by river @ 12:19 AM**

Saturday, May 22, 2004

EN KINT TEDRI . . .

Remember your first box of crayons? Probably not. Ok—remember your first box of REAL crayons—you know, not the silly eight colors, but the first real BIG box of crayons with four bewildering rows [of] colors and six different shades of brown that you never needed? Well, can you remember that mysterious color—burnt sienna—that was never brown enough for trees, and never really orange enough for flowers? That was the color of Chalabi's tie yesterday as he gave his phenomenal post-raid interview on Al-Arabia.

He sat, looking smug and supercilious, in a grayish suit with a tie that could only be described as "burnt sienna." During the duration of the interview, a silly little smile played on his thin lips and his eyes flashed with a combination of indignation and impatience at the questions.

I always enjoy a good Chalabi interview. His answers to questions are always so completely antagonistic to Iraqi public opinion that the whole thing makes a delightful show—rather like a vicious Chihuahua in the midst of a dozen bulldogs. There were several amusing moments during the interview. He kept waving around his arms and made numerous flourishing movements with his hands to emphasize some key points. A few interesting things I noted about the interview: he was suddenly using the word "occupation." During past interviews, he would never use the word "occupation." He used to insist on calling the invading army et al. "coalition" and the whole fiasco was persistently labeled a "liberation" by him and his cronies.

He made several insipid comments about the raid and his falling out with Bremer and the rest. My favorite comment was his "I've won the prize! I've won the Iraqi nationality prize . . ." Followed by a large grin (with several gaps between the teeth). The prize he was so proudly referring to was the disapproval of the CIA and "occupation." Apparently, he thinks that now that he has been blacklisted by the CPA, he will be enfolded by the tender arms of the Iraqi public. It's almost exhausting to see his endless optimism. At the same time, it's amazing to see his "about-face" regarding his American popularity. A few months ago, his value to the Bush administration was the personal achievement he was proudest of—he never failed to flaunt his American connections.

Of course, several things occurred to us, after hearing of the raid. The first thing I thought was, "Well, it's about time . . ." Then, as the news began to sink in, it made less sense. Chalabi was America's lapdog—why is he suddenly unsuitable for the new Iraq? He was convicted in Jordan several years ago and everyone knows he's a crook and a terrible politician . . . I'm also convinced that the Bush administration knew full well that he was highly unpopular in Iraq. He's not just a puppet—he's a mercenary. He encouraged the sanctions that killed hundreds of thousands of Iraqis and maimed the country itself. He supported the war and occupation vehemently and fabricated lies about weapons and threats to further his cause. He's a criminal—and a lousy one at that.

In the end, America had to know that Chalabi was virtually useless. Why this sudden change of heart towards Mercenary #1? People are saying that it is a ploy to help him rise in popularity, but I can hardly believe that. Could the decision-makers currently mulling over the Iraq situation be so ridiculously optimistic? Or could they have really been so wrong in the past? We have a saying in Arabic, "En kint tedri, fe tilk musseeba . . . in kint la tedri, fa il musseebatu a'adham" which means, "If you knew, then that was a catastrophe . . . and if you didn't know, then the catastrophe is greater."

Meanwhile, a couple of days ago, 40 people were murdered in western Iraq while they were celebrating a wedding—an American helicopter fired at the civilians, killing women and children. Apparently, the guests at the wedding were shooting klashnikovs into the air. You'd think that the Americans would know by now that shooting klashnikovs into the air is a form of celebration and considering the fact that the party was far from any major town or city, the shots were virtually harmless. No one did anything about the shots being fired when Saddam was caught—in spite of the fact that Baghdad was a virtual firestorm of bullets for several hours. That was ok—that was "acceptable" and even amusing to the "authorities." I can see how dozens of women, children and celebrating men would be a "threat" though. Yes, it makes perfect sense.

In a written statement the Pentagon said last night: "Our report is that this was not a wedding party, that these were anti-coalition forces that fired first . . . ("Wedding Party Massacre," The Guardian Unlimited, May 20, 2004, http://www.guardian.co.uk/Iraq/Story/0,2763, 1220750,00.html)

No. Of course not—it couldn't have been a wedding party. It was a resistance cell of women and children (one deviously dressed in a wedding gown!). It wasn't a wedding party just as mosques aren't mosques and hospitals are never hospitals when they are bombed. Celebrating women and children are not civilians. "Contractors" traveling with the American army to torture and kill Iraqis ARE civilians. CIA personnel are "civilians" and the people who planned and executed the war are all civilians. We're not civilians—we are insurgents, criminals and potential collateral damage. Check out mykeru.com to read some thought-provoking commentary on the whole sadistic incident.

Mykeru.com, http://www.mykeru.com/weekly/2004_0516_0522.html#052104, May 21, 2004

New details emerge in the wedding massacre at Ramadi which establish a gaping time interval between the wedding festivities and the American attack. According to news accounts in papers not approved by the American corporate media, naive and not-with-the-program enough to do some actual reporting, such as the Globe and Mail:

> Revellers at the wedding party said they began worrying when
> they heard aircraft overhead at about 9 p.m. With jets still over-
> head two hours later, they told the band to stop playing and
> everyone went to bed.
>
> The American attack came almost six hours later. You can read the
> accounts of this bloodbath yourself. I don't think I have to argue that
> blowing up women and children because lunatics, heavily armed
> lunatics, are in charge of the asylum is a bad thing. We should know
> that in this country, but the point seems to be lost in the midst of
> really pressing issues, such as American Idol voting scandals (unlike
> the real voting scandals that put the resident White House idiot in
> office) and, of course, Martha Stewart (not, oddly enough, Ken Lay).
> Go figure.

In conclusion, some words of advice to Chalabi—you are a mercenary
to be bought and sold . . . it's time to put you up on the market again
and hope for bidders. Get the car ready, make the trunk as comfortable as possible and head for the borders.   **posted by river @ 5:16 PM**

BACK IN IRAQ . . .

Chris Albritton is back in Iraq—check out his site. Check out his
reporting on the Chalabi debacle.

Back to Iraq, http://www.back-to-iraq.com/archives/000768.php
May 20, 2004

> By now, many of you know about the raid today on Ahmed Chalabi's
> house and two offices of the INC in Baghdad at about 9:30 a.m. local
> time. Some evidence and weapons were confiscated, senior Coalition
> officials said, and "several" people were arrested. There was no
> resistance, officials said, but footage after the raid showed that the
> place had been trashed.
>
> The official line is that this was an Iraqi police procedure, with
> search and arrest warrants handed down by an Iraqi judge after CPA
> head Paul Bremer referred an allegation 10 months ago to the Cen-
> tral Criminal Court of Iraq. The charges include fraud, kidnapping and
> "associated matters." (No expansion on that.) . . .

> *So if there was ever any doubt that Chalabi was now persona non grata with the Americans, today should dispel any confusion. First there was the bogus WMD information he peddled to the United States. Then it was his disastrous idea to Bremer to disband the Iraqi Army. Next, it was his seizure of tens of thousands of records from Saddam's era. He's involved in dozens of dirty little contracts and a corrupt oil-for-food investigation—Chalabi hand-picked the auditors!—may finally have caused the United States to cut the strings of its puppet/puppet-master . . .*

posted by river @ 5:23 PM

Tuesday, June 01, 2004

THE ROOF . . .

Hot. It's hot, hot, hot, hot.

The weather is almost stifling now. The air is heavy and dry with heat. By early noon, it's almost too hot to go outside. For every two hours of electricity, we have four hours of no electricity in our area— and several other areas. The problem now is that the generators in many areas are starting to break down due to constant use and the bad quality of the fuel. It's a big problem and it promises to grow as the summer progresses.

I have spent the last two days ruminating the political situation and . . . washing the roof. While the two activities are very different, they do share one thing in common—the roof, and political situation, are both a mess.

The roof of an Iraqi home is a sacred place. As much planning goes into it as almost anything else. The roofs are flat and often surrounded by a low wall on which one can lean and look out into the city. During this last year, a certain sort of special bond has formed between your typical Iraqi and the roof of his or her home. We run out to the roof to see where the smoke is coming from after an explosion; we gather on the roof to watch the helicopters flying over head; we reluctantly drag ourselves out to the roof to fill the water tanks when the water is low; we hang clothes to dry on the clotheslines strung out haphazardly across the roof; we sleep on the roof during the endless, powerless nights.

That last one, sleeping on the roof, was a tradition my parents once fondly talked about. They used to tell us endless stories about how, as children, they used to put out mats and low beds on the roof to sleep. There were no air-conditioners back then . . . sometimes not even ceiling fans. People had to be content with the hot Baghdad air and the energetic Baghdad mosquitos. Now my parents get to relive their childhood memories like never before because we've gone back a good fifty years. It's impossible to sleep inside of the house while the electricity is off. The darkness and heat descend upon you like a heavy black cloak and the mosquitos suddenly make a rush for any exposed bits of skin.

And so Riverbend and E. were sent to the roof a few days ago to do some cleaning.

We agreed to begin the cleaning process at dusk, half an hour after the harsh sun began its trip west. I met E. up on the roof, he holding a pail of luke-warm water and me armed with a broom and mop. The roof, upon examination, was a disaster. Dust everywhere. We had several dust storms these last few weeks and all the particles of dust that were swirling around Baghdad seemed to have agreed to rendezvous upon our roof.

It took almost 2 hours, 600 sneezes and around 15 buckets of water . . . but the roof is finally ready to sleep on. In an hour, we will drag out the mattresses and pillows. We were supposed to be out there, asleep, a couple of hours ago but the electricity came back on suddenly and I refuse to leave the computer.

The new governmental set is quite interesting. Some of the ministers are from inside of the country (not exiles) and the rest are from abroad and affiliated with different political parties. This will, naturally, determine the types of employees in the various ministries. You can't get a job these days without the proper "tazkiyeh" or words of approval from somebody who knows somebody who knows someone who knows someone else who has a friend who has a relative who . . . well, you get the picture.

I'll discuss the whole situation tomorrow . . . and this time I mean tomorrow. I haven't felt like blogging lately. The heat has been heavy and oppressive and I find myself reluctant to spend the few hours of electricity staring at the monitor. **posted by river @ 10:54 PM**

Friday, June 18, 2004

EXCUSES, EXCUSES . . .

I have had neither the time, nor the inclination, to blog lately. The weather is, quite literally, hellish. The heat begins very early in the morning with a blazing sun that seems unfairly close to our part of the earth. You'd think, after the sun has set, that the weather would be drastically cooler. This is not the case in Baghdad. After the sun has set, the hot sidewalks and streets emanate waves of heat for several hours, as if sighing in relief.

The electricity has been particularly bad these last two weeks in many areas. For every four hours of no electricity, we get two hours of electricity. And while we should be taking advantage of these two hours to do such things as wash clothes, get the water pump going and blog, we find ourselves sitting around in front of the air conditioner for a couple of hours of bliss, procrastinating and making empty promises to no one in particular.

School is out for most of the kids—both in grade school and in college. Everyone is just generally sitting around at home. It's a huge relief for parents and teachers alike. There was a time when, according to many frazzled parents, sending one's kids to school was the highlight of the day . . . now it has come to mean more anxiety and worry. While having them virtually trapped inside of the house is something of a trial on everyone involved, it is also a relief.

The new government isn't very different from the old Governing Council. Some of the selfsame Puppets, in fact. It's amusing to watch our [Hamid] Karazai—Ghazi Ajeel Al-Yawer—trying to establish himself. It's a bit of a predicament for many an Iraqi, and possibly foreigners too. Here he is—your typical Arab—the dark skin, dark hair and traditional "dishdasha" wearing an "iggall" on his head and playing the role of tribal sheikh quite well.

Beyond these minor details, however, he remains an ex-member of the Governing Council and was actually selected by the Puppets, supposedly over the American preference—Adnan Al-Pachichi (who is adamantly claiming he is *not* the American preference at this point). That whole charade is laughable. It has been quite clear from the very start that the Puppets do not breathe unless Bremer asks them, very explicitly, to inhale and exhale. The last time I checked, Puppets do not suddenly come to life and grow a conscience unless a fairy godmother and Jiminy the Cricket are involved.

He is, purportedly, one of the heads of one of the largest tribes in the region—Al-Shummar. This tribe extends over parts of Iraq, Syria and Saudi Arabia. They are largely Sunni but have several Shi'a clans. During and after the war, they were largely responsible for the northern and western borders. They are landowners, farmers, and—occasionally—smugglers of everything from sheep, to people, to arms . . .

Now, Yawer is our Karazai. He sits exuding all the outward signs of the stereotypical Arab (almost down to the camel) and yet, he seems to support Bremer et al. in almost every decision. Sure, he gives an interview now and then and says he doesn't agree with this decision or that one, but the first major meeting he attends, he calls for NATO forces inside of the country—as if Americans, Italians, Brits and the rest aren't already enough. There are also rumors that he is married to a certain lady who is a personal friend and adamant supporter of none other than Ahmad Chalabi . . . I'm still looking into that.

His image, admittedly, bothers me. I'm getting visions of corrupt Gulf emirs, oil wells, and shady business dealings.

Iyad Allawi is completely America and Britain's boy. He has been on the CIA's payroll for quite some time now and I don't think anyone was particularly surprised when he was made Prime Minister. The cabinet of ministers is an interesting concoction of exiled Iraqis, Kurdish Iraqis who were in the northern region and a few Iraqis who were actually living inside of Iraq. Of the 37 members of the new government, 11 were actually living inside of Iraq. Of those 11, one or two are known to be quite competent. The rest are either unknown or generally infamous.

Several of the new government actually have more than one nationality. Now don't get me wrong—I hold nothing against people with dual or triple or whatever number of nationalities. I do, however, have something against people with dual nationality being a part of government. It makes one wonder how many Americans would actually agree to having a senator or minister with, say, a French or German passport along with the American one.

While I don't have any definite numbers, I can assure the world that we have *at least* 20 million Iraqis, both inside and outside of Iraq, who have only a single nationality. I can even go further to assure the world that the majority of those Iraqis with a single nationality actually have lived inside of Iraq for most of their lives. However bizarre the statistics may seem, I do believe that out of those millions of Iraqis, 37 competent ones could have been found. True, they might not have CIA alliances, bank accounts in Switzerland, armed militias or multimillion dollar companies in Saudi Arabia . . . but many of them actually have a sense of national pride and an anxiety for their country and for the future of their children and their children's children inside of said country.

My favorite minister, by far, is the Defense Minister, Sha'alan Hazim. According to American newspaper Al-Sabah, Mr. Sha'lan Hazim "received a Masters degree in business administration from the UK before returning to Iraq to run a Kuwaiti bank. After being forced to leave Iraq by the former regime, Mr.Sha'alan became the head of a real-estate company in London until he returned to Iraq last June and has since worked as the governor of Qadisiya."

Now this is highly amusing. I must have missed something. If anyone has any information about just *how* Mr. Sha'alan Hazim qualifies as a Defense Minister, please do send it along. At a point when we need secure borders and a strong army, our new Defense Minister was given the job because he . . . what? Played with toy soldiers as a child? Read Tolstoy's War and Peace six times? Was regional champion of the game Commandos?

Beyond the unsure political situation, I have spent the last few days helping a relative sort things out to leave abroad. It is a depressing situation. My mother's cousin is renting out his house, selling his car and heading out to Amman with his three kids where, he hopes, he will be able to find work. He is a university professor who has had enough of the current situation. He claims that he's tired of worrying about his family and the varying political and security crises every minute of the day. It's a common story these days. It feels like anyone who can, is trying to find a way out before June 30. Last summer, people who hadn't been inside of Iraq for years were clamoring to visit the dear homeland that had been "liberated" (after which they would clamor to leave the dear homeland). This summer, it is the other way around.

The Syrian and Jordanian borders are packed. A friend who was returned at the Jordanian border said that they were only allowing 20 cars to pass per day . . . people were being made to wait on the borders for days at a time and risked being rejected at the border guard's whim. People are simply tired of waiting for normality and security. It was difficult enough during the year . . . this summer promises to be a particularly long one. **posted by river @ 9:06 PM**

IRAQI CIVILIAN WAR CASUALTIES . . .

Raed, of Raed in the Middle (raedinthemiddle.blogspot.com), has come out with a fantastic site: Iraqi Civilian War Casualties (civilians.info/iraq). Check out the "terrorists" and "collateral damage" killed and injured during the war. I'm sure many supporters of the "War on Terror" will feel mighty proud.

Iraqi War Casualties, http://civilians.info/iraq

> *I was the country director of the first (and maybe only) door-to-door civilian casualties survey. Marla Ruzika was my American partner, the fund raiser, and the general director of CIVIC. Unfortunately, she didn't have the chance to publish the final results until now.*
>
> *Decided to publish my copy of the final results of the Iraqi civilian casualties in Baghdad and the south of Iraq on the 9th of this month in respect to the big effort of the 150 volunteers who worked with me and spent weeks of hard work under the hot sun of the summer, in respect to Majid my brother who spent weeks arranging the data entry process, and in respect to the innocent souls of those who died because of irresponsible political decisions.*
>
> *Two thousand killed, Four thousand injured.*

posted by river @ 9:15 PM

AND WE'RE BACK . . .

An insurmountable combination of heat and family issues has kept me from blogging and I'm feeling terribly guilty. I have actually started to avoid the computer which seems to look at me reprovingly every time I pass by.

The heat is unbearable. It begins very early in the day and continues late into the night. You'd think that once the sun has set, the weather would cool appreciably—no such thing in Baghdad. Once the sun sets, the buildings and streets cease to absorb heat and instead begin to emanate it. If you stand a few centimeters away from any stucco or brick wall, you can feel the waves of heat coming at you from every crack and crevice.

The electricity has been quite bad. On some days, we're lucky to get 12 hours—3 hours of electricity for three hours of no electricity—but more often than not, it's four hours of no electricity and two hours of electricity. A couple of weeks ago, there was a day when our area had only one hour of electricity out of 23 hours with no power. The hellish weather had everyone out in their gardens by sunset, trying to find a way to stay cool.

Incidentally, one of man's greatest creations is definitely the refrigerator. I've made it a habit to rush into the kitchen every time anyone shows any inclination for a cool beverage. It gives me a great excuse to stand in front of the refrigerator for a couple of moments and let the cool—albeit slightly odorous—refrigerated air surround me. When we have some generator electricity, we keep the refrigerator working. At night, the refrigerator not only provides chilled air, and cold water, but it also offers that pale yellow light which falls like a beacon of hope across the darkened kitchen . . .

The family issues include the death of an older aunt. She had a stroke shortly after the war and has been deteriorating ever since. A combination of bad security, lack of the necessary health facilities and general stress and tension finally took its toll. We've been quite busy with the funeral process which can be extensive and drawn-out in Iraq. The deceased is buried after the proper preparation rituals, which shouldn't take longer than a day. The first problems we faced occurred in the graveyard. Upon visiting the graveyard, my uncles discovered that the family plot which had been purchased years ago had very recently been occupied by some strangers who could find very little room elsewhere in the overcrowded cemetery. The grounds keeper apologized profusely but said that they were bringing in an average of almost 100 bodies a month this year to his graveyard alone—where was he supposed to bury the bodies?

After some negotiations, the uncles were directed to some empty spaces on the outer borders of the cemetery and the aunt was resignedly buried there. Immediately after began the 7-day mourning ritual in the deceased aunt's house. For seven days—from morning until evening—friends, family and neighbors all come to give the family their condolences and mourn the dead. This is called a "fatiha" or a wake. Another wake is simultaneously held at a local mosque and this one is attended by the men—it lasts for only three days. Scheduling the mosque wake was also an issue because so many of the mosques are booked for wakes lately.

Lately, the condolences from neighbors and friends come in the form of, "She was much too young for such a death, but you should thank God—it's a better death than most these days . . ." And while death in general is still regarded as unfortunate, it is preferable to die of a stroke or natural causes than to die, say, of a car bomb, gun shot, beheading or under torture . . .

Security-wise, the situation is both better and worse all at once. The streets feel a little bit safer because you can see policemen standing around in the more crowded areas and even in some residential areas. There aren't nearly enough to keep things secure, but just seeing someone standing there is a little bit comforting. At the same time, kidnappings have multiplied. It's an epidemic now. Everyone seems to know someone who was abducted. Some are abducted for ransom while others are abducted for religious or political reasons. The abduction of foreigners is on the increase. People coming and going from Syria and Jordan tell stories of how their convoy or bus or private car was stopped in the middle of the road by men with covered faces and how passports and documents are checked. Should anything suspicious surface (like a British or American passport), the whole thing immediately turns from a "check" or "tafteesh" to an abduction.

I get emails by the dozen from people crying out against the abduction of foreigners. Endlessly I read the lines, "But these people are there to help you—they are aide workers . . . " or "But the press is there for a good cause . . . ," etc. What people abroad don't seem to realize is the fact that everything is mixed up right now. Seeing a foreigner, there's often no way to tell who is who. The blonde guy in the sunglasses and beige vest walking down the street could be a reporter or someone who works with a humanitarian group—but he could just as likely be "security" from one of those private mercenary companies we're hearing so much about.

Is there sympathy with all these abductees? There is. We hate seeing them looking frightened on television. We hate thinking of the fact that they have families and friends who worry about them in distant countries and wonder how in the world they managed to end up in the hell that is now Iraq . . . but for every foreigner abducted, there are probably 10 Iraqis being abducted and while we have to be here because it is home, truck drivers, security personnel for foreign companies and contractors do not. Sympathy has its limits in the Iraqi summer heat. Dozens of Iraqis are dying on a daily basis in places like Falloojeh and Najaf and everyone is mysteriously silent—one Brit, American or Pakistani dies and the world is in an uproar—it is getting tiresome.

Politically, things seem to be moving slowly. Maybe it's the heat. Everyone is waiting for the up and coming National Conference that is being debated so much. The problem is that it seems all of the same parties are going to be running—SCIRI, Da'awa, INC, PUK, etc. There does seem to be an interesting political resistance movement building up against them. Many of the parties that weren't involved with the CPA and Governing Council are currently trying to get their collective acts together.

Word on the street has it that email, internet access, and telephone calls are being monitored closely. We actually heard a couple of reports of people being detained due to the contents of their email. It's a daunting thought and speaks volumes about our current "liberated" status—and please don't bother sending me a copy of the "Patriot Act" . . . this last year it has felt like everyone is under suspicion for something.   **posted by river @ 8:53 PM**

Saturday, August 07, 2004

CLASHES AND CHURCHES . . .

300+ dead in a matter of days in Najaf and Al Sadr City. Of course, they are all being called "insurgents." The woman on tv wrapped in the abaya, lying sprawled in the middle of the street must have been one of them too. Several explosions rocked Baghdad today—some government employees were told not to go to work tomorrow.

So is this a part of the reconstruction effort promised to the Shi'a in the south of the country? Najaf is considered the holiest city in Iraq. It is visited by Shi'a from all over the world, and yet, during the last two days, it has seen a rain of bombs and shells from none other than the "saviors" of the oppressed Shi'a—the Americans. So is this the "Sunni Triangle" too? It's déjà vu—corpses in the streets, people mourning their dead and dying and buildings up in flames. The images flash by on the television screen and it's Falloojeh all over again. Twenty years from now who will be blamed for the mass graves being dug today?

We're waiting again for some sort of condemnation. I, personally, never had faith in the American selected proxy government currently pretending to be in power—but for some reason, I keep thinking that any day now—any moment—one of the Puppets, Allawi for example, will make an appearance on television and condemn all the killing. One of them will get in front of a camera and announce his resignation or at the very least, his utter disgust, at the bombing, the burning and the killing of hundreds of Iraqis and call for an end to it . . . it's a foolish hope, I know.

So where is the interim constitution when you need it? The sanctity of private residences is still being violated . . . people are still being unlawfully arrested . . . cities are being bombed. Then again, there really is nothing in the constitution that says the American millitary *can't* actually bomb and burn.

Sistani has conveniently been flown to London. His "illness" couldn't come at a better moment if Powell et al. had personally selected it. While everyone has been waiting for him to denounce the bombing and killing of fellow-Shi'a in Najaf and elsewhere, he has come down with some bug or other and had to be shipped off to

279

London for check-ups. That way, he can remain silent about the situation. Shi'a everywhere are disappointed at this silence. They are waiting for some sort of a fatwa or denouncement—it will not come while Sistani is being coddled by English nurses.

One of the news channels showed him hobbling off of a private airplane, surrounded by his usual flock of groupies and supporters. I couldn't quite tell, but I could have sworn Bahr Ul Iloom was with him. E. said that one of the groupies was actually Chalabi but it was difficult to tell because the cameraman was, apparently, standing quite far away.

The thought that Sistani is seriously ill does make everyone somewhat uneasy. Should he decide to die on us now, it will probably mean a power struggle between the Shi'a clerics in the south. Juan Cole has a lot more about it.

Informed Comment, http://www.juancole.com, August 7, 2004

Before I go over the details, here is my reading of what is going on in Najaf. The truce between the Mahdi Army and US/Iraqi forces broke down because they had different ideas of what the truce entailed. US-appointed governor Adnan al-Zurufi had demanded that the Mahdi Army disarm and/or leave Najaf. Moqtada al-Sadr on the other hand interpreted the truce to entail limiting his militia's activities to certain areas of the city and to have them avoid clashes with police and US troops.

In the past few weeks, the Mahdi Army has ensconced itself in the vast cemetery in Najaf, the crypts and stone walls of which afford excellent cover, and it has been stockpiling arms there . . .

One problem with an all-out attack on the Mahdi Army was that it might endanger the life of, or meet opposition from, Grand Ayatollah Ali Sistani. He was therefore spirited out of Najaf on the pretext that he had heart problems. But Al-Zaman reports today that Sistani stopped off in Beirut on his way to London, where he met with moderate Shiite leader Nabih Berri of the AMAL party, who serves as Speaker of the Lebanese Parliament. Sistani then went on to London, but is not in hospital and won't be for at least a week. This story just does not square with him being so ill that he had to be airlifted to London for emergency heart treatment. It would not have been easy for al-Zurufi and the Americans to convince Sistani to leave, but they could have simply shared with him their plans to have an all-out war in Najaf, and told him they could not protect him. That would have left him no choice but to leave. If you think about it, he could not possibly have been gotten out of Najaf to Beirut and London without US military assistance, though he flew a private plane from Baghdad airport.

Al-Hayat reports that Sistani's reason for leaving at this juncture was to remove himself from the scene of the fighting and to lift the mantle of his authority from the Sadrist movement. It was alleged that his distance from Muqtada, always substantial, had widened further in recent weeks. Al-Hayat suspects that if Sistani has ceased trying to protect Muqtada, it could mean that a decision has been made to put an end to him . . .

Last week churches were bombed—everyone heard about that. We were all horrified with it. For decades—no centuries—churches and mosques have stood side by side in Iraq. We celebrate Christmas and Easter with our Christian friends and they celebrate our Eids with us. We never categorized each other as "Christian" and "Muslim" . . . It never really mattered. We were neighbors and friends and we respected each other's religious customs and holidays. We have many differing beliefs—some of them fundamental—but it never mattered.

It makes me miserable to think that Christians no longer feel safe. I know we're all feeling insecure right now, but there was always that sense of security between differing religions. Many Iraqis have been inside churches to attend weddings, baptisms, and funerals. Christians have been suffering since the end of the war. Some of them are being driven out of their homes in the south and even in some areas in Baghdad and the north. Others are being pressured to dress a certain way or not attend church, etc. So many of them are thinking of leaving abroad and it's such a huge loss. We have famous Christian surgeons, professors, artists, and musicians. It has always been an Iraqi quality in the region—we're famous for the fact that we all get along so well.

I'm convinced the people who set up these explosions are people who are trying to give Islam the worst possible image. It has nothing to do with Islam—just as this war and occupation has nothing to do with Christianity and Jesus—no matter how much Bush tries to pretend it does. That's a part of the problem—many people feel this war and the current situation is a crusade of sorts. "Islam" is the new communism. It's the new Cold War to frighten Americans into arming themselves to the teeth and attacking other nations in "self-defense." It's the best way to set up "Terror Alerts" and frighten people into discrimination against Arabs, in general, and Muslims specifically . . . just as this war is helping to breed anger and hate towards Westerners in general, and Americans specifically. A person who lost their parent, child or home to this war and occupation will take it very personally and will probably want revenge—it won't matter if they are Muslim or Christian.

I always love passing by the churches. It gives me a momentary sense that everything must be right in the world to see them standing lovely and bright under the Baghdad sun, not far from the local mosque. Their elegant simplicity is such a contrast with the intricate designs of our mosques.

There's a lovely church in our area. It stands tall, solid and gray. It is very functional and simple—a rectangular structure with a pointy roof, topped by a plain cross or "saleeb," simple wooden doors and a small garden—it looks exactly like the drawings your 7-year-old nephew or daughter would make of the local church. This simplicity contrasted wonderfully with its stained-glass windows. The windows are at least 30 different colors. I always find myself staring at them as we pass, wondering about the myriad of shapes and colors they throw down upon the people inside. It hurts to pass it by these days because I know so many of the people who once visited it are gone—they've left to Syria, Jordan, Canada . . . with broken hearts and bitterness.
posted by river @ 10:57 PM

Wednesday, September 15, 2004

FAHRENHEIT 9/11 . . .

August was a hellish month. The heat was incredible. No one remembers Baghdad ever being quite this hot—I think we broke a new record somewhere in mid-August.

The last few days, Baghdad has been echoing with explosions. We woke up to several loud blasts a few days ago. The sound has become all too common. It's like the heat, the flies, the carcasses of buildings, the broken streets and the haphazard walls coming up out of nowhere all over the city . . . it has become a part of life. We were sleeping on the roof around three days ago, but I had stumbled back indoors at around 5 am when the electricity returned and was asleep under the cool air of an air-conditioner when the first explosions rang out.

I tried futilely to cling to the last fragments of a fading dream and go back to sleep when several more explosions followed. Upon getting downstairs, I found E. flipping through the news channels, trying to find out what was going on. "They aren't nearly fast enough," he shook his head with disgust. "We're not going to know what's happening until noon."

But the news began coming in much sooner. There were clashes between armed Iraqis and the Americans on Haifa Street—a burned out hummer, some celebrating crowds, missiles from helicopters, a journalist dead, dozens of Iraqis wounded, and several others dead. The road leading to the airport has seen some action these last few days—more attacks on troops and also some attacks on [the] Iraqi guard. The people in the areas surrounding the airport claim that no one got any sleep the whole night.

The areas outside of Baghdad aren't much better off. The south is still seeing clashes between the Sadr militia and troops. Areas to the north of Baghdad are being bombed and attacked daily. Ramadi was very recently under attack and they say that they aren't allowing the wounded out of the city. Tel Affar in the north of the country is under siege and Falloojeh is still being bombed.

Everyone is simply tired in Baghdad. We've become one of those places you read about in the news and shake your head thinking, "What's this world coming to?" Kidnappings. Bombings. Armed militias. Extremists. Drugs. Gangs. Robberies. You name it, and we can probably tell you several interesting stories.

So how did I spend my 9/11? I watched Michael Moore's movie, Fahrenheit 9/11. I've had a [a] bootleg CD version since early August. (Grave apologies to Michael Moore—but there's no other way we can see it here...) The copy has been sitting in a drawer with a bunch of other CDs. One of my cousins brought it over one day and said that while it was brilliant, it was also quite depressing and distressing all at once. I had been avoiding it because, quite frankly, I cannot stand to see Bush for five minutes straight—I wasn't sure how I'd cope with almost two hours.

Three days ago, I took it out while the house was relatively quiet—no cousins, no cousins' children, parents busy watching something or another, and E. asleep in front of the air conditioner for the next three hours.

The CD was surprisingly clear. I had expected some fuzziness and bad sound quality—it was fine. Someone had made the copy inside a movie theater. I could tell because in the background, there was a ringing mobile phone a couple of times and some annoying person in the front kept getting up to adjust his seat.

I was caught up in the film from the first moment, until the very last. There were moments, while watching, when I could barely breathe. I wasn't surprised with anything—there was nothing that shocked me—all of the stuff about the Bush family and their Saudi friends was old news. It was the other stuff that had an impact—seeing the reactions of Americans to the war, seeing the troops in Iraq being interviewed, seeing that American mother before and after she lost her son in Iraq.

Ah, that mother. How she made me angry in the beginning. I couldn't stand to see her on screen—convincing the world that joining the army was the ideal thing to do—perfectly happy that her daughter and son were "serving" America—nay, serving, in fact, the world by joining up. I hated her even more as they showed the Iraqi victims—the burning buildings, the explosions, the corpses—the dead and the dying. I wanted to hate her throughout the whole film because she embodied the arrogance and ignorance of the people who supported the war.

I can't explain the feelings I had towards her. I pitied her because, apparently, she knew very little about what she was sending her kids into. I was angry with her because she really didn't want to know what she was sending her children to do. In the end, all of those feelings crumbled away as she read the last letter from her deceased son. I began feeling a sympathy I really didn't want to feel, and as she was walking in the streets of Washington, looking at the protestors and crying, it struck me that the Americans around her would never understand her anguish. The irony of the situation is that the one place in the world she would ever find empathy was Iraq. We understand. We know what it's like to lose family and friends to war—to know that their final moments weren't peaceful ones . . . that they probably died thirsty and in pain . . . that they weren't surrounded by loved ones while taking their final breath.

When she asked why her son had been taken and that he had been a good person . . . why did this have to happen to him? I kept wondering if she ever gave a second thought to the Iraqi victims and whether it ever occurred to her that Iraqi parents perhaps have the same thoughts as the try to dig their children out from under the rubble of fallen homes in Falloojeh, or as they attempt to stop the blood flowing out of a gaping hole in the chest of a child in Karbala.

The flashes of the bombing of Iraq and the victims were more painful than I thought they would be. We lived through it, but seeing it on a screen is still a torment. I thought that this last year and a half had somehow made me a little bit tougher when it came to seeing Iraq being torn apart by bombs and watching foreign troops destroy the country—but the wound is still as raw as ever. Watching those scenes was like poking at a gash with sharp stick—it hurt.

All in all, the film was . . . what is the right word for it? Great? Amazing? Fantastic? No. It made me furious, it made me sad and I cried more than I'd like to admit . . . but it was brilliant. The words he used to narrate were simple and to the point. I wish everyone could see the film. I know I'll be getting dozens of emails from enraged Americans telling me that so-and-so statement was exaggerated, etc. But it really doesn't matter to me. What matters is the underlying message of the film—things aren't better for Americans now than they were in 2001, and they certainly aren't better for Iraqis.

Three years ago, Iraq wasn't a threat to America. Today it is. Since March 2003, over 1000 Americans have died inside of Iraq . . . and the number is rising. In twenty years time, upon looking back, how do Americans think Iraqis are going to remember this occupation?

I constantly wonder, three years after 9/11, do Americans feel safer? When it first happened, there was a sort of collective shock in Iraq. In 2002, there was a sort of pity and understanding—we've been through the same. Americans could hardly believe what had happened, but the American government brings this sort of grief upon nations annually . . . suddenly the war wasn't thousands of kilometers away, it was home.

How do we feel about it this year? A little bit tired.

We have 9/11's on a monthly basis. Each and every Iraqi person who dies with a bullet, a missile, a grenade, under torture, accidentally—they all have families and friends and people who care. The number of Iraqis dead since March 2003 is by now at least eight times the number of people who died in the World Trade Center. They had their last words, and their last thoughts as their worlds came down around them, too. I've attended more wakes and funerals this last year than I've attended my whole life. The process of mourning and the hollow words of comfort have become much too familiar and automatic.

September 11 . . . he sat there, reading the paper. As he reached out for the cup in front of him for a sip of tea, he could vaguely hear the sound of an airplane overhead. It was a bright, fresh day and there was much he had to do . . . but the world suddenly went black—a colossal explosion and then crushed bones under the weight of concrete and iron . . . screams rose up around him . . . men, women and children . . . shards of glass sought out tender, unprotected skin . . . he thought of his family and tried to rise, but something inside of him was broken . . . there was a rising heat and the pungent smell of burning flesh mingled sickeningly with the smoke and the dust . . . and suddenly it was blackness.

9/11/01? New York? World Trade Center?

No.

9/11/04. Falloojeh. An Iraqi home. **posted by river @ 2:49 PM**

CREDITS